CRITICAL TEACHING AND THE IDEA OF LITERACY

CRITICAL TEACHING
AND THE
IDEA OF LITERACY

C. H. KNOBLAUCH
LIL BRANNON

Boynton/Cook Publishers
A Subsidiary of
Reed Publishing (USA) Inc.
361 Hanover Street
Portsmouth, NH 03801
Offices and agents throughout the world

"Are My Hands Clean" by Bernice Johnson Reagon. Copyright by
Songtalk Publishing. Reprinted by permission.

Library of Congress Cataloging-in-Publication Data
Knoblauch, C. H.
    Critical teaching and the idea of literacy / C.H. Knoblauch, Lil
Brannon.
        p. cm.
    Includes bibliographical references.
    ISBN 0-86709-317-X
    1. Critical pedagogy—United States.   2. Literacy—United States.
3. Teaching.   I. Brannon, Lil.   II. Title.
LC196.5.U6K58 1993
370.11'5'0973—dc20   92-37899
                                                                      CIP

Cover design by Twyla Bogaard
Printed in the United States of America
93 94 95 96 97 10 9 8 7 6 5 4 3 2 1

Contents

Foreword

This book reads some stories from the educational world that are currently narrating the lives and circumstances of American citizens, particularly in their roles as parents, students, and teachers. It's a story about stories, and about the critical ways in which we should all be rewriting them, this one included.

For reading with us and helping to get our story straight, or perhaps we should say crooked, we thank Bob Boynton, certainly. He has encouraged us for lo these many years. More than anyone else, after Bob, we thank three Capital District teachers: Ann Connolly from Bethlehem Central, John Danaher from Shaker High, and Carol Forman-Pemberton from Burnt Hills/Ballston Lake. If the story had made no sense to them, it wouldn't have been worth the telling. Finally, we thank Jimmy Britton, Nancy Martin, Rosemary Hennessy, Ruma Chawla, Jim Collins, Suzanne Miller, and Glenn Hudak, all of whom have helped more than they know.

It seems proper for a story about stories to start with a story and we want to tell one about our daughter, Meta Susan. At the time of this writing, Susan is three years old and has just begun nursery school. One of the daily rituals of her nursery class is show-and-tell. Each day she brings a different item to class, as all the children do, and places it in a box outside the door of her classroom. After the singing, and crafts, and games, the children all go out to the box, bring in their special objects, toys, books, dolls, and talk about them, each in turn, with their classmates.

Coincidentally this fall, Susan underwent an operation to remove a birthmark from her leg, which left her in a cast from ankle to hip for three weeks while the incision healed. On the morning, three days after the operation, when she was to return to school, while sitting at breakfast, we all began to talk about what she might bring for show-and-tell—and naturally her parents both agreed that the best object she could show her classmates would be her new cast. Surely it would provoke everybody's interest. Susan, however, was quite solemn about the idea, not nearly as eager as we thought she'd be. After a moment, she announced to us, firmly, that she couldn't possibly use the cast for show-and-tell. We were surprised at the rejection of such inspired advice and tried to press our case. Finally, exasperated at her parents' obtuseness, Susan explained that if she wanted to talk about her cast, she would first have to stand outside in the show-and-tell box all morning long and would miss a whole day's school!

No doubt various readings of this story are possible, but one that stays in our minds is the power of conventional, routinized thinking to control people's lives. We all forget at times that the world contains more possibilities than any particular construction of it preserves, that we can recover unconsidered choices if we have the imagination and strength to do it. Of course, a child has that yet to learn. Had Susan's teachers reinforced her innocent conclusion, this story would not be as affectionately amusing as it is. And we all know the bureaucratic mind whose slavish devotion to uncontextualized rules has led to real suffering and harm. Or the still more sinister mind that aims to enforce convention just because it reminds everyone of who has power and who doesn't. Susan will learn about such people and figure out how to make accommodations. But this is a simpler story than that, about a child's understanding, and it includes, in the background, caring teachers whom we admire and trust. We know that the most important thing Susan will learn as she grows is that you don't have to stand in the show-and-tell box, even if someone tells you it's the rule.

This book, of course, is for Susan.

Chapter One

"Representation"
Naming the World in Schools

What's in a name? That which we call a rose by any other name would smell as sweet.

Shakespeare,
Romeo and Juliet

To exist, humanly, is to name *the world, to change it. Once named, the world in its turn reappears to the namers as a problem and requires of them a new* naming. *[People] are not built in silence, but in word, in work, in action-reflection.*

Paulo Freire, *Pedagogy of the Oppressed*

Our city newspaper recently ran an advertisement on behalf of the local shopping mall, an ad plainly aimed at stimulating business for Father's Day. Half a page in length, the ad features a letter from a young boy to his father, composed by hand in a print evidently meant to evoke the image of a child not quite in control of letters and struggling at a labor of love. The word "signed" at the bottom of the letter is spelled "singed." The text reads, "Dear Dad, Somebody told me Father's Day was invented by some merchants to hype sales during the slow June selling season. [Paragraph] But that somebody also thinks that the Easter Bunny and Santa Claus are marketing strategies. [Paragraph] I think that Father's Day is another chance to say I love you to you. [Paragraph] Singed, Your son." We ask ourselves, what are the messages here? An affectionate child, bravely postponing the cynicism of adulthood, rises above troubling charges that are at once true and false about Santa Claus and the Easter Bunny in order to communicate something of value to his father. The reader naturally hopes that the child will preserve his innocence, that he will remain unpersuaded by that "someone" sneering at commercial motives behind public holidays. The reader may even indulge a fleeting recollection of her own former innocence, her childhood with beloved parents, reading the letter with a complicated adult mix of amusement, sympathy, remembrance, sentiment, and skepticism. Nothing in the ad aims directly to sell merchandise or even to encourage people to shop for Father's Day: it could be read as nothing more than a public-spirited reminder of an opportunity for children, whatever their ages, to reaffirm parental bonds. One almost forgets who is responsible for the ad, how expensive one of this size must be, and how useful a shopping mall might find the identification, among consumers, between the love of children for parents, the official designation of a day to reassert that love, and the opportunity to purchase goods. Almost.

In a collection of essays titled *The Feminist Critique of Language*, the editor, Deborah Cameron, reflects on the way in which two English newspapers describe an incident involving a married couple whose house had been broken into. One newspaper is the respected *Daily Telegraph*, the other a tabloid, the *Sun*. The lead in the *Telegraph* reads, "A man who suffered head injuries when attacked by two men who broke into his home in Beckenham, Kent, early yesterday, was pinned down on the bed by intruders who took it in turns to rape his wife." The lead in the *Sun* reads, "A terrified 19-stone husband was forced to lie next to his wife as two men raped her yesterday." What strikes Cameron in these accounts is that in both "the act of rape is being represented as a crime against a man rather than a woman" (17). The first emphasizes, both grammatically and rhetorically, the man's head injuries, the violation of "his" home, the loss of his freedom—having been "pinned down," and the attack on him by "intruders," who also, as a last indignity directed at the man, raped "his" wife. The second emphasizes the man's terror, insinuating an incongruity between that emotion and his large size, and the horrifying, yet also perhaps luridly titillating image of him "lying next to his wife," a position implying not just sexual encounter but also ownership, while two other men stole from him his sexual prerogative. In both, the issue of rape, here plainly a crime against a woman, is framed exclusively in terms of the violation of a man—his body and his "property." The only distinction between the reports is the greater willingness of the tabloid to capitalize on barely suppressed sexual imagery; the "respectable" paper no less than the tabloid takes it for granted that rape is a form of theft, that the woman who is raped becomes "damaged goods" (17).

For us, the issue that relates the shopping advertisement and the two newspaper stories is *representation*: how things are named, who gets to do the naming, what motives are involved, what consequences follow, what possibilities for alternative naming have been forgotten, or gone unrecognized, or been ignored, hidden, or suppressed. Is it just unhappy accident that two editors, serving two quite different audiences, reveal the same misogyny in their representations of rape? Does it matter that both editors are male? Would a woman editor necessarily have told the story in a different way? Or is there something much broader, subtler, unconscious, systemic, and historically situated at work—a cultural propensity to "represent" women as property? How is treatment of women in English culture—and beyond—affected by, even conditioned by, such a structural representation at some given historical moment? What are the chances that the representation might be changed, and that the life circumstances of women in English society might be changed as well through its critique and a deliberate recomposing of "woman" as subject rather than object (rhetorically as well as grammatically) within public discourse? And what of the advertisement? Past the pleasurable sentimentality of its representation of Father's Day, what less sanguine economic motives might be entailed in a shopping mall's manipulation of our images of children, fathers, and family love? What motives underlie the use of secular signs—Santa Claus, Easter Bunny—that have reconstituted formerly religious representations, considering that both refer to creatures who give things to others, a noble gesture to be sure but one that is typically accomplished in this culture by first purchasing whatever is given?

The issue is representation, the practices by which people name and rename the world, negotiate the substance of social reality, and contest prior namings in favor of new or different ones. Naming can appear relatively straightforward: what's the difference between calling someone a freedom fighter or a terrorist, a confidential informant or a stool pigeon, gay or queer? What's the difference in calling a social practice "equal opportunity" as opposed to "reverse discrimination"? Naming can also be subtle and complex, as our previous examples illustrate, where more is at stake than a choice of nouns or adjectives, where entire habits of expression or textual statements are involved in multilayered significations. (Actually, "representation" is always more complex than we're suggesting here, but that's a story for Chapter 7.) And naming is inevitably political, entailing a struggle among opposing interests and competing possibilities, where the power to name, and also to enforce the subordination, even silence, of alternative voices, figures crucially in the distribution of cultural standing and social privilege. A recent news item, for instance, reports that women with AIDS have more difficulty receiving government disability payments than men do because the standard definition of AIDS does not include many of the symptoms that women uniquely experience. The problem lies in determining when an HIV infection becomes "AIDS" and therefore disabling in the eyes of the law. Health agencies list Kaposi's sarcoma as part of the definition, but women with AIDS rarely get this form of cancer. Meanwhile, cervical cancer, which HIV-infected women do get, is not included in the definition, so that women with this disease cannot claim AIDS disability that would entitle them to benefits for themselves and their children. The issue here is precisely one of representation, how something is named and what consequences attend that naming; it is also evidently political, with clear social advantages at stake for those who maintain as well as those who critique and work to change the current definition of AIDS.

Representation is a function of the verbal, visual, and other signs by which naming is achieved. Signs are the raw materials of cultural production, the means by which social reality is constructed: they include, for instance, the Declaration of Independence and the U.S. Constitution; the American flag; architectural styles; money and credit cards; novels and newspapers; television and movie images; paintings and sculptures; rock music and jazz; Reeboks and loafers; Bloomingdale's and Sears; the Cross and the Star of David; biographies and family albums; fairs, parades, and funerals; the physical spaces of factories and schools; dolls and cap pistols; yachts and canoes; everything from hair styles to the layout of neighborhoods (tenements here, ranches there) to salary scales (the auto worker, the CEO of General Motors). The world is thick with signs and their variegated meanings; the world is a human production in continual change as signs are composed, fought over, insisted upon, marginalized, resisted, and altered. Examining and critiquing signs as they function within concrete social and historical settings is the project of a discipline that has come to be called "cultural studies." The intent of cultural studies, according to Patrick Brantlinger, is to learn about "the lived experience of people producing meanings and values through everyday social interaction." Its intent is also to promote, as a responsible "goal of all serious intellectual work," the achievement of a fully democratic "common culture" (38), where all people have equivalent authority to engage in the production and negotiation of signs—the practices of representation. Precisely at the intersection between cultural studies as an academic pursuit and any classroom full of students who deserve rich opportunities to learn and grow and become productive citizens lies the educational practice that we will call "critical teaching," borrowing the name (the "representation") from Ira Shor (*Critical Teaching and Everyday Life*). Our principal theme throughout the arguments that follow will be the goals and means of critical (also called "radical" and "liberatory") teaching, specifically in the domain of reading and writing instruction in high schools and colleges. Liberatory pedagogy can occur in any academic discipline—physics, history, mathematics—in any educational setting—the inner-city vocational school, the suburban prep school, the adult community workshop, the labor union literacy program—and at any academic level from elementary through graduate school. Our choice of literacy instruction in high school and college reflects our interests and professional experience, but critical teaching is a more encompassing activity, just as cultural studies is a broader intellectual domain than "English." Our concern is for "representation" in the school world, specifically that portion of the school world given over to the teaching of reading and writing. We propose to look at how things are named in that world, who has authority to do the naming and who doesn't, how representations frame parents, teachers, and students, cast them in certain kinds of roles or "subject positions" (note in such language our own tactics of representation, the academic discourse that informs our statements). We want to look at definitions of literacy in particular, as they range across the political as well as intellectual spectrum of American life, in order to offer parents, teachers, and students a way to examine the rhetoric of those definitions, acknowledging the power but also the potential for revision of "stories" imposed upon them through the authoritative discourses of public life, the privileged languages of politicians, university researchers, and school administrators. To see these stories as rhetorical constructions, historically situated, is effectively to see "through" them to their ideological designs. To see "through" them is to exercise the power to think critically and to act upon the school world, as parents, students, and teachers deserve to act upon it, in transformative capacities.

Critical teaching aims to transform. That ambition is both subversive and entirely common, akin, that is, to the aim of any teaching. Schools, after all, accept the burden of assisting the nation's young people to become responsible and productive citizens. Hence, teaching is always a transformative act: students aren't expected to leave their classrooms thinking, knowing, judging, living in the ways they did before they entered them—fundamentalist students encounter evolution in biology class; students raised on television read literature; students from "liberal" backgrounds study growing crime rates in sociology and the cost of assistance programs in economics; "conservatives" study the women's movement in history class or Marxism in philosophy. The choices teachers make in their classrooms are always, in part, choices about what children "ought" to become, what the nation "ought" to aspire to through the productive action of succeeding generations. These are political choices: the question is, what indeed *should* students become and who should have the power to say so? What indeed *should* the nation aspire to, and who should compose the stories about that aspiration? Critical teaching differs from other sorts primarily in its answers to these questions and in its self-consciousness about the political nature of schools (including its own practices). It presumes that American citizens should understand, accept, and live amicably amidst the realities of cultural diversity—along axes of gender, race, class, and ethnicity—that are the hallmarks of American society. It presumes that people are entitled to fairness in their social and economic lives. It presumes that a critical citizenry, willing as well as able to take responsibility for the nation's future, is preferable to a passive, unengaged citizenry that lets government, business, and mass media do its thinking. Finally, it presumes that no one group is exclusively entitled to the privilege of representation, but that each has a right to tell its story, critique other stories, and participate in forming a community responsive to the needs of all its members.

Since politics is the essence of social life—people negotiating the terms of free and fair collective existence—and since schools are social formations, critical teaching accepts the political character of schools and educational practice while attempting to encourage a politically intelligent and alert citizenry. Disciplinary knowledge—mathematics, history, a foreign language—becomes more than a neutral "content" to be transferred to passive students for narrowly selfish credentialization or other gain. That knowledge becomes, instead, a means to productive living, an opportunity to develop forms of understanding and ability that make for informed social practice. Studying biology offers the capacity to discuss issues of reproductive freedom and responsibility or the damage of environmental pollution, not just the opportunity to enter medical school. Studying mathematics offers the capacity to challenge deceptive statistics on the costs of welfare to taxpayers or determine the fairness of a bank's interest rate or an oil company's profits, not just to manipulate the junk bond market. But disciplinary knowledge is also subject to critique in its own right, along with the institutional arrangements that have assigned its priorities (so that science, for instance, is "represented" as more "important" than art appreciation, more "objective" and hence more "truthful"; so that sociology is a "real" subject while African American studies is not). The school world itself, in other words, is as much an object of attention as any of its disciplines, because that world (including its disciplines) has been formed in response to social and economic, not just intellectual, interests. The organization of school life—principals superior to teachers, teachers superior to students, parents on the sidelines; study apportioned in particular allotments of time; some activities required, others optional or unavailable; curricula fixed according to age, ability, or class affiliation; placement and competency testing; class sizes, attendance requirements, dress codes, rules of behavior— reflects the socioeconomic purposes of schooling and determines the circumstances, not always for the better, of everyone living in the school world. For critical teachers, therefore, the school and what it "represents" become objects of discussion along with academic subjects, because the quality of life for teachers and students is very much at stake in the organization of the school, just as it is at stake in the surrounding world on which the school patterns itself and to which it contributes.

Plainly, critical teachers accept a more complicated and burdensome responsibility in educational life than those colleagues who remain content, either out of apathy or a commitment to less presumptuous obligations, to teach what they are told, in the authorized ways, without change through the years and without concern for any larger context of public action. Critical teachers develop an informed reflectiveness about the conditions both within and outside schools that impinge on their quality of life and that of their students—for instance: American socioeconomic hierarchies reproduced in schools through "tracking" policies; or factory models of work reproduced in regimented, clock-punching, mind-numbing school days; or manager/worker distinctions reproduced in relations between school administrators and faculty. They remain similarly reflective about their instructional practices, so that they stay responsive to the fullest range of student needs as well as the ethical imperatives of social justice—so that issues of gender, race, and class, for instance, along with other cultural realities of American life, are woven self-consciously into pedagogy, not subordinated to a myth of disciplinary neutrality or a myth of the American melting pot. Finally, they undertake to translate these forms of reflectiveness into pedagogical action that both serves their students and, over time, changes the very character of American schooling, making it more responsive to democratic ideals amidst the complexities of socioeconomic life.

In short, there is both a theoretical and a practical dimension to critical pedagogy, an interrelationship between reflection—thinking about the world, one's own positions in it as well as those of others, the nature of a teacher's responsibilities—and action—doing work that affects the world, alters it in the service of productive living. Paulo Freire, a leading exponent of critical pedagogy whose work we will explore later, refers to this reciprocity as "praxis," a sustained, directed, thoughtful effort, grounded in lived experience, to name the world and to change it (*Pedagogy of the Oppressed*, 60–61). Praxis entails a theorizing of the "work" of teaching, but also a continual reconstituting of theory by appeal to the concrete experience of practitioners. We're not talking here about that other notion of "theory" to which high school teachers, for instance, are regularly exposed when outsiders, typically from universities, drone on about "residual learning outcomes" or "the acquisition of decoding skills" during sterile in-service meetings designed to colonize the working class so that Madeline Hunter or the publishers of basal readers can make more money. We don't mean theory that is purchased with federal funding and "disseminated" to docile faculties, theory prepackaged with color-coordinated transparencies and imposed by local superintendents. This kind of theory merely allows "managers," whether politicians or principals or university researchers, to retain control of education by subordinating teachers, parents, students to a jargon, an esoteric body of knowledge, and an agenda all essentially foreign to the school world. Praxis doesn't descend from above (although much "theory" does); it emerges from within. Praxis entails teachers' own "representations" of what they do, standing at a critical remove both from the hectic, daily routine of the classroom and also from the alternative representations that cast teachers (students and their parents too) exclusively as characters in other people's stories rather than as subjects coauthoring the narrative. In true praxis, teachers scrutinize for themselves the choices they make in the classroom, remembering that they are constantly deciding what to do and how to do it, albeit so routinely that they might well forget the agency that suffuses their work. Theory reminds teachers that they're acting by design—never merely their own design, too often indeed mainly that of others, but hopefully in some measure a design that they have helped to negotiate. Theory involves wondering about practice (Steven Mailloux calls theory "practice about practice"), mulling over alternatives, questioning motives, reassessing values and purposes. If theory unresponsive to practice is at best empty talk and at worst an academic power trip at the expense of other people, teaching without theoretical articulateness is a product of unthinking custom, accident, and the impositions of others, with no less potential (perhaps more, in fact) for taking advantage of the powerless. Praxis incorporates the dimensions of reflection and of action, the process of naming reality (theorizing, "representing") and the process of changing reality (directed action in the material, historical world). Teachers know the power of representation in the school world all too well because they are habitually on the losing end of a struggle over who gets to name the realities of that world. Consider the representations of "student ability" that are imposed upon teachers. Most of what counts as knowledge about the classroom comes from the educational research establishment and the testing industry (which maintain mutually beneficial ties that the public ought to regard with more suspicion than it does). For them children are often "represented" quantitatively as scores that fall in standard deviations above or below the mean. Students are placed on the basis of these scores in remedial, regular, or advanced categories, which "represent" their abilities and prospects while offering rationales for public expenditures and focuses of educational attention. The scores are used, too, in comparisons across cities, states, even countries, offering "representations" of success and failure (frequently against the backdrop of dire warnings about cultural decay) while stimulating an atmosphere of competitive hostility and suspicion (crystallized in militarist sloganeering like "the war against illiteracy"). Sometimes they are used to judge how well teachers teach, so that if reading scores decline in a district over a couple of years the cry is soon enough heard that teachers aren't doing their jobs. Always they have the effect of driving curriculum, since teachers are compelled, as a matter of job protection, to ready students to pass tests before they engage them in learning disciplinary content. Quantitative assessment is a dominant representational practice in American schools.

Anyone who has taught in this setting knows how limited and limiting assessment can be, how deadening it is to the possibilities of creative teaching and learning, how degrading for large numbers of people. Teachers know (and name) their classrooms differently, know that students aren't as tidy a reality as numbers are, that student performance varies over time, that students' abilities aren't necessarily equivalent to their performances (especially on tests), that the places they occupy because of previous testing aren't necessarily best suited to their development, that teaching whatever the tests mandate isn't necessarily the appropriate pedagogical decision given a particular group of students and a concrete educational moment. Teachers know these things but know too the power of the assessment-driven school world to enforce their participation in its assumptions and practices. So, they dutifully divide children by "ability"—calling them red birds and blue birds, perhaps, since these names are more palatable than bright people and stupid people—and assign grades that are supposed to have measured all the complex activities and processes that constitute learning. But what if teachers claimed the authority to offer their representations of school life as challenges to those of the testing industry? And suppose teachers, acting collectively alongside like-minded parents, school administrators, and university colleagues, were to use that authority to critique the power and economic self-interest of the testing establishment? What if teachers' stories of classroom trauma resulting from assessment practices helped to create a more reflective American public that began to realize the culture, class, and gender biases in testing; began to worry about the power of testing to stereotype children at very early ages in ways that will stamp the rest of their lives; began to consider how test results reify, and therefore falsify, human potential; began noticing the frequency of technical error in testing—all the intellectual mistakes and abuses documented, but with little public reaction, in Stephen Jay Gould's *Mismeasure of Man*? What if Americans were to take seriously the story (portrayed in the movie *Stand and Deliver*, Warner Brothers, 1988) of Jaime Escalante's Hispanic students in East Los Angeles whose math scores, as a result of his and their effort, were dramatically higher than they "should have been," occasioning ETS charges of cheating? Suppose these were the dominant themes of an American educational story about quantitative evaluation?

Critical pedagogy aims to retheorize testing—tell a different kind of story about it than the one preferred by the assessment industry—then to envision alternatives to the mass testing practices that dominate American curriculum (portfolio evaluation is a modest instance) and to change the unimaginative school world that results from the sterile quantification of its community. A delightfully readable book by our colleague Peter Johnston, titled *Constructive Evaluation of Literate Activity*, will help in the conceiving of those alternatives. Meanwhile, a practical example of change is the work of the Center for Educational Improvement Through Collaboration at the University of Michigan, whose projects include writing instruction in the public schools of Saginaw and Detroit, Michigan. The CEIC has worked successfully to persuade teachers, administrators, and school boards in these districts that quantitative measures offer inadequate representations particularly of students classified as "nonachievers," leading to unresponsive curricula. It has sponsored a series of pilot courses for "nonachievers" in which the "measure" of success, in each instance, was a student publication of stories and poems, including most recently *Reflections: Expressions From Inner City Detroit*, published by the Dewey Center Community Writing Project (1990), and *Struggles and Celebration: Voices From the City*, published by the Northern High School Community Writing Project (1990).

Jay Robinson (*Conversations on the Written Word*) and the many teachers who have developed and engaged in the Michigan efforts have been able to look into the ideological conditions of schooling, including standard representations of achievement, in order to argue effectively for more responsive principles of curriculum as well as evaluation. Other teachers can do the same through reflection and action: critiquing dominant representations, posing alternatives, undertaking transformations. Without reflection, teachers (parents too) are trapped as objects in other people's stories, making active engagement impossible to imagine. Hence, most teachers as well as parents accept the "fact" that students must be tested and conspire to make testing a permanent feature of schooling, often against their own best instincts. They may complain about assessment but they find it hard to ask the explosively simple question, "Why do it this way?" But critical educators (including "official" teachers but also parents) do ask, and then struggle in their praxis to conceive and create a different kind of school world.

Competing representations of literacy seek to dominate school life much as stories about assessment do, and indeed in even greater variety. The critical teacher of reading and writing is obliged to examine stories about literacy in order to engage in productive action. We'll look at some of the stories in detail shortly, since they constitute, along with the idea of critical teaching, a crucial theme in everything that follows. But we want to offer a preview here in order, initially, to emphasize the ideological complexities that have always been entailed in the idea of literacy and that continue to surround it today. In a culture dominated by scientific objectivism, it is anything but a self-evident assertion that "literacy" is an ideological or political construction. Indeed, the stories about literacy that currently dominate American attention have given considerable effort to concealing their political agendas in order to insist that their definitions are natural and right, along with the particular curricular recommendations, ways of conceiving teachers, students, and parents, means of judging success and failure, that are implied in their definitions. The issue, as with everything else in the school world, is control—power—the gains that accrue to those who have the standing and will to conceive the world in ways that maintain their interests. There need be nothing consciously malicious in those interests or in the struggle to keep control: indeed, more often than not, the motives are benign, are represented as a concern to "do something for" those who are less skilled and (therefore) less fortunate. The controllers are barely aware, if at all, of any paternalistic or colonizing tendencies in their "good will"—scarcely aware of what Elspeth Stuckey has called "the violence of literacy" as a weapon of subordination. These tendencies always exist, however, whenever those with power set out to "do something for" those without it, including even critical educators who must be particularly vigilant, given their philosophical pretensions as well as their explicit utopian agendas, not to romanticize a benevolence that masks yet another bid for power.

Some historical anecdotes will make the case plainly enough that literacy is an ideological construction. Plato explains in the *Phaedrus* that King Thamus of Egypt was unenthusiastic about the "value" of literacy. When informed by the god Theuth, "father of written letters," that writing "will make the Egyptians wiser and will improve their memories," the king replies that, on the contrary, "this invention will produce forgetfulness in the souls of those who have learned it" because "they will not need to exercise their memories, being able to rely on what is written." Worse, young people will end up "widely read without benefit of a teacher's instruction," entertaining "the delusion that they have wide knowledge, while they are, in fact, for the most part incapable of real judgment." Socrates is quick to reinforce Thamus's unmasking of Theuth's attempts to democratize knowledge by taking it out of the control of wise teachers like himself and placing it, irresponsibly, in the hands of the uninitiated: "writing has this strange quality about it," leading us to imagine that its words speak "as though they made sense, but if you ask them anything about what they are saying, if you wish an explanation, they go on telling you the same thing, over and over forever." The trouble with writing is that it may fall "into the hands of those who have no concern with it just as easily as under the notice of those who comprehend: it has no notion of whom to address or whom to avoid" (68–70). Imagine the chaotic consequences, Plato implies, the destabilizing effect on institutional arrangements, educational and otherwise, the threat to established interests, if freely accessible documents and a broadly achieved capacity to read them were to encourage unregulated learning among the ignorant masses. A recent cartoon echoes Plato's point: it shows a king (less astute than Thamus) and his adviser looking from a balcony down on a crowd of marching citizens. The rabble is carrying signs that read "Question Authority" while the king says to his adviser, "You and your literacy programs!"

"Clerks" in medieval England were more inclined to appreciate literacy, and for reasons as predictably self-interested as Plato's in opposing it. They were taught reading and writing in grammar schools controlled by the Church so that they could write papers and keep accounts for merchants, landowners, and public officials. Though there was no educational concern for the literacy of the general population, the Church understood the crucial economic function that clerks fulfilled in maintaining records, correspondence, and other documentation in businesses as well as state and legal offices. Accordingly, as one dividend of their social standing, these clerks enjoyed immunity from the jurisdiction of the civil courts. When convicted of a felony crime, stealing sheep for instance, which ordinarily carried a capital sentence, they were entitled to plead "benefit of clergy," thereby enabling the disposition of their case in the more lenient ecclesiastical courts (Trevelyan, 65–66). The literate sheep-stealer might endure a short imprisonment, a whipping, or a branding of the left hand, but he (the masculine pronoun is deliberate: women could not be clerics and therefore had no need to be literate) would at least escape the gallows. Benefit of clergy, which required displaying one's ability to read in the dock prior to sentencing, remained a principle of English law through the eighteenth and into the nineteenth century, gradually becoming more limited in the kinds of felonies to which it applied but also more broadly available to people, in Holy Orders or not, who could demonstrate language proficiency and thereby the privilege due them. During the seventeenth century, for instance, anyone who could read or recite the first verse of Psalm 51 (even with the book open to the wrong page) could beat the hangman: "Have mercy upon me, O God, according to thy loving kindness: according unto the multitude of thy tender mercies blot out my transgressions." Appropriately, these lines were known at the time as "the neck verse" (MacKinnon, 303–4), a palpable sign to actual and aspiring miscreants alike of the social importance of literacy.

Why does Plato, himself literate, choose to rationalize so earnestly the continued illiteracy of others? Why would British law, so obsessed with the right to own and protect property that it made theft and robbery (over a shilling's worth of value) punishable by death, be willing to set aside felony convictions merely because a person could read? Any answer entails a consideration of ideological questions rooted in a particular time and place: how the literate distinguish themselves from the illiterate, how and why power, wealth, and prerogatives are distributed on the basis of particular "skills" or attainments defined in particular ways, and how the (variable) ability to read and write allies itself to sociopolitical hierarchies, to judgments about superiority of class, gender, or ethnicity, and to the shaping of social institutions in concrete historical circumstances. Our point emerges straightforwardly enough in the posing of these alternate images of the purpose and importance of reading and writing: it's that the issue of literacy can never be separated from the issue of ideology. "Literacy" is one of those mischievous concepts, like "virtuousness" or "craftsmanship," that appear to denote capacities but that actually convey value judgments.

Dictionary definitions of the term are, to be sure, beguilingly direct: according to the *American Heritage Dictionary*, literacy is "the condition or quality of being literate, especially the ability to read and write." But the meaning of the word is not bounded by its ostensible reference: "to be literate" does not *mean* the same as "to be able to read and write": people understand that a statement such as, "students these days are no longer literate"—a common enough sentiment—does not mean that students are radically unable to read and write. Moreover, the notion of "ability" is no more stable than the notion of literacy itself: minimal capacity is not some sort of objective baseline, as the wildly divergent estimates of numbers of "illiterates" in the current American population plainly show (see Hunter and Harman, 24–30). Instead, it varies in accordance with the idea of literacy that conditions its measure (the ability to sign one's name is "minimal" from one point of view; the ability to read and quote from the Bible from another; the ability to critique government proclamations from still another, perhaps that of the cartoon marchers who "question authority"). The idea of "minimum ability" also varies with ideas of intellectual, economic, or sociopolitical stratification: hence, from some perspectives, Plato's for instance, the welder need not be literate in the same way or to the same degree that the business executive is. These differences of meaning and value are precisely a function of ideology.

Of course, "ideology" is itself a vexed concept, variously defined even within a single intellectual or political perspective, let alone across competing points of view. Raymond Williams has distinguished three definitions within Marxism alone: (1) "a system of beliefs characteristic of a particular class or group"; (2) "a system of illusory beliefs—false ideas or false consciousness—which can be contrasted with true or scientific knowledge"; and (3) "the general process of the production of meanings and ideas" (55). For Williams, the first definition seems preferable, for he explains elsewhere that "the normal sense" of ideology is "a relatively formal and articulated system of meanings, values, and beliefs, of a kind that can be abstracted as a 'world-view' or a 'class-outlook' " (109). Our own preference is more for the third, which appears to be a broader definition that could readily include the first as a special application. As we use the term, we do not intend the second definition, nor does Williams in his work, although traditional Marxism tends to prefer it. In fact, we repudiate it as ultimately antithetical to the position we are taking on the question of literacy. And we find support for our sense of the word's significance (though we agree with Williams that any insistence on a "true" meaning would itself be ideologically situated) in Volosinov's argument that "the domain of ideology coincides with the domain of signs"—that semiotic activity is always essentially social, that the making of meaning in the relationships of social life constitutes ideological action, and that "everything ideological possesses semiotic value" (9–15). When we say, therefore, that the concept of "literacy" is and must always be ideologically situated, we are saying that its reference to reading and writing abilities is always qualified by the context of assumptions, beliefs, values, expectations, and related conceptual material that accompanies its use by particular groups of people in particular sociohistorical circumstances. We agree, then, with Linda Brodkey's assertion that literacy is properly viewed "as a social trope" and its various definitions "as cultural Rorschachs" (47).

The labels "literate" and "illiterate" almost always imply more in common usage than a degree or deficiency of skill. They are, grossly or subtly, sociocultural judgments, laden with approbation, disapproval, or pity, about the character and "place," the worthiness and prospects, of persons and groups of people. The scholarship on literacy supports, and no doubt helps in part to account for, this popular understanding. Alternative representations motivate scholarly judgments about who the literate as well as the illiterate are and how many there are in each group, why literacy is important and whether it is more or less important than other attainments, what should be done "for" or about those who are not literate or are "less" literate than others and who gets to say so. It will be quickly apparent that there is no single, or self-evident, definition of literacy since the values that surround reading and writing abilities differ from argument to argument. There are instead multiple and competing definitions, responsive to the agendas of those who characterize the ideal. Invariably, that is, definitions of literacy are also rationalizations of its importance. Furthermore, they are invariably offered by the literate, constituting therefore implicit rationalizations of the importance of literate people, as well as literate societies, who are powerful, the reasoning goes, *because* they are literate and as such deserving of their power.

The concept is embedded, then, in the ideological dispositions of those who employ it, those who profit from it, and those who have the standing and motivation to enforce it as a social requirement. It's obviously not a cultural value in all times and places: when Sequoyah brought his syllabic writing system to the Cherokee, their first inclination was to put him to death for dabbling in an evil magic. The majority of the world's languages have lacked alphabets, though they have nonetheless articulated rich oral traditions in societies which have also produced many other varieties of cultural achievement. To be sure, there are various rationalizations advanced for the necessity of literacy in the "modern" world, "explanations" that typically imply a more "developed" mode of existence among the literate. I. J. Gelb proclaimed in 1952, for instance, that "as language distinguishes man from animal, so writing distinguishes civilized man from barbarian," going on to point out that "an illiterate person cannot expect to participate successfully in human progress, and what is true of individuals is also true of any group of individuals, social strata, or ethnic units" (221–22). This argument offers a pernicious half-truth, representing the importance of literacy, which is unquestionable, in terms of absolutist concepts of "progress" and the prerequisites of civilized (as opposed to "barbarian") life, which are, at best, ethnocentric.

If literacy today is perceived as a compelling value throughout the world, the reason lies not in such rationalizations but in its continuing association with forms of social reality that depend on its primacy—forms which reading and writing abilities have historically played a significant role in constituting. Not accidentally, for instance, as Richard Bailey has pointed out in "Literacy in English: An International Perspective" (Bailey and Fosheim, 30–44), the international preoccupation with literacy is frequently specified to emphasize literacy in English—a colonizing language that, like Latin before it, has for centuries intruded upon and reconstituted non-English-speaking and nonliterate societies so as to advance Western political, religious, and technological priorities that continue to depend on literacy for their achievement. There can be no question, therefore, that literacy is truly necessary to survival and success in the contemporary world—a world that enjoys its authority to set the terms of survival and success, a world that reading and writing abilities have significantly shaped in the first place. But it's important to regard that necessity in the context of ideological conditions that have accounted for it, or else we sacrifice the humanizing, not to say humbling, understanding that life can be otherwise than the way we happen to know it—and that people who are measured positively by the yardstick of literacy enjoy their privileges in life because of their power to choose and apply that instrument on their own behalf, not because of their intelligence, point of "development," or other innate worthiness. Possessing that understanding, educators in particular, but other citizens as well, may advance their agendas for literacy with somewhat less likelihood of being blinded—in the light of their own benevolence—to the imperial designs that lurk in the midst of their commitments.

In the United States today several distinct and conflicting arguments about the nature and importance of literacy, each reflecting an alternate ideological disposition, vie for power in political and educational life. Reviewing them quickly (for they are well established) will show how definitions of the concept arise from the social agendas of the definers—conservative, liberal, or radical—and serve the ends of diverse political groups (see Knoblauch, "Literacy"). Literacy never stands alone in these perspectives as a neutral denoting of skills: it is always literacy *for* something—for professional competence in a technological world; for civic responsibility and the preservation of heritage; for personal growth and self-fulfillment; for social and political change. The struggle of any one definition to dominate the others entails no merely casual or arbitrary choice of values, nor does it allow for a conflating of alternatives in some grand compromise or list of cumulative benefits. At stake are fundamentally different perceptions of social reality, the nature of language and discourse, the importance of culture, history, and tradition, the functions of schools, as well as other ideological convictions, few of which are regarded as negotiable. At the same time, since no definition achieves an absolute and permanent authority, their dialectical interaction offers a context of choices within which continually changing educational and other social policies find their stimulation, resources, and justification. The process of choosing is visible every day, for better and worse, in legislative assemblies, academic conferences, television talk shows, school board meetings, newspaper editorials, and classrooms throughout the country.

Surely the most familiar, and probably the most popular, "representation" of literacy in this country comes from the functionalist perspective, with its appealingly pragmatic emphasis on readying people for the necessities of daily life—writing checks and business letters; reading sets of instructions, street signs, and warning labels—as well as for the professional tasks of a complex technological society. Language abilities in the functionalist argument tend to be characterized by the mechanistic metaphors of information theory so well suited to a culture that values technical know-how: language is a "code" that enables the "processing" of "information"; speakers and writers are "encoders" and "senders" of information-bearing "messages," while hearers and readers are "receivers" and "decoders." According to Donald MacKay, "In communication between human beings . . . the problem is ultimately the production in one reasoning-mechanism of a representation—a pattern—already present in another reasoning mechanism" (46). The concern of a functionalist perspective is the efficient transmission of a content from someone who possesses it to another who doesn't by means of a medium that contains the pertinent information and enables its transfer. "Basic-skill" and technical writing programs in schools, many on-the-job training programs in business and industry, and the literacy training programs of the U.S. military, which prepare soldiers to comprehend field manuals or other writings pertinent to their job specialties, all typically find their rationalization in the argument for functional literacy, in each case presuming that the ultimate value of language lies in its utilitarian capacity to pass information back and forth for economic or other material gain.

The functionalist argument has the advantage of tying reading and writing abilities to explicit contexts of use, appealing to concrete needs rather than to generalized exhortations about self-improvement, the joys of a cultivated life, or the possibility of changing an unfair world. It appears to promise socioeconomic benefit, a measure of personal freedom and success available from the mastery of marketable tools, to anyone who will strive to achieve the appropriate "minimal competency." Hunter and Harman define functional literacy as "the possession of skills perceived as necessary by particular persons and groups to fulfill their own self-determined objectives as family and community members, citizens, consumers, job-holders, and members of social, religious, or other associations" (7). The functionalist argument has a more hidden advantage as well, at least from the standpoint of those whose literacy is more than minimal: it safeguards the socioeconomic status quo. Whatever the rhetoric of its advocates concerning the "self-determined objectives" of people seeking to acquire minimal competence, functionalism serves the world as it is, inviting "outsiders" to enter that world on the terms of its insiders by fitting themselves to roles that they are somewhat free to choose but that have been preprepared as a range of acceptable alternatives. The soldier will know how to repair an MX missile by reading the field manual but will not question the use of such weapons because of her reading of antimilitarist philosophers; the renter will be able to read at least the dark print on a lease and sign at the bottom but will not necessarily be able to write a letter of grievance to, or still less a legal document bringing suit against, a powerful, self-interested landlord; the clerk will be able to fill out and file his order form but will not therefore be "qualified" for a position in "upper" management.

In short, the tendency of a functionalist perspective is to accept a given social order, to perceive it as right if not as inevitable, and to insist sincerely on the necessity of "training" individuals to take useful places in it. Just as workers were once prepared for specific tasks on the assembly lines of the industrial economy, they are now prepared for suitable jobs in the information economy; the skill has changed but the pecking order and the worker's field of vision have not. American functionalists are prone to an aggressive defense of their conservative reality, often reminding fellow citizens of their obligation to beat the Russians to satellite warfare (if the Russians are still interested) and the Japanese to better televisions, or warning citizens of the economic peril they face if workers are unqualified, or scolding teachers who are ignoring "basic skills" and "higher order reasoning," thereby contributing to incompetence, waste, and inefficiency in the marketplace. Functionalist arguments, frequently mounted by leaders of business and industry, and therefore also by congressional panels and government commissions, leaven a rhetoric of technological progressivism (as in Boyer's *High School*) with a mixture of fear and patriotism (as in *A Nation at Risk*) in order to defend a social program that maintains managerial classes—whose members are usually far more than just "functionally" literate—in their customary places at the top of the economic pyramid, while outfitting workers with the reading and writing "skills" that have lately supplanted the tool-press, hammer-and-nail, smelting, and welding skills of a now outmoded industrial age.

"Cultural literacy" constitutes a second "representation" of the importance of reading and writing abilities, one frequently offered by traditionalist university educators but popularly sustained as well among individuals and social groups who feel insecure about their own standing and future prospects when confronted by the volatile mix of ethnic heritages and socioeconomic interests that make up contemporary American life. The argument for cultural literacy aims to move beyond a limited conception of "basic skills" and toward an affirmation of supposedly stable and timeless cultural values inscribed in the verbal memory, in particular the canonical literature, of (primarily) Western European society. Its reasoning is that "true" literacy entails more than technical proficiency and also more than a minimal ability to earn a living and make one's way in the world: that literacy also includes an awareness of cultural heritage, a capacity for "higher-order" thinking, a contemplative ability and some aesthetic discernment, a feel for the richer meanings of literature and philosophy (meanings that depend on artistic, religious, historical, and other areas of knowledge not immediately accessible to the reader who is merely able to "decode" the words on a page without grasping their context). Language is no mere tool or instrument in this view, but is regarded reverently as the repository of cultural values and a source of social cohesion as long as it remains undefiled by the insidious erosions of vulgar usage and dialectal variation. In its populist versions, cultural literacy features a protectionist regard for English as the "proper" American language, exhorting the citizenry to write "correctly" as well as functionally, the way George Orwell ("Politics and the English Language") and William Strunk (*Elements of Style*) would wish, to read the "best" works of the English-speaking world (and of Western civilization generally, but in English translation as a rule), and to insist on English as the language of commerce and political life. Spanish, Chinese, and other "alien" tongues need not be altogether excluded from American life, but they are to have no public legitimacy and are therefore to be discouraged in schools and other institutional settings. The economic self-interest that pervades the functionalist perspective gives way here to a broader, and potentially more alarming, ethnocentrism, presuming that the salvation of some set of favored cultural values lies necessarily in the marginalizing or even extinction of others.

The argument for cultural literacy frequently wins support by enfolding itself within a myth of the Fall from Grace. Language, and by extension culture, though they once enjoyed the perfection of an Eden-like existence, are currently in danger of collapse because of internal decay and sundry forces of barbarism. People no longer speak, read, write, or even think with the genius, the strength of insight, the majesty of which they were once capable. As serious, they no longer *remember*, and therefore no longer venerate. The age of High Culture has passed, an illustrious classical period of which the present (elder) generation is a last, faint imitation and the forthcoming (youthful) one a dismal parody. Minds and characters have been weakened by television, or rock music, or the automobile, or permissiveness, or the sixties, or narcotics, or the disintegrating family. The reasons for this present lapsarian condition vary but the message is clear: unless heritage is protected, moral fiber recovered, the former purity of language reconstituted, the (past) life of art and philosophy retrieved, we stand in jeopardy of cultural disintegration, the final descent into chaos and desolation. Whatever the plausibility of such gloomy projections, there's no mistaking the melancholy energy of contemporary proponents of cultural literacy or, judging from the recent best-seller lists, the numbers of solemn citizens, anxious perhaps about new influxes of Mexicans, Vietnamese, and other "outsiders," who take their warnings to heart.

Arguments for cultural and functional literacy plainly dominate the American imagination at the moment, and for predictable reasons. In the main, they articulate the needs, hopes, anxieties, and frustrations of conservative ideology. They reveal in different ways the means of using an ideal of literacy in order to maintain the world as it is, a world in which the interests of the United States, and indeed particular groups within this country, dominate the interests of others, both within and without. Schools understandably reflect that conservatism, viewing themselves as agencies of socialization in accordance with the hierarchical requirements of a capitalist economy. But there are also other representations of literacy, on the margins of American educational life, which reflect the tendencies and agendas of liberal and even radical ideology—reflecting as well, therefore, the internal stresses and potentialities for change that characterize any social reality. The liberal argument emphasizes literacy for personal growth, finding voice in the so-called process-writing movement in American high schools, in such reading programs as Daniel Fader's Hooked on Books, and in arguments for educational reform that emphasize collaborative learning, "schools without walls," Montessori techniques, and other practices aimed at personalized learning. The liberal argument has been successful, up to a point, in schools because it borrows from long-hallowed American myths of self-determination, freedom of expression, and supposedly boundless personal opportunity, romantic values to which schools remain willing to pay at least lip service even when promoting more repressive curricula otherwise (hence the care to include a few moments of "free writing" in the classroom that spends much of its time laboring over grammar drills and business letters).

The assumption of a literacy-for-personal-growth argument is that language expresses the power of the individual imagination, so that nurturing reading and writing abilities offers a way to develop that imaginative power, thereby promoting the progress of society through the progress of the individual learner. The political agenda behind this story, therefore, tends to be educational change, since it places personal learning ahead of rigid socialization, inevitably drawing attention to school practices that thwart the needs of individual learners or disenfranchise certain groups in the interest of maintaining values of the status quo. Other forms of social change are also encouraged, through a belief that institutions naturally repress imagination in their own defense, so that the freeing of imagination through learning cannot help but lead toward a reconstituting of those institutions. The kinds of change that the personal-growth argument recommends are, on the whole, socially tolerable (albeit uncomfortable for some) because they are basically moderate in character. Using the rhetoric of moral sincerity, the argument speaks compassionately on behalf of those who have not fared well in American socioeconomic life. Meanwhile, it avoids, for the most part, the suggestion of any fundamental restructuring of institutions, believing that the essential generosity, adventuresomeness, and fair-mindedness of American society will accommodate some liberalization of "outmoded" curricula, even an improved quality of life for the less fortunate, as long as general political and economic interests are not jeopardized. Frequently, Americans do hear such appeals, though always in the context of an implicit agreement that nothing very important is going to change. Accordingly, advocates of "expressive writing," personalized reading programs, "whole language" curricula, and "open" classrooms have been given modest room in schools to carry out their educational programs, with politicians and school officials quick to realize the ultimate gain in administrative control that comes from allowing the illusion of self-determination to release any pressures of dissatisfaction that can build up in otherwise oppressive school settings. Such programs have become, in effect, the coffee breaks of the educational workplace.

A fourth argument, substantially to the left of personal-growth advocates, is one for "critical literacy," a radical perspective whose adherents, notably Paulo Freire (*Pedagogy of the Oppressed*), have been more influential to date in the third world, especially Latin America, than in the United States. As our statements—representations—have already made plain, we sympathize with this story in particular, but not without the reservations that properly derive from habits of "critical" reflection. Strongly influenced by Marxist philosophical premises, and more recently reconceptualized in feminist and postmodern theory, critical literacy is not a particularly welcome perspective in this country and finds voice currently in only a few university enclaves, where it too often exists more as theory than practice, and an even smaller number of community-based literacy projects, typically concerned with adult learners. Its agenda is to identify reading and writing abilities with a "critical consciousness" of the social conditions in which people find themselves, recognizing the extent to which language practices articulate—objectify—and rationalize those conditions, as well as the extent to which those with the political power to "name the world" come to dominate those whose voices they have been able to silence, marginalize, or appropriate. Literacy therefore constitutes a means to "empowerment," a way to voice discontent and seek political enfranchisement, not in the naive belief that merely being literate is sufficient to change the distribution of power, but in the knowledge that the ability to speak is dialectically related to the authority to speak, and that the authority to speak alone enables entrance to the public discourses in which power is negotiated. In parts of the world where "illiteracy"—in the sense of rudimentary incapacity to read and write—is widespread, the achieving of literacy among populations that have been economically oppressed has entailed social revolution on a scale unknown and probably unattainable in more broadly literate Western nations. But the potential for radical social change, specifically for a reconstituting of economic practices and institutions that assist the hegemony of certain groups and the oppression of others, remains an ideological commitment of the argument for critical literacy as much in the United States as elsewhere. For that reason, if for no other, it will remain suspect as a theoretical enterprise and will be considered dangerous, perhaps to the point of illegality, in proportion as its American adherents attempt to implement it conspicuously either in schools or in other social contexts. The scholarly right has signaled this institutional hostility in attacks on Jonathan Kozol's *Illiterate America*, the most popular American rendering of critical literacy arguments, for its alarming (opponents say wildly inaccurate) statistics about illiteracy, calculatedly patronizing Kozol's "enthusiasm" for radical change. The National Association of Scholars has, more recently, mounted some aggressive campaigns against critical teachers— Linda Brodkey, for instance, whose writing program at the University of Texas, Austin (which featured critical readings of legal and legislative documents pertaining to equal rights as well as other social issues) was challenged effectively enough to cause a weak-kneed University administration to back away from approvals that had already been recommended in its own governance committees. Meanwhile, although critical literacy is trendy in some left-leaning academic circles, those who commend it also draw their wages from the capitalist economic system it's designed to challenge. Whether those comfortable academics will, with Kozol, take the risks of bringing so volatile a practice into community schools (that is, beyond their well-protected university classrooms), whether they will take their political values past the threshold at which powerful counterinterests tell them they must stop, is a matter still in doubt. At the same time, if such a practice were to find its way into educational contexts—local literacy projects, community action groups, labor unions—in which the dispossessed themselves, with considerably less to lose, have opportunity to set educational priorities, and the solidarity to enforce them, a fully politicized literacy might well become a more plausible goal. Moreover, if social equality (which will always entail struggle for change) through literacy is conceived of, not in melodramatic revolutionary terms, but in the pragmatic terms of stubborn advocacy, continuing conversation, and small gains, the possibility that critical literacy will come to have a measure of influence in American educational and political life may be less fantastic than its least temperate advocates have made it appear.

We could multiply examples indefinitely. The variety is astonishing and it serves to underline our point, that definitions don't tell with metaphysical certainty what literacy is, but only what somebody with the power to speak wants or needs it to be. What makes any such representation powerful is the ability of its adherents to make it appear invisible, or at least transparent, a window on the world, revealing simple and stable truths, so that the only problem still needing to be addressed is one of implementation: how best to make the world—other people—conform to that prevailing vision. The reverse is true as well. What makes any ideology visible as such, and therefore properly limited in its power to compel unconscious assent, is scrutiny and critique, the only safeguards human beings have if they are to participate freely in negotiating the world. To the extent that literacy advocates of one stripe or another, or teachers of reading and writing, remain unconscious of their ideological dispositions, their "offerings" of skills constitute a form of colonizing, a way of making others more like themselves, a paternal act that rationalizes the control of others by representing it as a means of liberation (see Stuckey). To the extent that the nonliterate allow themselves to be objects of someone else's "kindness" instead of subjects who articulate, and demand the right to articulate, their realities, they will find no power in their literacy, however it is defined, but only altered terms of dispossession. When, for instance, the memberships of U.S. English and English First, totaling around half a million citizens, argue for the compulsory English "literacy" of the American population, they may well intend the enfranchisement of those whose lack of English language abilities has depressed their economic opportunities; but they also intend the extinction of cultural values inscribed in languages other than their own and held to be worthwhile by people different from themselves. In the case of this, or any other, position on literacy, its advocates, no less than its intended beneficiaries, need to hear, for all our sakes, a critique of whatever assumptions and beliefs are fueling their passionate benevolence.

Chapter Two

The Real Political Correctness

It is common in universities today to hear talk of politically correct opinions, or PC for short. These are questions that are not really open to argument. It takes real courage to oppose the campus orthodoxy. To tell you the truth, I was a student during the days of McCarthy, and there is less freedom now than there was then.

Donald Kagan, Dean of
Arts and Sciences,
Yale University, quoted in
D'Souza

Our university campuses are now islands of repression in a sea of freedom.

Abigail Thernstrom,
political scientist, formerly
at Harvard University,
quoted in D'Souza

Because universities have exhausted the patience of the most sympathetic advocates of the victim's revolution, the backlash against preferential treatment and sensitivity education will continue to get worse. Nobody will say so, but the truth is that a large number of students and faculty have had it with minority double standards and intimidation. Until they change their policies, universities are likely to see a dramatic increase in racial tension and racial

*incidents, with a corresponding upsurge of violence. The
worst is yet to come.*

Dinesh D'Souza,
Illiberal Education

There are two stories abroad about the concept of "critical teaching"—two "representations" of its assumptions, values, purposes—
and the stories couldn't be more at odds. The version told by
proponents holds that the aim of liberatory pedagogy is social justice,
a democratic society in which diversity along axes of gender, race,
class, and ethnicity is allowed to flourish, differences all intact,
instead of being repudiated by appeal to fictions of "the melting pot,"
or attacked by appeal to monolithic definitions of culture, or unfairly
regimented by appeal to meritocratic and other hierarchical social
orders. Critical teaching, so this story goes, seeks to enfranchise
historically subordinate, and therefore oppressed, groups by means
of instructional emphases and tactics that focus the attention of
students from all backgrounds on the value of "difference" as well as
on the social practices (like discrimination in the workplace) and
institutional arrangements (like segregated schools) responsible for
subordination. It also accepts a curricular obligation to encourage
people of good will, both those who have enjoyed privilege and those
who haven't, to challenge inequities that have demonstrably harmed
portions of the community. The story related by opponents, however,
proceeds in another way. According to its account, critical teaching
is an "illiberal pedagogy" whose goal is "political correctness" (a
restrictive, dogmatic fidelity to "*au courant*" prescriptions of leftist
ideology) and whose advocates are "thought police" or "tenured
radicals," political activists formed in the naive and/or unscrupulous
sixties who have lately come of age, are threatening to take over
higher education, and have begun, in their uncompromising zeal for
dramatic social change, to pose a serious threat to free speech, tolerance, and other democratic virtues. Radical teachers and administrators, enacting crudely political agendas, are pushing "diversity" and
"multicultural" curricula, so this story goes, at the expense of traditional emphases on the intellectual and aesthetic achievements of
Western civilization. They are also compromising time-honored
standards of excellence by opening student admissions and faculty
hiring policies in order to bring "minorities," whether able or not,
into colleges and universities. Ultimately, they are feathering their

own nests, fattening their paychecks and resumes, by climbing onto the "sensitivity" bandwagon, instead of offering real economic or social advantage to the groups they claim to sponsor.

We're obliged to read this second, negative story with all seriousness, because we must respect its influence even though we reject its themes and characterizations. Two facts seem to us unmistakable. One is that the negative story speaks authoritatively to large numbers of American citizens who regard themselves as politically moderate and generally sympathetic to values of educational excellence. The negative story has pushed all the right buttons to ensure its success: patriotism, freedom of speech, individual opportunity, free enterprise, objective standards, intellectual rigor, the supremacy of Western culture, the dangers of creeping radicalism. But it's the other fact that is really important: most citizens haven't been permitted to judge for themselves the comparative merits of the stories because they haven't heard both of them. The two neither exist on an equal footing nor compete fairly with each other in any forum of public appraisal. Instead, one of them has silenced—or more accurately has appropriated the telling of—the other, so that its success offers a dramatic illustration of the politics of representation, the means by which powerful groups construct their versions of "real life," suppress or manipulate alternatives, and maintain their authority over public consciousness. The first story has been framed for Americans almost exclusively in the terms of the second, so that it has been made to appear from the outset, not merely wrongheaded, but unpatriotic, extremist—indeed, un-American.

The key to effective representation in American culture is media control. As advertising agencies, special interest groups, and campaigns for public office have long recognized, the most persuasive storytellers in American life today are the popular media, television in particular but also radio, magazines, newspapers, and commercial publishers. Whoever has access to the media controls thereby the production and distribution of images, the composing of arguments (preferably in simplified, memorable "sound bites"), and the endorsement of conventional truths. If anyone doubts which of the two stories about critical teaching is more compelling to ordinary Americans, which more substantially "names the world," let that person look to media depictions, from television talk shows to books on the best-seller lists. There can be no serious dispute that the second story narrates the beliefs of mainstream America, not only in what it attacks but more importantly in what it implicitly affirms along the way. To be sure, the media don't present an ideological monolith: the *Washington Post* and the *New York Post* don't speak with one voice. But occasional op-ed liberalism notwithstanding, the media are corporately owned, dependent on commercial advertising, and broadly responsive to a climate of public opinion in which "moderate" and "conservative" are virtually indistinguishable political values. Not surprisingly, therefore, the media have effectively ensured that their "customers" encounter alternative stories about critical teaching primarily in bastardized versions within the dominant story. We want to argue, therefore, that this second story sponsors the real "political correctness" in educational life today, even though its representational privilege has enabled it to claim otherwise. We want to spell out that other, "real" correctness here because the range of popular attitudes that it encompasses offers material grounds on which to argue the compelling need for a critical pedagogy in American schools.

No one who has read a newspaper editorial page, watched a Sunday morning television news program, or seen a popular magazine devoted in some part to educational issues could have failed in recent years to come across arguments opposing what Dinesh D'Souza has effectively labeled "illiberal education" and what pundits across the American ideological spectrum from George Will to Sam Donaldson have called "political correctness." Throughout the 1980s, coincidentally or not paralleling eight years of Reaganite reactionary politics, increasing numbers of ugly, sometimes violent race- and gender-related confrontations occurred on college campuses, ranging from a fraternity "slave auction" at the University of Wisconsin, Madison, to a hate letter directed to black students at the Yale Law School (signed "Yale Students for Racism"), to a rising incidence of gay bashing and date rape. Several universities, Wisconsin, Michigan, Brown, among others, implemented legislation, not always wisely, intended to curb and punish the violence of prejudice, including the linguistic violence of derogatory speech. A great many schools began quickening efforts, often already underway, to introduce curricular changes that emphasized issues of diversity and multiculturalism in the name of intellectual no less than social responsibility. These legislative and curricular actions served as principal catalyst for a media show, beginning at the end of the decade, that soon encompassed far more than just local efforts to combat intolerance. The actual incidents behind both the legislation and the new urgency of curricular reform were speedily erased as mass-media attention, reflecting public impatience with gender and race "oversensitiveness," began giving free play to pent-up conservative fears, grievances, and frustrations regarding equal opportunity and the (seemingly) changing face of the American socioeconomic no less than educational scene. Criticism broadened gradually from issues of free speech (the most legitimate ground of dispute since some school legislation certainly did err in its attempts to strong-arm bigotry into silence) to include equal-opportunity hiring practices in the academy, "minority" admissions policies, new forms of curricula, including African American, Hispanic, and Women's Studies programs, assaults on the canon of Western "great books," forms of literary theory that entail challenge to the assumptions of classical hermeneutics, and pedagogical styles that make visible the broadly political nature of schools and teaching.

Between the winter of 1990 and spring of 1991, mass media began to devote unprecedented effort to "naming" a range of "liberal" (meaning leftist) educational beliefs and practices in blatantly reproachful terms that they could reasonably assume would appeal to the public at large. In December 1990, *Newsweek* gave extensive coverage to criticism of "political correctness" (PC), as did *The New Republic* in February of 1991, *The New York Times Magazine* during the same month, and *The Atlantic* in March. Two books from commercial presses, one published in 1990, the other a year later, gave substantial focus, if not primary impetus, to this media attention, the first by Roger Kimball titled *Tenured Radicals*, the second by Dinesh D'Souza titled *Illiberal Education: The Politics of Race and Sex on Campus*, which the columnist James Kilpatrick called "the most important work of non-fiction in many months" (Albany *Times Union*, April 15, 1991). Popular news programs, such as *This Week with David Brinkley*, featured "extended" discussion (five minutes or more, a lifetime by television standards), syndicated columnists from Cal Thomas to Alan Derschowitz weighed in with their views, and, late that spring, President Bush entered the fray with remarks as commencement speaker at the University of Michigan deploring PC and any legislative effort on campuses to restrain racist and other degenerate forms of free speech. Through the same period, the National Association of Scholars, a political lobby of conservative academics based in Princeton but with a national membership, undertook watchdog responsibilities on college campuses to ensure that the educational values of the ideological right continued substantially unopposed in matters of university governance as well as curriculum.

What was conspicuously, but not surprisingly, missing in all the media brouhaha was any sustained public argument from people who actually practice critical pedagogy or can claim some part in elaborating its theory. With the possible exception of Jonathan Kozol, who hinted at some of the activities of liberatory teaching in *Illiterate America*, published for general audiences in 1985, the American public is altogether unfamiliar with the actual work of critical educators, never having read, or even heard of, Paulo Freire, Bell Hooks, Ira Shor, Maxine Greene, Henry Giroux, the work of the Ontario

Institute for Studies in Education or the Birmingham Centre for Contemporary Cultural Studies, or *Radical Teacher*, published by the Boston Women's Teachers' Group. Just as well, perhaps, since the combination of alienating Marxist or postmodern rhetoric and perversely inaccessible prose that are, it seems, the unhappy hallmarks of most critical teaching theory would do little to persuade, or even mollify, average Americans whose commonsense knowledge about everyday life is wholly at odds with what they would find in that theory. But our point is that the popular "debate" about critical teaching has never been truly a debate at all, although there has been abundant talk. Critical teachers and theorists have had little if any access to the popular media except as objects of its attention.

To be sure, a handful of "spokespersons" have been occasionally named as characters within the negative story. Favorites include the self-promoters at Duke, sometimes called "the Fish bowl" after Stanley Fish, the head promoter. Fish is especially titillating, therefore popular in the media because he demonizes the left with his wickedly trivial intellectual anarchism. Now and then, these characters are allowed a limited opportunity to say something—whenever the storyteller could gain from remarks that appeared either inflammatory or stupid or both. But just as often such theorists and teachers assume a mute background presence, as in the case of Linda Brodkey, who is named in a November 1990 *Chronicle of Higher Education* attack on her critical practices at the University of Texas but never allowed to explain their purpose (opponents had plenty to say). When David Brinkley hosted a program on "political correctness," he included three college presidents (among them Leon Botstein, whose bow tie and eccentricities make him a media darling like Fish), along with the ubiquitous William Bennett and of course George Will, Sam Donaldson, and the other regulars, all of whom naturally deplored it, but no nationally recognized advocate of critical pedagogy. When a *Firing Line* hour-long special offered "debate" on questions regarding free speech on college campuses, Stanley Fish was back (again), among others, opposed by William Buckley and John Silber (admittedly, as much a caricature of the right as Botstein is of the left), among others, but no practitioner of critical pedagogy appeared. What transpired was a parody of discussion, a ritual combat of empty, slogan-filled positions and sadly comic images: Silber stuttering indignantly at the impropriety of words like "chair" for "chairman" ("a woman is not a chair," he said) and a haughty and melodramatic Catharine Stimpson scolding diminutive Dinesh D'Souza like a wicked school boy. And so our point: whether given a limited speaking role, or only allowed a walk-on appearance, or never being named at all except in such malevolent corporate refer-

ences as "thought police," critical teachers don't tell their own stories; they are spoken of and spoken for, rendered evil or pious or silly,
but otherwise silent. Of course, they *have* told their stories elsewhere,
outside the popular media, in the pages of academic journals, in
books published by relatively obscure presses such as Bergin and
Garvey or Boynton/Cook. They might reach an audience of several
hundred or even a few thousand over several years. Meanwhile,
Dinesh D'Souza, whose critique of PC was published by Macmillan,
has reached the best-seller lists (along with Allan Bloom and E. D.
Hirsch, of whom more later). His acknowledgments offer thanks to
his book agent, who "defended my pecuniary interests."

The politics of mass-media representation couldn't be more conspicuous. Much of what critical teaching stands for, in its positive
depiction, is antithetical to the values and commitments of the corporate sponsors of American storytelling. The ideology of the mass
media is saturated with what Edmund Sullivan has called the "social
mythology of capitalism," which includes an allegiance to passive
consumerism, rather than active engagement in the construction of
social life, and a long-standing hostility to practices of critical inquiry, certainly including liberatory pedagogy but also, historically,
the challenges of labor unions, feminists, gays, environmental activists, and anyone else posing a conceivable threat to economic interests and managerial hierarchies that the media help to maintain. The
media create images of needs and desires, images of status and social
expectation, images of benevolent producers of goods showering the
fruits of free enterprise on hungry and grateful citizens. Its programming serves its advertising, enforcing notions of The Good Life and
the values of The American Way. Sanitized sitcom representations of
the family, game-show celebrations of greed and easy money, violent
dramas legitimizing mayhem when the cause is "just," sports con-
tests showing off a misleading handful of black millionaires, electronic preachers asking donations from the poor and elderly, are
framed on all sides by deodorants, sports cars, lite beers, and hemor-
rhoid treatments. News programs on television, regardless of political slant, are small islands dotting the sea of consumer
acquisitiveness; commercial sponsors pay for them and pay also,
indirectly, the large salaries of glamorous talking heads who "give"
the news to passive viewers in small, digestible nuggets between
commercial breaks. Other media—radio, magazines—are successful
primarily in their ability to approximate the standards of television
as a preeminent sales and entertainment vehicle.

Meanwhile, critical teaching aims to redress grievances by directing attention toward institutions and practices, including the mass
media themselves, that have produced grievances. It aims to promote

an active citizenry that might question whether every American really has, or should even want, equal access to the fantasies of The Good Life that the media strive to sell. Little wonder if newspapers, magazines, and television find liberatory pedagogy a jeopardizing presence; and little wonder, given their substantial (though not absolute) control of public information, that they would take full advantage of their authority to represent the world in terms favorable to their interests. Because of the power of mass media to constitute simplified images of "reality" and sell them to the American public, terms such as "political correctness" and "illiberal education" have quickly won acceptance as the normal and proper ways of referring to critical pedagogy, without the slightest suspicion, amidst all the talk, that public dialogue has never actually occurred. Nor is there any suspicion that the "PC" of media manufacture might be a falsification projecting onto critical teaching the practices of "thought control" at which the media themselves are so subtly adept, while also deflecting attention from the real substance of "political correctness," the "common sense" of American life that explains all the negative media attention.

Since "political correctness" has been by far the most successful sound-bite-size nugget fed to consumers as representation of critical teaching, it merits the closest scrutiny. D'Souza alone, grasping the potential in sound-bite rhetoric, has become a cottage industry for producing additional nuggets—"the victim's revolution," "the new censorship," "tyranny of the minority," "the new racism"—but nothing else has the cache of "PC." The term refers ironically to left-wing "right thinking," making clear that it's actually "wrong thinking," while hinting at coercion among those who engage in it. The term intends to disparage in a vague, comic way that allows the issues of critical pedagogy to be dismissed without the discomfort of having to engage them. So the term has essentially a preemptive function: it casts the advocates of critical teaching in a sneering light that enables opponents, by rote evocation, to sabotage the potential for seriousness in attempts to explain what the issues actually are. This tactic is not, of course, used only against the political left; the expression "star wars" has had a similar function, used to depict Ronald Reagan's efforts to subsidize a "strategic defense" technology. In effect, the question becomes negatively loaded from mere mention of the phrase—and loaded not by allusion to counterargument but by a comic or sarcastic connotation that makes it intrinsically silly as well as wrongheaded. We don't fault the tactic in itself (nor will we shrink from turning it, presently, back on its users). We fault the abuse of power that underlies its use by those who have the authority and standing to dismiss questions that require serious address.

In its darkest employment, after all, the catchphrase "political correctness" enables the still unspeakable, even for the political right, to move quietly closer to articulation: it names the mollycoddling of academically "incompetent" students of color (who "should never have been admitted to colleges in the first place"); it names the mollycoddling of annoyingly "aggressive" feminists, as well as embarrassingly visible gay men and lesbians, who think that colleges ought to make space for people who are insufficiently male and/or heterosexual; it names attempts to foster on college campuses more respect for human diversity than exists in American life at large; it names the use of political power by progressive faculty and administrators—who have just a little—to implement their views, as though the use of power by the Department of Education, the National Endowment for the Humanities, state legislatures, local school boards, and the National Association of Scholars were their own exclusive prerogative. These are the kinds of meanings that can lurk behind references to PC, a phrase intended to end conversations before they start; to ridicule what is and ought to remain quite serious; to preempt, override, and regulate—all in the name of repudiating "thought police."

At base, PC is a representation that serves the same kind of function that "reverse discrimination" serves: in its critique, it lays claim to a set of values historically underlying certain ameliorative practices in order to underwrite opposite, reactionary practices, thereby appearing to seize the moral high ground in defending positions that have long been convicted of immorality. Where "reverse discrimination" appeals to values of fairness and equality in order to maintain the economic privileges of white, male, middle-class society despite widespread understanding of race- and gender-motivated disparities in employment practices, so PC appeals to values of free speech and pluralism in order to ensure that universities (in particular) retain their character as protectors of a meritocracy established by and created for certain favored groups. The *topos* underlying PC arguments is substantially the same as that underlying "reverse discrimination" arguments: namely, the abuser claiming to be abused. The historical makeup of American higher education—its privileging of some groups of people over others, its responsiveness to the cultural heritages of some over others, its ignoring of intellectual and aesthetic traditions outside its mainstream—is a matter of extensive public record and hardly a disputed question (even PC critics like D'Souza feel pressure to admit that there are rudimentary issues of fairness at stake in college admissions and employment policies, though they do so mainly to retain rhetorical advantage). Yet the opponents of liberatory pedagogy press on regardless to insist that changing the situation will undermine "intellectual integrity," "differential merit," and "programmatic quality," as these have been defined by historically favored groups, in effect "abusing" those groups by altering fundamental educational values (which "everyone" should cherish) along with their privilege. The consequence of PC and reverse discrimination arguments alike is preservation of the status quo. The crude reasoning is: if changing an unjust situation can only be bought at the price of making those who have profited from it less comfortable, better not to change it. If somebody has to be privileged, better white guys than anyone else.

What, then, is the "real" political correctness that lurks underneath and directs the charges against critical pedagogy? A close reading of D'Souza's Illiberal Education reveals it clearly enough. D'Souza's principal rhetorical tactic is to manipulate scale, making small issues look like large ones and large like small, a tactic consistent with the pattern of logical reversals on which PC arguments are built. One trick, for instance, is to detail a steady procession of inflammatory anecdotes (effective, as television is, at persuading by means of simplified, concrete images): in one chapter, students of color receiving preferential treatment; in another, school administrations enacting unwise rules against free speech; elsewhere, incidents of black students' intolerance toward whites; in another place, faculty arguing poorly about the importance of multicultural curricula; and in yet another, radical students making sophomoric demands to dismantle Western culture. The point is to create an implication that these events, remarks, policies are happening everywhere, are normative, are always justified as foolishly as they are in the examples. Meanwhile, smaller numbers of anecdotes (revealing, for instance, the hostility of white students toward those of color) are included to create the impression of fairness to both sides but are quickly overwhelmed, both in size and detail, by those that help to make D'Souza's case. There is, of course, nothing wrong with marshaling evidence for one's own position: D'Souza is frequently correct about the abuses he details—they happen and they shouldn't. He is also correct about the complexities that attend admitting nontraditional students, hiring by affirmative action, legislating democratic conduct, introducing new curricula, and generally making space where none existed before for people whose cultural, social, and educational backgrounds ensure a difficult "fit" with the traditional collegiate population. Where he's wrong—but cleverly so—is in manipulating scale to suggest that the abuses, errors, and faulty reasoning that have attended good-faith efforts to recognize and allow for cultural diversity in schools are more serious, in kind as well as number, than the abuses that those efforts have been struggling to remedy. The historical subjugation of black and Hispanic people, and of women as well, within institutions of slavery and servitude is more pervasive, more harmful, and less conscious of its own error than the excesses that D'Souza has found in equal-opportunity hiring or multicultural curricula. One wouldn't know that, however, from reading him. Where he's also wrong is in supposing that a bad situation should be left the way it is until the alternatives achieve perfection. He's wrong in these views, but he speaks a majority opinion: these subtly prejudicial attitudes are part of the *real* political correctness (RPC) that informs American life.

We would state the first, most general tenet of RPC this way: demonstrably harmful practices or institutions—the preferential hiring of white males, let's say—should nevertheless remain in place if a proposed solution appears to take some privilege away from those who have traditionally enjoyed it. Alternative practices or institutions, like equal opportunity, that have some flaws but that nonetheless respond to greater abuses should be discarded rather than critiqued and steadily improved. Problems should stay as they are until perfect solutions to them can be found. D'Souza continually falls back on this first principle of American "correct thinking." In a chapter on admissions policy at Berkeley, he details, over several pages, an incident in which an Asian student was denied entry to the University because he didn't rank as highly within the category of Asian applicants as other students did in their own "minority" categories (usually meaning black and Hispanic students), even though, in terms of straight individual merit, his "test scores and grades" were higher than those of some students who were admitted. "Here was an extraordinary state of affairs," D'Souza exclaims. "While professing its commitment to 'equal opportunity,' Berkeley seemed to operate separate racial tracks in its admissions process, resulting in the University 'putting a lid on the number of Asians' " (25). As a result, D'Souza concludes, "a preferential treatment program instituted to help minorities appeared to be hurting a minority group.... Quotas which were intended as instruments of inclusion now seemed to function as instruments of *exclusion*" (29). D'Souza is skilled in discovering the paradoxes, contradictions, unresolved difficulties, and bureaucratic clumsiness in equal-opportunity admissions projects. He may have found a good instance here (it's certainly more effective than a humdrum example of some white student losing out at Berkeley); and even if he hasn't, we'd concede that he would eventually come across more than one. But since he invests all his energy in finding such examples and no energy at all in preserving the goals of such projects while remedying their deficiencies, we must assume that he labors the difficulties exclusively in order to discredit the projects. His intent is not to find creative solutions to admissions problems but rather to reject the idea of affirmative action.

Another of D'Souza's manipulations of scale is to spend thirty-four pages complaining about the decision at Stanford to introduce a sequence of three required courses on "Cultures, Ideas, and Values" that would offer some attention to non-Western perspectives, so that readers are left with the impression that the lights of Western civilization are winking out on American college campuses (59–93). He concedes that the Stanford approach "would include Western perspectives" but points out that limitations on the number of texts treatable in a semester means that "the relative importance of Western thinkers would be . . . reduced" (61). All true enough, of course, in the narrow context of the CIV program. But what he leaves out is the fact that undergraduates in American universities typically take around forty courses, 120 credits, over four years; that "general education" programs of the sort Stanford has implemented range from a half-dozen courses, eighteen credits, to perhaps a dozen, thirty-six credits, only a few of which involve diversity or multicultural issues (like the nine credits at Stanford); that the Stanford program offers eight course options under the CIV requirement, only one of which includes the reading list that particularly offends D'Souza; that university curricula, including general education, are steeped in the values, beliefs, assumptions, historical periods, major texts, and intellectual as well as aesthetic achievements of Western civilization; that nearly all "major fields" assume a Western orientation; and that the vast majority of university faculty have done most of their learning, and continue to do all of their teaching, from the disciplinary and methodological vantage points of the West. Diversity and multicultural programs are almost embarrassingly modest efforts to include non-European and nonpatriarchal perspectives: at our institution a single course in "human diversity," three credits, is required in an undergraduate preparation of 120 credits—less than three percent of a student's intellectual experience. Meanwhile, more ambitious offerings such as Women's Studies or African American Studies remain relatively small enterprises at most schools, including our own, compared with departments of English, history, physics, or philosophy. They frequently exist on grants and other "soft money," frequently have no independent hiring lines or tenure authority, frequently can't offer a major or a graduate curriculum, and nearly always borrow many of their faculty as well as courses from more firmly established programs. In the face of all this, D'Souza wants his audience to believe that CIV at Stanford signals the decline of the West. The process is "already far advanced," he says, "of downplaying or expelling the core curriculum of Western classics in favor of a non-Western and minority-oriented agenda" (247).

This leads us to a second principle of RPC: established institutions and practices, favoring the dominant white, Eurocentric, middle-class, masculinist culture, are natural and just; anything else is eccentric, erroneous, and biased toward particular groups. More specifically, the historically dominant curriculum in schools exists because of the intrinsic merit of its subject matter, while alternative curricula exist because of special pleading and political pressure. Any attempt, however modest, to encroach upon the settled, predominantly Western focus of collegiate curricula is to be resisted as a dangerous precedent heralding the collapse of Western values, the compromise of intellectual standards, and the introduction of clearly inferior academic materials. D'Souza offers a blizzard of arguments for maintaining the dominance of the West: many other cultures (certainly African, for instance) lack the developed intellectual and ethical traditions of the West (79; 83–84; 115–21); some other cultures have merit but Western faculty don't know enough about them to introduce them well (81); false claims of superiority are being put forward in the name of non-Western cultures (115–21); faculty are viewing these cultures through prisms of Western ideological bias (81); other cultures are just as racist and sexist as Western society, if not more so (79)—Mohammed, after all, was a polygamist who owned slaves (84); other cultures have legitimate intellectual achievements but multicultural curricula are introducing bad or mediocre examples as canonical reading (73–75); Western culture has espoused all the best values that other societies have, so there's no reason not to emphasize its achievements (89–91). The bottom line is that "core curricula" should introduce the legacy of Western civilization, that there are fixed "standards of merit" (87) available to explain why *Othello* belongs in the canon while *The Color Purple* and *I, Rigoberta Menchu* do not, that "great" non-Western books, like the *Analects* of Confucius or the *Tale of Genji,* might have a modest place, though not at the expense of Shakespeare and Euripides, and that any more serious effort to cater to "the victim's revolution" would represent, in the words of William Bennett, a curriculum "brought low by the forces of ignorance, irrationality and intimidation" (68).

But the real issue for D'Souza is not poor teaching, infected by ignorance or ideology; if it were, his position would be that Stanford and other like-minded institutions need to hire smarter, more diverse, more open-minded, more scholarly faculty for the good of the CIV course and the rest of the curriculum alike. Even less is the real issue poor text selection from the heritage of other cultures; if it were, he would argue for Confucius over Elisabeth Burgos-Debray and have done with it. These issues together would hardly take up the two chapters he devotes to abuses in multicultural education. It isn't even all that important to D'Souza that multicultural curricula are offering "myths" in the service of enhancing the self-images of minority students, such as the problematic claim that Egypt has an African rather than Middle Eastern culture whose philosophical tradition anticipates the achievements of Greece and Rome (115–20). If it were, he would be as relentlessly critical of the dominant Western curriculum, with its myths about the superiority of European culture over the others it has colonized, of men over women, of science over art, rationality over emotion, technology over nature, Christianity over "paganism." In fact, he would be more critical of the Western curriculum because it has misled larger numbers of people over a longer period of time with more apparent damage. What's really on his mind is none of these; it is instead the insistent demand coming from women and "minority" groups for representations of them-selves in a curriculum that has traditionally excluded them. What's really on his mind is the provocative questioning of familiar, time-honored, and evidently biased images of people and the world that traditional, exclusively Western academic narratives have been offer-ing students through the years. Bad enough, in his view, that Shake-speare should be read for issues of gender or racial insensitivity; but when non-Western texts are also invoked in the name of coun-terimages of subordinated peoples, the "forces of ignorance, irration-ality, and intimidation" are truly knocking down the walls. And what ingratitude at a time when the West has provided "the developing world" its "first" tastes of freedom and capitalism, a time when democracy is spreading at last through Latin America, "a continent habituated to dictatorship." Today, D'Souza says with evident satis-faction at the triumph of the West, "most of Latin America is demo-cratic, largely due to human-rights policies begun by President Carter and continued by Presidents Reagan and Bush" (86–87). The good guys are winning, thanks mainly to Republicans, and he wants to keep it that way.

Finally, of course, there would be no struggle over the nature of school curricula, or fair hiring practices, or open admissions policies were it not for the awkward reality of differences among people—men, women, black, brown, gay, straight, Hispanic, Asian—all of whom seek entitlement to represent their experience and to find it fairly represented in the communities they form and join. The "real" political correctness includes many assertions about the nature and significance of human differences, as well as the values and preroga-tives attached to them, and D'Souza offers them with compelling clarity. Plainly, the most important is the view that these differences don't actually matter, so that there really shouldn't be any struggle. "Individual merit" is the first and last measure of difference in American life regardless of someone's affiliations in terms of gender, race, class, or other "group" identification. D'Souza, like many Americans, not only dismisses the social constitution of reality but finds, in arguments about group rather than individual status in U.S. society, the principal villain responsible for the decline of collegiate education. According to RPC, American life comprises, simply, large numbers of individual citizens, each of them either measuring up or not measuring up to the challenges and opportunities presented to them. By definition, then, there is no possibility either of collective preference or of collective discrimination. The historical makeup of student populations in colleges has resulted from nothing more than the surfacing (like cream) of the natural abilities of individuals, as impartially discerned by the testing industry. Some minority students, inevitably, have come to college through merit, and more power to them, but the large numbers who have been admitted in recent years have entered unfairly through political pressure, including "group" quota systems, discounting the undeniable "fact" that the individual Hispanic student doesn't ordinarily measure up to the abilities of the individual white student and needs to accept the consequence of that limitation in the free market of American higher education.

"The problem at Berkeley," D'Souza writes, is that "admissions policies have in the past been based on principles of merit or achievement," while today they are wrongly grounded in "proportional representation," which mandates distributing certain numbers of seats to previously underrepresented groups (26). D'Souza doesn't pause to wonder whether the traditionally white, European, male character of American colleges might suggest "group" favoritism in the past rather than the innocent accident of individual talent. He fails even to consider the less abstract political reality that colleges have always regularly reserved seats for children of alumni (according to the Department of Education, such "legacies" at Harvard are admitted at a 36 percent rate as against a 17 percent admissions rate for applicants as a whole), and for children of substantial donors or other "well-situated" citizens, with less regard for merit. For him, efforts to create equality in schools by an appeal to group identifications are a recent product of the cult of victim sensitivity, leading to the admission of underqualified students, correspondingly high dropout rates among them, the development of political (that is, nonintellectual and nonacademic) special interest groups like African American Studies masquerading as curricula, and increased tension across diverse constituencies, reflecting the "often bellicose group consciousness" nurtured in social organizations and clubs catering to separate genders, ethnicities, or races. Such divisions are "the natural consequence of principles that exalt group equality above individual justice" (50–51). Democracy, D'Souza insists, "does not entail group representation but rather expects that individuals will serve the shared community which transcends these narrower interests." Any concept of "group justice," he concludes, is "hostile both to individual equality and to excellence" (55), two values that are supposed to work in comfortable harmony for all individual Americans.

D'Souza is so preoccupied with "individuality" in the service of his particular concerns that he fails to acknowledge even the most obvious networks of affiliation that have always characterized American social life—families, neighborhoods, cities, states, churches, schools, clubs, political parties, labor unions, special interest organizations, and more. Democracy *always* "entails group representation," the struggle among competing interests defended by different communities of people. Of course D'Souza knows this, his zeal for stark individualism notwithstanding. What's at stake for him is the organizing principles that underlie different affiliations. What he opposes are groupings based on gender, race, class, or ethnicity—the differentiating characteristics that are supposed to have melted in the American pot. Perhaps his critique of group reality is simply naive, since it entails ignoring the fact that such characteristics haven't actually melted, that the "white consciousness" underlying segregation or the "male consciousness" underlying sexism remains very real indeed. But pieties about the undifferentiated American family appear disingenuous when they apply only to newly emergent ethnic or gender-related identities and entail no accompanying critique of the dominant group identities placing these at hazard. If the pieties are disingenuous, then an argument about social reality that is merely untrue when innocently advanced becomes an argument that is tactically suited to domination. Its effect, after all, is to deny to historically disadvantaged "groups" the solidarity they require to gain a positive self-image, a collective voice, and ultimately the political power they require in order to redress grievances. If D'Souza had equality in particular on his mind, he would concede that American life must retain two concepts at once, that of group rights as well as that of individual rights, because inequality has been, historically, very much a group issue. The individual white, managerial-class male has rights because of these affiliations, while the individual black, underclass woman lacks equivalent rights because of hers. A stark emphasis on individualism in the face of this social reality naively or cynically furthers the interests of favored groups because that black, working-class woman has no power alone to insist on her entitlements. She must either turn to a group that has power (which then may or may not intercede on her behalf, with little fear of retaliation if the decision is negative) or join a group of the powerless who are nonetheless willing to struggle for their interests. The only authentic challenge to discrimination aimed at groups is group resistance.

This is not complicated reasoning, and D'Souza is not naive. But he isn't altogether cynical either: he's willing to accept historical facts of oppression, as indeed most Americans are, and even willing to recommend steps to combat unfair privilege, for instance by targeting economic need rather than race in admissions policies or by allowing campus groups featuring shared intellectual or cultural interest while prohibiting those based on gender or ethnic identification (251–54). But he isn't nor are many Americans willing to recognize relationships between group identity and power (no individual woman could have won the right to vote), or to face the root causes of historic discrimination (Europeans didn't end up exterminating Native Americans simply because Sitting Bull and Custer had personal differences), or to recognize the strategic place of collective protest and other pressure in civil rights movements (King didn't challenge segregated transportation in Birmingham either by himself or by appeal to the inherent generosity of the governor of Alabama). At the same time, neither D'Souza nor most Americans would concede the inherently political (that is, social) nature of educational life, which has always entailed admissions considerations beyond "merit" (including regional distribution, athletic talent, extramural interest, special ability, and unusual background), always entailed changing conceptions of what "merit" or "excellence" is (yesterday's "good character" and family; today's SAT scores), and always entailed struggle over appropriate curricula (rhetoric was once a mainstay of the liberal arts; British literature did not exist as an academic subject until the late nineteenth century). Furthermore, D'Souza is unwilling to accept the discomfort, awkwardness, messiness entailed in aggressive political challenges of injustice on college campuses— the "bellicose group consciousness" that signals an unwillingness to allow the status quo to remain unexamined. He wants purity, tranquility, reasonableness, unwilling to consider whether the expression "let's be reasonable" has the same political substance when used by the powerless that it has when used by the powerful. He is content to place his hopes for social justice on a myth of American individualism that denies both history and any promise of serious social change. Little wonder if excluded persons, noting the convenience of such a belief for those not similarly excluded, react cynically to this fragment of the real political correctness. But there's more. The next step in the reasoning of RPC is that since equality is never anything but parity between two individuals in the context of shared, neutral standards of evaluation, there is also no basis for challenging discriminatory practices beyond appeal to those standards. If a black student posts 1200 on the SAT and a white student 1150, the black student wins a place in college: that's the meaning of fair play. And of course, should the situation ever be reversed, the white student posting 1200, then the same rule innocently applies. If the white student with 1150 is allowed to enter ahead of the black student with 1200, that's discrimination; if the black student with 1150 enters ahead of the white, that's *reverse* discrimination, which vaguely acknowledges the likelihood that situation one has occurred rather more frequently than situation two while insisting that each is as wrong as the other. According to RPC, historical discrimination has not existed since the sixties (that low, dishonest decade) as a matter of law or economic fact, so there's no need to counteract it in law by appeal to "unfair" considerations of individuals (let alone groups) whose forebears had been oppressed. Everyone starts even; to give someone an edge is not sporting; to favor the black student isn't justice, it's vengeance. To be sure, D'Souza is willing to consider extenuating circumstances, where residual socioeconomic differences have helped one student and hurt another. A score of 1150 from an economically deprived black student might, after all, be worth more than a 1200 from a white student living in the suburbs. What D'Souza objects to, again, is the "group" appeal of race (or gender or ethnicity): the advantaged black student shouldn't get a break just because of color. The trouble with this reasoning, once again, is that it is altogether abstract and utopian, supposing a condition of American life that even commonsense awareness would concede to be false were it not for the more compelling knowledge that facing up to discriminatory practices would entail imperatives for unacceptably dramatic social change.

For D'Souza, if the most grotesque economic inequities have been dealt with, so that some blacks now earn more or less what some whites do, and live in more or less the same sorts of neighborhoods, discrimination is ancient history. Give some consideration to a handful of deprived students, who are also accidentally Hispanic, and the problems will be solved. Never mind that women today earn only around seventy cents for the same work that earns men a dollar, and that 80 percent of the female work force is concentrated in the twenty lowest-paying job titles. Never mind that there remains a high correlation between economic deprivation and factors of race as well as gender, so that infant mortality rates are twice as high among black families as among white, while the percentage of blacks living in poverty is proportionately higher than the percentage of whites (though numerically more whites are poor). Never mind that rates of illiteracy for women around the world are consistently higher than those for men, or that the number of illiterate women rose by more than fifty million between 1970 and 1985 (*The World's Women*). Finally, never mind that there are dimensions of discrimination that extend beyond economic issues, important as those are. With rape statistics on the rise, it should be clear that women are more than underpaid: they are also demeaned and degraded. Given the continuing awkwardness of race relations, it should be clear also that "minorities" aren't just frequently pressured out of some neighborhoods or denied bank loans; they are also feared and despised. Discrimination is psychological as well as economic; subtle as well as overt. The point of representational admissions policies in colleges is larger than economic parity: they aim at a nurturing of tolerance for difference in a culture that is undeniably pluralistic, not a melting pot, and undeniably not yet tolerant; they accept the fact that discrimination will not end, that real democracy can't be achieved, as long as jobs and other social perks are distributed by the "managers" of the dominant culture on the implicit understanding that everyone in America is "basically" white and male.

There are still other links in the chain of "correct" thinking. If only individuals, not groups, are the significant players in American life, and if only merit is the determiner of success, and if discrimination has been lately rooted out so that "everyone" starts equal, then noisy political posturing from "groups" claiming discrimination and asking special favors are going to annoy all the "individuals" who make up the balance of the population. Those individuals will rightly feel indignant at the special pleading and they are bound to develop a new form of gender and race hostility that will be more understandable than the old form, even perhaps appropriate, because it's a righteous reaction against unfair "victim rhetoric." To the extent that this "new racism" (236–42) comes to pass, D'Souza believes, the pressure groups will have only themselves to blame. Here we find easily the most ominous claim of RPC, a validation and encouragement of white backlash given respectability in a book ranked in the top ten on the best-seller list in 1991. The quote from D'Souza that heads this chapter is a frank warning from the powerful to the powerless: cross the establishment and there will be consequences. Continue to cry "victim" and you will be made victims—and it will be your own fault. The new racism exists, D'Souza says, because the

dominantly white population of college campuses recognizes "a re-
gime of double standards that divides and balkanizes" university life.
"However well-intended," policies that allow for "preferential treatment, minority cultural centers, sensitivity training," and the like,
"generally supply the oxygen with which the new racism breathes
and thrives." As he sees things, "this is why incidents of bigotry are
confined predominantly to northern progressive campuses" (242).
The only options D'Souza will allow the country are the melting pot
or balkanization; either everyone pretends to be male and white or
else colleges must factionalize into warring special interests as
American society slouches toward a new Dark Age. Better, he suggests darkly, to accept the terms of the white male establishment
because that is the "group" with power to put everyone else in its
pot, the group that distributes economic rewards—and punishments.
Meanwhile, eliminate the problem of northern progressivism and
most "individuals" will happily jump into that pot: American life
will be free and fair at last.

RPC is quite clear about where this "northern liberal" rabble-
rousing is coming from, the character and quality of those who
sponsor it. There is an unholy alliance in American education
between radical students defending feminist and "minority" special
interests and radical faculty, weaned in the degenerate sixties, who
mumble "*au courant*" Marxist, deconstructive, and feminist discourse theory while fantasizing about oppositional culture as they
approach what would otherwise be the blandness of middle age.
Activist students make abrasive, iconoclastic demands ("Hey, hey,
ho, ho, Western culture's got to go" [59]), uninformed claims
("Socrates, Herodotus, Pythagoras, and Solon studied in Egypt"
[66]), persistent, unreasonable, and often fraudulent allegations of
racial or sexual insensitivity (149–50; 192–204; 134–35), impetu-
ous, generalized indictments ("The class 'perpetuates a racism that's
in the university as a whole' " [150]), and provocative comments
("Students were amazed by the power they had. . . . It's like
someone who suddenly has a gun, and realizes what he can do
with it" [111]) as they intimidate other students and school administrators, disrupt business, manipulate the media, and foist their
demands on the rest of the community. Meanwhile, normal students
do the best they can to stay above this bullying, remaining generally
calm, amiable, and open-minded, but also growing increasingly
exasperated at all the radical posturing. D'Souza devotes a paragraph to excusing conservative students who destroyed antia-
partheid shanties erected by demonstrators on the Dartmouth green
in 1986, explaining that "some of these antics are sophomoric, but
we must remember that they are largely carried out by sopho-

mores." Conservative students, he goes on, "are not powerful enough to stall the victim's revolution," and so "some of their attacks are reflexive, ill-considered, unkind, and lacking in historical perspective" (19). Meanwhile, he piles up examples of similar but typically far less dramatic behavior on the part of campus radicals without extending the same generosity to the sophomores who equally make up their ranks. Leftist students are powerful forces of unrest and social disintegration; conservative students are generally benign but can occasionally indulge in juvenile behavior out of their bewilderment at the abuses of radicals.

A conversation D'Souza has with two "moderate" students at the University of Michigan reveals his view of normal and proper campus attitudes—habits of mind and speech that carry, for D'Souza, no hint of ideological valence, so perfectly woven are they within the fabric of American correct thinking. Blacks, one student tells him, "are the most talked about subject at the university." Of course, people say "minorities," but "everybody knows that the term minorities means blacks." This student is Palestinian and claims a particular sensitivity to discrimination. But he says that most white students like himself don't consider blacks today to be victims of racism any longer. "To many people, the racial incidents seem like hype, you know, crybaby stuff." The student explains that blacks are no longer "legally persecuted," that, on the contrary, blacks are treated these days with "excessive deference," that admissions policies favor them, that they are "anything but disadvantaged." This student doesn't buy the argument that aptitude and achievement tests are racially biased, adding that most whites go along with this judgment "because they don't want to be racist," meaning they don't want to be accused of bias. Affirmative action, he says, "in its most blatant form . . . is a form of racism," a product of the "Black Power movement," which "celebrates Malcolm X rather than Martin Luther King." According to radical black advocates, "you don't need to do well in university"; the real agenda is "to promote separatism and Black Power." For these radicals, "whites are now Public Enemy Number One." Concerning the disc jockey at the University radio station who had recently told racial jokes on the air, this student hazarded the view that "definitely the person was being insensitive," adding apparently without a trace of self-consciousness that "you usually save jokes like that for your friends," and concluding that blacks who protested the jokes were less interested in justice than political gain: "It's a power grab. . . . They've found out that it's easy to get a bunch of people together and get the president jumping" (128–31). These opinions, by D'Souza's standards, are ordinary, commonsensical, easygoing: he offers many of them himself in more polished form. But a student activist's complaint about institutional racism or gender bias is extreme, biased, and incendiary.

Finally, of course, faculty are more responsible than students for campus rabble-rousing, according to the real political correctness. Marxist, feminist, and postmodern philosophical arguments, which D'Souza persistently refers to as "*au courant*" (that is, faddish, superficial, and ephemeral), have created fertile ground for relativism, the degeneration of intellectual and ethical standards, the sabotage of cultural values, the defeat of meaningfulness in "interpretive nihilism" (175). D'Souza characterizes these philosophical perspectives but doesn't explain them, doesn't cite from their arguments, doesn't explore their complexities, and may not know very much about them judging from his characterizations. We won't try to explain them either, not at least until a later chapter, because it's important in the context of RPC *not* to know much about their intricacies, the more readily to demonize them as sources of radicalism and cultural decay. By D'Souza's reading, nihilistic faculty use these arguments to justify irresponsible social criticism and, like pied pipers, lead impressionable students to emulate their own Nietzschean excesses. By denying ontological standards of truthfulness in literary texts, in cultural productions of all sorts, these *au courant* theories reduce everything to politics: "the critic . . . is free not just to create literary meanings, but also to impose his or her political views on the general understanding of culture. The traditional norms of scholarship no longer rein in the activist instinct." The consequence is "uninhibited ideological proselytization" (183–84). He cites the always helpful Stanley Fish to support his case. Speaking of reader-response theory and the concept of "interpretive communities," Fish says, "The political left loved it. They began to say: once you realize that standards emerge historically, then you can see through and discard all the norms to which we have been falsely enslaved" (175). Just the sort of ranting that RPC expects to find among college teachers.

D'Souza concludes that "it is truth itself which the *au courant* critics spurn, or more precisely, by reducing all truth to the level of opinion they spurn the legitimacy of any distinctions between truth and error" (179). By rejecting objective truth, these critics can challenge the integrity of Western canonical literature while elevating the status of third world and other texts; they can make women's issues appear on a par with men's issues; they can challenge standardized competence testing as relativistic and prejudicial; they can turn intrinsic merit into mere favoritism; they can question the authoritativeness of established disciplinary knowledge and offer equivalent status to "Hispanic Studies"; above all, they can write new books in a publish-or-perish academic marketplace, get tenure, talk a clever "deconstructive" lingo, affect glamorous Marxist poses, and enjoy the power trip of manipulating students and university administrations into reorganizing curricula or hiring black faculty. All at cost to the educational responsibilities and the intellectual credibility of the academy. "What is the goal of liberal education," D'Souza asks, "if not the pursuit of truth? If education cannot teach us to separate truth from falsehood, beauty from vulgarity, and right from wrong, then what can it teach us worth knowing?" (179). Good questions these, but not in the overheated climate of RPC, where they are intended only to close discussion rather than to open it. We would say that the goal of liberal education is *liberality* of a sort that PC critics have not envisioned: a liberality that recognizes different kinds of "truth"— that of science but also that of art, that of *The Iliad* but also that of an American Indian folk tale; a liberality that welcomes cultural difference and explores the various conceptions of truth, beauty, or right that different times and places have afforded; a liberality that wishes to make the fact of human diversity a proper consideration in matters of curriculum, student admissions, and faculty hiring; a liberality that expects educators, as responsible citizens, to take active roles in support of social change when conditions of prejudice and oppression require it. These assumptions and the values behind them are not "political correctness." They are in theory the substance of a democratic country. And they are in fact the substance of critical teaching.

Chapter Three

Images of Critical Teaching

Radicalteachers have a relatively coherent set of commitments and assumptions from which they teach, and they are aware of it; this awareness distinguishes them from rocks, mollusks, and nonradical teachers. . . . Radicalteachers believe that theory and practice are not separable. . . . (Their) teaching assumes that minds do not exist apart from bodies and that the bodies or material conditions, in which the potential and will to learn reside, are female as well as male and in a range of colors; that thought grows out of lived experience and that people come from a variety of ethnic, cultural, and economic backgrounds; that people have made different life choices and teach and learn out of a corresponding number of perspectives. . . . Radicalteachers work with themselves, their classes, and their colleagues to discover, name, and change sexism, racism, classism, and heterosexism. . . . (They) demand a lot from their students. . . . Radicalteachers do not assume they know it all.

Pamela Annas, in O'Malley,
Politics of Education

The arguments of Dinesh D'Souza and the American ideological right, specifically their implicit naming of the real political correctness, effectively represent the sociocultural conditions in the United States today that necessitate a critical pedagogy in schools. There *is* a "new racism" abroad, not all that different from the old in its consequences but alarmingly different in the self-righteousness of its hostility, its astonishing claim that "victims" have brought it on themselves by asking for more democracy than dominant groups are willing to tolerate. Students today *are* influenced, if not quite consumed, by greed and self-interest in a capitalist marketplace where brute competition and other Darwinian values combine with an ethic of consumption to set the terms of "winning" and "losing" in American life. Structures of domination and repression are alive and well, as poverty and unemployment statistics, the growing gap between rich and poor, housing and lending practices, government funding priorities (defense high, social programs low), Supreme Court attitudes toward the rights of women and minorities, (un)ethical practices in business, management/union relations, and the factory organization of schools all make clear. The purpose of a critical pedagogy is to help alleviate unethical and oppressive conditions— to further the utopian project that has been at the philosophical heart of the "American experiment" from its beginnings. The critique of oppression does not imply "un-American activity," that neurotic, still-potent representation from fifties McCarthyism, nor does it suggest (Marxist intellectual roots notwithstanding) a violent revolutionary dismantling of cultural institutions. There is nothing un-American about social justice, about steadfast self-examination or public work in the service of a still imperfectly achieved democracy. Critical teaching presumes nothing more sinister—or trendy—than an active social conscience. But it's also quite uncompromising about the centrality of social conscience in educational practice.

Critical teaching is about the willingness of people to inquire and change and make changes, to accommodate themselves to difference, to read the social world, in its complexity, for the promises it makes about the quality of its members' lives and the extent to which it delivers on those promises. Critical teaching doesn't politicize education; it recognizes the political nature of education and works to make students, no less than other citizens, aware of the consequences of that recognition. Critical teaching doesn't aim at polarizing people by its emphasis on multiculturalism and human diversity; it aims to repudiate harmful myths of the melting pot, because they are neither true nor helpful. More important, it aims to establish difference as a *legitimate* feature of community, so that the cultural identities and histories of Hispanic or black people, for example, are allowed to flourish in their difference from other such identities and histories, just the way differences among other kinds of groups—political parties, families, churches, clubs—deserve equally to flourish. Groups nurture their members while also cooperating with other groups in larger public projects. Members of such groups have more than one affiliation in their lives; they move from one to another and back again. People are as entitled to be African American or gay as they are to be Republican, North Carolinian, Baptist, and fans of the Dodgers. Within and through these shifting identities, they are American too and entitled equally to the privileges of citizenship, just as they are entitled to resist group-based denials of those privileges by appeal to collective action. Critical teaching is not directed toward minorities, as religion is imposed upon primitives. It intends to provoke disciplined thinking in all students, from whatever background, in the interest of political awareness, civic duty, and a tolerance of cultural pluralism. Finally, critical teaching doesn't intend abrupt, violent, social revolution, as melodramatic representations of its praxis, from both the political right and the left, imply. It accepts values of dialogue and negotiation, but it also expects that historically powerful groups will accommodate themselves to the rights of others to claim entitlements that the powerful have long maintained for themselves. It advocates a gradual but determined, responsible but ethically committed intervention in American sociopolitical life, when demonstrably unfair or dehumanizing conditions require.

The best way to become familiar with the theory of critical teaching, the other representation that media depictions have ignored or appropriated, is to look at the praxis of actual teachers. We propose here to tell some stories. Anne Fausto-Sterling is a biologist, a feminist, and a critical teacher who has told of her classroom practices in an essay titled "The Myth of Neutrality: Race, Sex, and Class in Science," originally published in the journal *Radical Teacher* and included in a recent collection of essays from that journal titled *Politics of Education*, edited by Susan Gushee O'Malley, Robert C. Rosen, and Leonard Vogt. Fausto-Sterling is a professor of Medical Sciences at Brown University. In this essay, she speaks of the difficulties she had experienced early in her career reconciling her several lives as scientist, teacher, and political activist—engaging social questions as a responsible citizen in "a world filled with sorrow and woe" while investigating "some minor aspect of the embryological development of the fruit fly," in the process "losing" valuable research time, according to her colleagues at least, by teaching undergraduates. She "lived like a juggler" until the balls in the air finally escaped her control and she was forced, "thank heavens," to integrate her lives, an effort that continues to this day. She still finds, of course, that public attitudes, which always affect "personal" beliefs and practices, create intimidating barriers to the integration: the view that science research is man's work, therefore important,

that teaching is woman's work, therefore unimportant, and that social change is an aspiration shared only by idealists, who are silly, or
communists, who ought to be illegal; the view that science is about
facts, that teaching is about the transmission of facts, and that ideology has no place in science or teaching. Fausto-Sterling's classes are
all about how wrong and damaging these opinions are for scientists,
teachers, and students alike.

Fausto-Sterling speaks candidly about how difficult it is to challenge the popular impression that scientific knowledge is objective
and detached, to persuade colleagues no less than students that
biology is politically valenced, a part of the social world rather than
perched neutrally above it. In her classes, which include Social
Issues in Biology and Biology of Gender, she argues that biological
theory is inevitably produced in the context of existing social relations. She explains, for instance, "how the cultural and ideological
framework of both the individual scientist and the historical period
translate into a particular scientific world view" (215). One intriguing
example she provides is research concerning the Daddy Water Bug,
a large predatory insect, "up to five inches in length," living in
freshwater ponds and streams "looking for all the world like a dead
leaf." Daddy Water Bugs baffled scientists of the later nineteenth
century because the behavior of some species failed to conform to
what biologists of the time assumed were "appropriate" sex roles.
The female deposits her eggs on the back of the male, leaving him to
care for them until they hatch. Male scientists of the time, observing
this insect through the distinctive tints of their social lenses, insisted
that the egg carrier must be female and developed theories to account
for how "she" managed to pull the eggs out of her reproductive tract
and deposit them on "her" own back. A woman scientist finally
determined that the male was the carrier, but even she felt the "grip
of societal ideology," concluding that the male "chafes under the
burden" of the eggs and willingly suffers blows, when attacked, as
though even death were preferable to "the indignity of carrying and
caring for the eggs" (214). The political framework of science in the
later nineteenth century "made it difficult in the first place . . . to
'see' that the bug with the eggs was the male," and then demanded,
once that fact had been established, "that the father water bug hate
being a parent."

Science today is no less bound by culture and no more exempt
from the interpretative biases that conditioned earlier scientific
knowledge (see Kuhn). Unfortunately, the ideological character of
that knowledge is more difficult to discern in the present because
the "common sense" of culture is largely unconscious, taken for
granted, not an object of critique. Yet, for Fausto-Sterling, it's

crucial to reveal that character because science in our time has such power to "justify and provide an underpinning for the status quo" (210). As example, following Stephen Gould, she points to modern research on IQ, particularly Arthur Jensen's, that has the effect of "explaining" the intellectual, hence social, inferiority of women and black people in terms of "natural" physiological differences (210–11). So she insists that students read about the political shape of scientific knowledge, while also enabling them to experience it firsthand through classroom exercises. One exercise invites students to interpret standards for reasonable amounts of asbestos in the air, first assuming that they worked for an asbestos company, second assuming they worked for a union's health and safety committee (215). Another asks them to observe "some sort of animal behavior, leading half of the class to expect one sort of activity (e.g., telling them that they're looking at a hyperactive strain of rats) and the other half of the class the opposite (e.g., telling them that the rats are genetically depressed)." Students can then experience "how their own expectations distort their power of observation" (215). Fausto-Sterling doesn't just want her students "doing science"; she also wants them to understand "that their world of facts and figures is not a hair more neutral than Ronald Reagan's" (210).

Marilyn Frankenstein is a math professor at the University of Massachusetts/Boston College of Public and Community Service, and another contributor to *Politics of Education*. In "A Different Third R: Radical Math," she explains that mathematical literacy entails "more than the ability to calculate," that it includes the "ability to reason quantitatively, the ability to use numbers to clarify issues and to support or refute opinions" (219). In her classes mathematics is a means of understanding the world at a time when prevailing beliefs about objectivity allow social practices to be powerfully justified through quantitative arguments (as we suggested earlier in connection with testing). Frankenstein believes that the widespread mathematical illiteracy among Americans is a product of bankrupt mathematics curricula that offer rote and passive computation drills, along with word problems detached from ordinary experience, in place of a critical positioning of mathematics in the daily lives of students. She challenges the pervasive educational practice of breaking knowledge "into separate, unrelated issues to be discussed only by specialists" (a way to mystify technical understanding, making it inaccessible to mastery or use except by a privileged technological priesthood), and aims in her teaching to help students see mathematics as a way of analyzing the social conditions that surround them, see it as part of the fabric of American life—where "even totalling a grocery bill carries the nonneutral message that paying for food is natural" (220). She argues that mathematical reasoning is necessary for full participation in our culture, that a citizenry lacking this ability becomes susceptible to "numerical lies and obfuscations" (220), not to mention domination by the technologically literate. Frankenstein describes a course for adults that aims to combat the timidity and negative self-images they've acquired from their prior mathematics instruction. She encourages students to work cooperatively with one another, to share their knowledge in accomplishing particular tasks, and to keep journals of their progress, recording their concerns and feelings as the course goes on. Her written comments on journal entries "offer encouragement, alternative solutions or perspectives, and explanations of how students' remarks on learning math often apply to learning in general" (226). She makes an interesting distinction between "explaining" and "teaching." Explaining a mathematical solution involves showing someone else the logic of what one did; teaching a math problem demands that one "be able to recognize all the correct methods of solving it as well as the logic behind incorrect methods" (226). Frankenstein wants her students to explain their work but also to teach one another, both at the board as she does and in working groups, because by teaching they are "arguing constructively and thinking creatively about solutions to the problems" that are offered (226–27). Her intent throughout is to situate mathematics in her students' lifeworlds, posing authentic economic and social issues—costs of food and housing, employment statistics among women and minorities, arguments about mortality rates and energy sources—that reveal the uses and also the abuses of quantitative analysis.

One problem illustrates how Frankenstein contextualizes mathematics in order to dramatize its impact on students' daily lives. In this instance she's teaching the operations of decimals. Figures are offered, taken from a *Boston Globe* article published in December 1980 and based on a Department of Energy study, as a resource for discussing questions about nuclear power. Since its beginnings, according to the (now dated) article, nuclear power has benefited from federal aid in five major categories—23.6 billion dollars for research and development; 237.4 million to promote foreign reactor sales; 2.5 billion for uranium market promotion; 7.1 billion in fuel enrichment pricing aid; and 6.5 billion for management of wastes, mining spoils cleanup, and unpaid decommissioning costs (222). She asks students first to compute the total federal subsidy to the industry, hoping to "help improve students' intuitions about large numbers." She offers charts that "give specifics on how much in human services our nuclear power and nuclear armament spending costs us." She then

asks them to write individual statements of view about the advantages and limitations of nuclear power, inviting students with similar
opinions to work together in small groups. They list the kinds of
numerical data that might support their views and they also do some
research to find "at least one of the facts" that they believe would be
helpful, in order to become more aware of how people discover and
use numbers to make arguments (222–23). Frankenstein observes
that when advocates of nuclear power point to the fact that nuclear
plants provide 12 percent of the country's electricity, "only a mathe-
matically sophisticated populace could counter" that nuclear energy
(at the time her article appeared) "provides just 3 percent of our total
energy needs" (220). Critical citizens in Frankenstein's classes aren't
mesmerized by numbers; they read them attentively, scrutinize their
uses and the motives of those who employ them, note their rhetorical
effects, frame them in alternative ways, introduce different numbers
or calculations, and never lose sight of the ideological dimension of
mathematical argument.

Illustrative stories of critical teaching are available from several
sources, including *Composition and Resistance*, edited by Mark
Hurlbert and Michael Blitz; *Critical Teaching and Everyday Life*,
written by Ira Shor; the books of Paulo Freire (though these emphasize the sociocultural conditions of third world peoples and have
limited practical relevance to American teachers); *Gendered Subjects*, edited by Margo Culley and Catherine Portuges; *Freire for the
Classroom*, edited by Ira Shor; and others. We find *Politics of Education* a particularly good one because of the breadth as well as depth
of the examples it provides. We'll summarize a final story from that
volume, though it contains many more, this time one written by a
high school teacher. Pam Sporn, teaching history at an alternative
high school in the South Bronx, used the prompting of a student,
who, after seeing *The Deerhunter* on TV, asked for a class on the
Vietnam War, to design a course that engaged her black and Hispanic
students, all dropouts or truants from traditional New York City high
schools, in the construction and examination of history. Rather than
filling her students with facts and dates and causes, the stuff of
history textbooks, Sporn invited her students to become historians,
composing their own questions about the war, interviewing veterans
and others affected by it, reading literature, seeing films, examining
documents and artifacts in order to immerse themselves in the cross-
currents and complexities of that moment in American history. The
students began to wonder what war was actually like and why so
many veterans, not much older than they, had such a hard time
adjusting afterward to life "back in the world." Students also came
to wonder at the disproportionate numbers of black and Hispanic

men and women sent to fight a war that had so little relevance to their own lives and prospects, sent to a war that young middle-class white people generally declined to attend. Students read Mark Baker's *Nam*, which consists of "testimonies" from veterans of different racial and economic backgrounds as well as political allegiances. They noticed parallels between recruiting strategies of the sixties and those used today, grew disgusted at the barbarities of war, the atrocities on all sides, debated what they might have done if ordered to shoot villagers. The most moving and provocative portion of the course came when six Vietnam veterans and the ex-wife of a veteran visited the class to talk about their experiences of the war. One veteran who grew up in a cold-water tenement in Spanish Harlem told of how he finally realized he was fighting people who were poorer than he was. Another, a Puerto Rican, discussed the terror of war and his growing awareness of how war was "legalized genocide." The ex-wife discussed the complexities of relationships that are interrupted by war, the difficulties of adjusting, the arguments, and in the end the dissolution of a marriage. After these stories, the students began talking to their parents, visiting the Vietnam Veterans Outreach Center, and interviewing as many people as they could find who had been affected by the war. They wrote social histories from this research offering kaleidoscopic images of the time and dispelling stereotypes not only about those who participated in the war but also about those who protested its continuance. Sporn's students discovered that history comprises stories of lived experience, not just textbooks of inert information, that they too make history in the living of their lives, that they have authority to compose their own stories while critically engaging those of others.

Important themes run through these accounts of critical pedagogy: teachers unwilling to deny or ignore the sociopolitical contexts of their disciplinary practices, their school lives, or their lives as American citizens; teachers accepting the responsibility to pose problems for students' critical attention, to cast students in positions of activity and responsibility themselves so they can't take refuge in more familiar roles as passive consumers of information; teachers attentive to the dynamics of gender, race, and class in the forming of their classrooms and their schoolwork; students challenged to think, not told how or what to think; students offered many opportunities to critique, but no imperatives of "political correctness"; students of the dominant culture, not just "minority" students, struggling with issues of diversity and fairness that are every bit as important to their quality of life as they are to those who have been historically oppressed. There's another theme, too, although not as fully developed as we think it needs to be: the necessity of *self*-critique, teachers aware of their own ideological commitments, aware of the failures in their classrooms (their own failures as well as those of their students), continuously monitoring their practice—retheorizing it—in order to change it in beneficial ways. Sporn notes that her students "were not very interested in . . . the anti-war movement" despite their expressions of "strong sentiments" against the conflict in Vietnam. She quotes a student explaining that "Politics just isn't that interesting to young people anymore." Sporn is led to speculate about the "wall" that exists between the classroom and the real world "even in the South Bronx," fully aware of the shared failure, finally, in her class to recognize any connection between "the imperialistic and exploitative nature of the war in Vietnam . . . and an understanding of the necessity for masses of people to act, and change such situations" (83). Fausto-Sterling concedes the difficulties she still encounters listing teaching "under the heading of real work" (209), admits the departmental political confrontations she encountered when trying to make Biology of Gender a course in the major, raises substantive questions about the relationship between such evidently political offerings as Biology of Gender and basic science courses designed to introduce students to concepts and methods of her discipline.

There are a great many problems to be addressed in teaching that aims so directly and profoundly to alter people's lives. What moral authority can the critical teacher claim for such an imposing classroom agenda (beyond the weak response that traditional pedagogy is even more insistent—backing up its designs on people with elaborate testing apparatuses that signal its power to define cooperativeness in terms of academic success and failure)? Suppose students don't want to be "enlightened" in the ways that critical teachers believe they must be? How far do teachers have a right to go in celebrating their values while critiquing others? What utopian vision lies at the end of a critical praxis: exchanging capitalism for socialism? transferring power from men to women, or from whites to Hispanics, or from more conservative faculty to more liberal ones? Does the freedom of speech that critical teachers might invoke to defend their interests extend also to those whom they oppose, even in such repugnant circumstances as racist diatribe? Who is "oppressed" in American life and who isn't? Who gets to say so? Who are the oppressors and who the liberators? How does one tell? One distinguishing mark of the critical teacher is an openness to self-critique, where these questions and others can be posed in the name of a praxis that is ethically responsible. Since no classroom succeeds (or fails) perfectly, no reflective teacher should wish to remain comfortable about what happened there, should settle carelessly or smugly or resolutely on fixed means or even ends. We want to tell two final stories ourselves

emphasizing the problems and failures of attempts at critical pedagogy in order to underline this need for sustained self-scrutiny while
also probing, in ways the previous stories don't, some representative
complexities of liberatory instruction in the specific circumstances
of American society.

Cy's story (which has appeared in somewhat different form in
Composition and Resistance): My students come, arguably, from the
comfortable middle of the American middle class. I'm as comfortable as they are. My students are white, as I am, their heritage
European and Judeo-Christian, as mine is. They are predominantly
from a suburban culture, not unlike mine, and many of them,
perhaps most, have grown up without substantial experience of
people different from themselves. More than half have spent their
formative years in the tranquil neighborhoods of Long Island, New
York; they drive their own cars between home and school on typical
weekends. My students have an average combined SAT score of
around 1150. Large numbers of them come to the University
expecting to major in business; most of the rest anticipate professional work in industry, medicine, law, the usual. Our English
department has over one thousand majors (in a population of twelve
thousand undergraduates), not because the humanities are intrinsically appealing but because the Business School restricts its enrollment and the word is out that English is a good preparation for
business and professional careers. Around 12 percent of our undergraduates are black and Hispanic; a substantially smaller percentage
of faculty come from these backgrounds. Occasionally, the University mounts efforts to recruit from groups outside its mainstream,
but it has been only modestly successful.

My students belong to what the educational left would call the
dominant culture, a misleadingly simple fiction, to be sure, but one
helpfully evocative of the privileges attending those in the United
States today who are (sub)urban, white, upper middle class, Eurocentric in outlook, and either male or willing to accommodate the norms
of patriarchal reality. My school has been substantially shaped by
that culture, in turn supporting and replicating its values. I too have
been constituted in its terms, and I help the school, even when I'd
prefer not to, in furthering its social and economic agendas. For the
most part, not surprisingly, my students accept without self-
consciousness the values that their home and school lives have
commended to them. They believe that their prosperity is a function
of natural merit matched with achievement, through hard work, in
the competitive academic marketplace. They believe that the disad-
vantages of others result from natural limitations (which schooling
has effectively "measured"), compounded not infrequently by lazi-

ness. They are confident that they deserve to be tomorrow's managers, though more anxious than they really need to be about the success that almost inevitably awaits them. They are also generally quite hostile to the idea that anyone who has not "achieved" as much as they have should be given "unfair" entry to the managerial hierarchy or even the collegiate training ground that their own superior effort has merited.

My students accept the stories about freedom and self-actualization, fair play and altruism, progress and prosperity that their history books have composed to portray the American experience. In accepting them they are not more naive than their parents or their teachers. They believe that Abraham Lincoln and Martin Luther King together emancipated black people, so that any disparity between black and white today results from causes other than the merely historical evil of racial prejudice. Many believe—with the Supreme Court—that equal opportunity is a liberal euphemism for reverse discrimination. My women students, no less than the men, believe that the patriarchal oppression of twenty, two hundred, and two thousand years ago (the eras all run together) has given way, conveniently within the last ten years or so, to gender equality, due to the efforts of Jane Fonda and a few other tastelessly but opportunely insistent older women. They believe that their challenge is now to measure up to their male counterparts (whose standards they do not question) according to the neutral scale of merit that properly ensures quality control in the workplace. My students have heard about oppression in other parts of the world, a natural consequence of dictatorship, communism, and Islamic religious fervor, but its unfortunate existence does not serve as a call for critical scrutiny either abroad or, still less, at home. Nor does it imply any responsibility to open our borders to "aliens" whose presence here might jeopardize the prospects of "our own" people. This is not to imply that my students are selfish or cynical: they are in fact generous, warm-hearted, and sympathetic to others, provided there is no specific threat to their own well-being and perceived entitlements. They are honest and likeable people. They resemble their parents and their teachers.

Nothing in this profile seems peculiar to the situation in my school. It could be substantially replicated for the majority of universities across the country, and indeed for many of the nation's children, whether in college or not. There are, to be sure, other kinds of students and educational settings: grade and high schools serving the underclasses of urban as well as rural poor; trade schools and community colleges comprising working-class students, many of whom are adults; neighborhood training centers and other nontraditional academic arrangements. There are also different kinds of students within universities, students from diverse cultures, students with working-class and other backgrounds, students whose instincts are liberal, even radical, despite their socioeconomic standing. But several points require emphasis. One is that university life preponderantly reflects the values and expectations of the dominant culture: it is a managerial training ground for the social elite. A second is that university research and curricular agendas have a powerful role in rationalizing, if not actually accounting for, educational realities in other school settings, so that the values of the dominant culture are effectively transmitted to other populations. A third, following partly on the second, is that more people accept those values than just the statistical minority who are readily identified with social privilege. The dominant culture defines how The Good Life is led, not only through its control of schools and other sites of political authority, but also through its control of popular media, where images of what constitutes The Good Life offer illusions of possibility to anyone with access to a television, a radio, a magazine, or a movie theater. Where The Good Life does not exist as social reality, it exists as an aspiration made concrete through the manipulations of mass culture.

I offer this profile of my students in order to resituate the practice of critical teaching on atypical and problematic ground: the circumstances of middle-class life familiar to many if not the majority of American teachers, even when their classes include students from other backgrounds. Historically, critical teaching has emerged in connection with literacy programs in countries, especially in Latin America and Africa, where conditions of profound illiteracy have helped to maintain a ruling elite to the evident detriment of other groups. Activist teachers working with oppressed populations, Freire in Brazil for instance, have been able to illustrate and make students conscious of sharp distinctions between rich and poor, landlord and peasant, owner and dispossessed. Some American teachers have appropriated the practices of critical pedagogy in the name of students perceived to be on the margins of school life, those in remedial programs, those from "minority" groups traditionally excluded from fast academic tracks, those who have dropped out of school. In these instances, the goal has been to find ways to enfranchise "outsiders," typically by making them more aware of the social realities that constitute their lives, more aware of the means by which power is gained, used, and distributed in the professional and other communities they may wish to enter, more aware of the ways simultaneously to acquire that power and also subvert the structures that objectify prevailing—and debilitating—power arrangements. Ira Shor's efforts in the community college setting and Jonathan Kozol's in community-based literacy projects are examples.

These are noble enterprises, but they are by no means invariably clear about the precise aims of liberatory education or the concrete praxis, the modes and means of resistance, that ought to characterize critical teaching in the specific circumstances of American life. Who is to be liberated from what? Who gets to do the liberating? Is the U.S. government an oppressor in the same sense that the South African government is? Are middle-class black persons as "outside" as underclass Hispanic? Is Elizabeth Dole an outsider? Where exactly is the inside? Is the goal to make the outsider into an insider? Is it to transform one inside into another? Is it to abolish capitalism? Does the moral commitment, and the political authority, of the critical teacher properly mandate a change in the consciousness of arguably disenfranchised students regardless of their own wishes, their own sense of what they might gain or lose from accommodating themselves to the dominant culture? Since American life does not readily resolve into conflicting images of the hacienda and the mud hut (though it has its versions of both), since profound illiteracy is less common here than in some places, since an alternative literacy in mass media and the myths they propagate is very high indeed even among so-called outsiders, since most Americans possess reassuring fragments of The Good Life, these questions are not simple. No less complex are the supplementary questions I want to pose in light of the fact that my students belong to the dominant culture, not to the margins by any definition. Is critical teaching anything more than an intellectual game in such circumstances? If not, what does it entail, how is it justified, what are the terms of its success in classrooms filled with literate, economically privileged, young suburbanites whose political consciousness, as of the most recent presidential election at least, extended only as far as the wearing of George Bush campaign buttons to class? Are these heirs to American wealth and power in fact the oppressor (re)incarnate, already too corrupted for Freirean dialogue since they have so much to gain from not listening? Can the university really serve as a site for radical teaching? What is the meaning of "radical teacher" for faculty in such privileged institutions—paid by the capitalist state, protected from many of the obligations as well as the consequences of social action by the speculativeness of academic commitment, engaged in a seemingly trivial dramatization of utopian thought that the university itself blandly sponsors as satisfying testimony to its own open-mindedness?

An example will make these questions concrete. Last semester I taught English 122, an introduction to shorter prose fiction. My over-enrolled class of forty-three included one Asian student and one black student. The latter, a woman, said nothing all semester, though the class was designed, through small and large group formats, to stimulate talk. The ironies of her mute presence haunt my recollection. I followed many of Shor's suggestions for a critical pedagogy, helping students reconstruct the ideological conditions surrounding the production of "literary" texts, involving them in debate, through talk and extensive writing, about the sociocultural tensions and struggles in their own lives by appeal to the mediating situations depicted in stories (*Critical Teaching*, 220ff.). Much of the class work was technically successful: these students know the drill, know how to interpret, know about "foreshadowing" and "plot" and "symbol," understand the conventions of "literary" chatter. At the same time, their readings of stories, their commitment to those readings even in the face of occasional resistance from me or from a few recalcitrant peers, spoke volumes about their own social standing and expectations. We read Toni Cade Bambara's "The Lesson," for instance, a story depicting the experiences of several black children from Harlem who travel to Manhattan, in the company of an adult mentor, Miss Moore, to visit F.A.O. Schwartz, an outrageously upscale toy store. Importantly, the narrator of the story is not an omniscient onlooker, and not even Miss Moore; it is one of the children, Sylvia, an obstreperous youngster who would much rather be swimming, who stiffs the cabbie bringing them downtown in order to keep Miss Moore's money, and who has no inclination at all to learn whatever it is this earnest adult is bent on teaching.

The children, Sylvia included, are awed by what they see, particularly by a toy sailboat that costs over a thousand dollars. They talk about what it might mean that some people spend more on a toy than others have to spend in a year for eating and sleeping. Various opinions are offered. "White folks crazy." "Equal chance to pursue happiness means an equal crack at the dough." But whatever the lesson is, Miss Moore doesn't spell it out for the children, nor do the children agree among themselves. Arguably, Sylvia, the narrator, grasps even less of it than others do. And so the question arises, what do readers think it is? A sampling of the initial written responses I requested from my students is revealing. "I think the lesson Miss Moore was trying to get across was that black people can be smart or rich if they work at it." "When the kids saw the tremendous prices for little toys, they got a sense of money and what it's like to be rich. In other words, if they studied or someway made it out of the slums, they could have such toys." "If you strive for what you want, you can receive it." "The children are living a lifestyle much different than those who are wealthy. Sometimes I got the feeling that the children were jealous of rich and white people." "There's rich and poor and there's ghetto and Park Avenue. You have to work your way up there to get what you want and be what you want." "They can voice their indignation at how the cost of one toy boat could feed an entire family, or they can become educated so as to afford that boat one day."

These responses are too predictable, too understandable, for me to suggest that anyone should feel surprise at their middle-class innocence. In any case, the substance of critical teaching does not lie in a co-opting of student readings in favor of one that is, presumably, more socially, ethically, or politically sensitive—namely, the teacher's. Nor does it lie in a mere juxtaposition of opposed readings, with the (naive) hope that students will "see" the merit in some over that in others. Freire observes that "one has to respect the levels of understanding that those becoming educated have of their own reality. To impose on them one's own understanding in the name of their liberation is to accept authoritarian solutions as ways to freedom" (*Literacy*, 41). Henry Giroux makes a similar but expanded point. The teacher doesn't set out to win converts to a personal ideology, even if it has to do with the evils of sexism or racism, through the manipulation of text as moral exhortation. To do so is to assume "an authoritative discourse which disallows the possibility for the students to tell their own stories, to present and then question the experiences they bring into play," (Introduction to *Literacy*, 19). Such an abuse of power, whether overt as lecture or disguised as "discussion," replicates the very structures of authority that the critical teacher aims to call into question, resulting either in students' disengaged assent for survival's sake or their sullen resistance.

Critical teaching begins, in this case, not with a power struggle over preferable readings, but with the *reading* of those readings, contextualized by the life experience of those who produced them. Teacher and students alike engage in self-scrutiny as joint participants in the processes of teaching and learning. I copied several responses to "The Lesson" on the blackboard, asking about the values implicit in the judgments we reached. Certain themes emerged from the talk. Running through these responses, for instance, is a belief that education is intrinsically liberating and also a belief that hard work leads inevitably to The Good Life. Why do we take these as true? If they are true for us, are they then true for everyone? Are they, in fact, always true for us? What does experience suggest? What documentation can we discover? Finally, can we reenter the story (since it introduces, at least potentially, some exotic "voices" in our conversation) to find alternative meanings, presuming that the scrutiny of our own beliefs has yielded problematic awarenesses of ourselves that the story itself can now serve to interrogate? Can we establish a critical dialogue between our own biographies and the voices of the text? Can we recompose our biographies by means of that critical effort? The answer might have been yes, given sufficient time and trust, given more courage on both sides. But I was obliged to confront the fact that students are not prepared in school to recognize a dialectical relationship between states of belief and acts of reading, where two sets of meanings interact to produce altered understanding. Instead, they are socialized to presume that the meanings of stories serve to ratify beliefs. Stories are taught in school, from early grades, in order to convey moral messages. They are not supposed to call a dominant morality into question; when they do, they are immoral themselves. My students diligently constructed the usual messages they expected this story to provide, as they had done often before. They agreed, sportingly, to look hard at their values. They made some verbal adjustments to deemphasize the class bias implicit in their initial pieties about "hard work" and getting an education. They even produced a new reading of the story—which upheld the very beliefs they had started with, only clothed (as students apparently guessed I wanted them to be) in the trappings of American liberalism.

The final, dismissive reading went something like this: in America every child deserves the same opportunity to purchase a thousand-dollar toy sailboat. Students did not want to address the issue of conspicuous consumption that the story invited them to consider; they felt intensely uncomfortable at the suggestion that class differences might be anything but superficial and finally surmountable with hard work; they could not imagine questioning the value system that produces an F.A.O. Schwartz in the first place. Despite the fact that many of them could no more afford a toy from this store than Sylvia or Sugar could, they fought for their psychological investment in its importance as a symbol of The Good Life. Other stories we discussed produced similar dismissals, similar defeats of oppositional images at the hands of deeply embedded commitments. They decided that the mother in O'Connor's "Everything That Rises Must Converge" is indeed a bigot, but that her son, Julian, having received a college education, is an enlightened man (he isn't) who rightly embarrasses her for her views. They did not consider their own self-righteousness in so easily condemning the mother. They believed that Mrs. Ames in Boyle's "The Learned Astronomer's Wife" wins her liberation upon discovering that only some men are dreamers like her husband (who ignores her), that others are practical like the plumber (who pays condescending attention to her) and to that extent validations of her own character and abilities. Most students pitied the woman in Tillie Olsen's "I Stand Here Ironing" too much to hold her accountable for her daughter's unhappiness; but they leveled aggressive criticism at her for being so irresponsible as to have more children than her economic condition allowed. They concluded that the Arab in Camus' "The Guest" goes to prison on his own, despite Daru's gift of a "choice" to return to his own people, because he respects the value of (French colonial) law and feels a (Western) obligation to Daru who has placed him "on his honor."

The issue here seems to go beyond tactics to a question of the real plausibility of liberatory teaching in circumstances where there is a powerful self-interest, rooted in class advantage, that works actively, if not consciously, against critical reflectiveness. What do my students have to gain from a scrutiny of values and conditions that work to ensure their privilege? Why should they struggle with the troubling self-awareness that one course aims to create when the culture of the university as a whole reassures them of their entitlements? Shor makes some pragmatic but discomfiting concessions. Since teachers can only create the conditions of democratic learning, cannot compel assent to a radical agenda (except at cost to the very democracy they seek to establish), there are real boundaries to what critical teaching can accomplish. The "consciousness in each class" will determine "the limits of egalitarian reconstruction." Moreover, "in each school or college, teachers need to assess what level of liberatory learning they can assert, given student consciousness and institutional politics." Shor's postscript to this debilitating admission is that "students are a mass of potential allies" because they have, finally, "the most to gain by the success of democratic learning" (*Critical Teaching*, 112–13). But Shor's students are working-class adults in the "community college," whose interests are not well served by their capitulation to the dominant culture, whose discovery of critical consciousness might be an enabling step in reconstituting their social reality. What do my students have to gain?

The question is a serious one, to which moral pieties will not serve as adequate response. But its difficulty must not imply an invitation to university teachers to accept the comfortable disengagement of fatalism, leaving the issue of educational transformation to those alone who work with marginalized populations. Giroux warns that applying the project of critical teaching restrictively to contexts of the disadvantaged and dispossessed falsely conceives of literacy in terms of a "deficit theory of learning." Schools, the reasoning goes, "unevenly distribute particular skills and forms of knowledge" in ways that benefit the middle class, and so the aim of radical pedagogy is merely to ensure that "outsiders" get the reading and writing skills necessary to live critically in the school world and eventually to gain economic equality. In this view, literacy becomes a "privileged cultural capital," with "minority" students deserving their fair piece of the pie. What this argument produces is a parochial, functionalist concept of literacy that ignores any pervasive commitment to name and transform "ideological and social conditions that undermine the possibility for forms of community and public life organized around the imperatives of a critical democracy." Composing such a democracy is not a matter of turning outsiders into insiders: it entails a pervasive, ceaseless, public negotiation of power arrangements in the interest of social justice; it implies the necessary participation of "those members of the middle and upper classes who have withdrawn from public life into a world of sweeping privatization, pessimism, and greed" (Giroux, Introduction to Freire and Macedo, 5).

I don't have a fully adequate answer to the question of what advantage my students might expect from the development of social responsibility. But I have reason to believe that a portrait of middle-class, upwardly mobile suburbanites consumed by nothing more than self-interest and opportunism would be a dishonest caricature, unresponsive to the complexities of life. My students are self-interested, but they are not only that. They do seek The Good Life, but not at any cost. They cling to their myths, but they also learn and change. Perhaps that is the starting point for reconsidering the plausibility of critical teaching in the university setting. There is a tendency to assume that its challenge is to overcome an inertial condition, but that assumption is false. Change, not stasis, is the condition of life: the instructional challenge, accordingly, is not to force open obstinately closed minds but to intervene creatively in processes of change that are already underway, making use of the intellectual disequilibrium that the university can foster in the interest of learning. There is also a tendency to assume monolithic conditions surrounding the enterprise of critical teaching: "students of the dominant culture" is such a monolith when conceived not as a helpful analytic abstraction but as a fact of social life. The university is as much a contested ground as other institutions are, one where alternative goals and methods, liberal, conservative, and radical agendas, teachers and students from assorted backgrounds are the stuff of dialectic. Any classroom is a site of conflicting beliefs, values, affiliations, desires, class and gender identities, the tapping of which can offer opportunity for critical reflection. There were moments of such opportunity, brief but potent, in my own class: women who felt authentic fear and anger after reading Lessing's "A Woman on the Roof," people arguing about the chauvinist narrator's prejudices in implying Margaret's murderous intent in "The Short Happy Life of Francis Macomber," students puzzled and frustrated over the paradoxical values in Singer's "Gimpel the Fool," students appalled at the money/success ethic behind the tragedy in Lawrence's "A Rocking-Horse Winner."

It may be that the rewards of critical teaching must always be found in such small, tantalizing moments of classroom encounter, not in measurable advances on the grand schemes that theoretically propel the enterprise. Whether the accumulation of those details is likely in the end to add up to the realizing of those schemes constitutes one of the many uncertainties, the many hopes or doubts, that teachers learn, and ought to learn, to live with.

Lil's story: Let me set the stage with a "critical" prefatory reading of Ira Shor's (Marxist) representation of liberatory pedagogy and the classroom practice that derives from it. Shor builds a forceful argument in *Critical Teaching and Everyday Life* about the stratifying function of American education and the particular circumstances of working-class students in the community college setting. Mirroring what Freire calls "the ladder of oppression," schools transfer responsibility for academic limits and failures experienced by working-class children from the educational system that actually produces them to the individual student (1–26), who has typically been tracked from early grades; who has suffered through years of authoritarian regimen, transfers of inert information, and unrewarding drills on decontextualized "basics"; who eventually fails to "measure up" to the demands of university education; and who finally comes to the community college classroom—where Shor worked—in a last, resigned bid to acquire the "credentials" of respectable employment. Along the way, this student has been effectively persuaded that her failures and setbacks are her own fault, that she has had unrealistic expectations, that she must now settle for the kinds of work that her limited talents enable, but that this last chance at schooling represents, as the hustler says, "a real opportunity." The consequence of this academic mind-game, Shor argues, is that corporate America gets from schools precisely what it wants—an undemonstrative work force, meekly satisfied with the limited "rewards" to which its modest efforts have entitled it and apathetic about its (continuing) socioeconomic manipulation.

I find Shor's argument plausible and his instructional recommendations, which are described in rich detail, a powerful source of ideas for teaching. But I want to pause a moment over his rhetoric, which entails a rationalist confidence in the inevitable correctness of his Marxist reading of educational life combined with a heroic representation of classroom success that not only conceals instructional errors and inadequacies (mustn't there have been some?) but also raises questions about the extent of his determination to bring students to the same conclusions as his own through the same rationalist inquiry. There may be no overt pressure on students to conform to his agenda, but power arrangements in the classroom make some pressure unavoidable, leading one to worry how significant the difference really would be between a student's enforced belief in her oppressed circumstances as opposed to an enforced belief in her "natural" academic limitations. Listen for a moment to Shor's explanation of critical study in his classroom: "Through rational analysis, the class not only reverses mysticism in its mind, but it simultaneously exposes the shape of social life and the unused powers of thought in every brain. By using their conceptual skills, students reverse their own disempowering consciousness. They gain an immediate sense of power which accompanies their emerging awareness of reality" (107). Both the theme of rationalist confidence and the theme of veiled coercion seem to me to be present in this account. "Analysis" exposes the "shape of social life," resulting in a new "sense of power." Reason is triumphant. Students who accept the challenge of rational inquiry (but what options do they have?) relieve themselves of "mysticism"—the condition of mind that prior schooling had imposed (including the belief that their oppression was really a form of success)—and recognize the world for what it is. Students eventually concede, in other words, that Shor's reading of that world is accurate. By implication, one must suppose, student resistance to Shor's rhetoric of rationalism can be nothing else but the continuing effect of false consciousness and mystification.

Shor represents the teacher as hero in the classroom (a common narrative tactic in stories of critical teaching) in order to create a necessary momentum for the praxis he urges. When, for example, he asks his students to explore the hamburger as a sign of "commodity culture" (162ff.), asking questions about where its ingredients come from, how it is made, and who profits from their "buying" it, both literally and figuratively, he says that the students, with minimal teacher intervention, begin to "read" the conditions of their life—the capitalist exploitation of their health, their living conditions, and their habits of mind. As a result, they are transformed. According to Shor, students find the hamburger, upon close inspection, to be greasy and noxious; presumably, they now look more critically upon the alleged benefits of the market economy that produced this object and persuaded them to consume it. If that's what happened, so be it—but I'm a little surprised at the extent of the success. I start to wonder about what isn't included in the account. Did *no one* confess a liking for hamburgers? To what degree, I wonder, has Shor's inventive questioning of his students increased their awareness of capitalist oppression and to what degree only their awareness of what a teacher wanted them to do and believe? He refers earlier in his account to a prior stage of instruction, a kind of prerational unsettledness, that he describes as the "common period of classroom anarchy that accompanies the transition from orthodox to liberatory structure" (113). That messier sort of engagement is more familiar to me than the later dramatic change of consciousness. What causes Shor's students to move beyond it—liberatory awakening or acquiescence to new rules of the game? Shor is almost certainly struggling here, as any critical teacher does, with the intellectual inertia that leads students to prefer established belief to the promise of altered understanding, attempting to prod students through course requirements to explore and challenge and see with new eyes. He well knows how thin the instructional line is between energetic encouragement and coercion. He recognizes the tendency to exempt one's own position from the scrutiny to which others are subjected, particularly in circumstances where resistant students might look for opportunities to escape serious engagement by satisfying themselves that a teacher won't push them past a certain point. I wish he had talked about these issues, because the responsibility to develop a literate, critical citizenry entails creating classrooms where every point of view is critiqued, including one's own, without implicitly coercive efforts to plead or imply the transcendence of any given perspective by appeal to ontological, positivist, or other rational necessity.

Which brings me to my story about a graduate course in the teaching of writing and literature required of all doctoral students in our English program. It's a story of struggle, an effort to understand the kind of teacher I am, an effort to read useful lessons in what happened during the three years I team-taught the course with my colleague, Judy Fetterley, an effort to define the kind of educator I'm inviting my students to become. Since mine is a story about uncertainties and at least partial failures, I'm working against the convention of the self-confident, heroic narrator, like Shor, who guides teachers through inventive sequences of classroom ideas that "work." Comparatively few stories of such struggle have been told, at least from the vantage point of teachers who continue to believe in, and recommend, the principles of liberatory education. They are, after all, rooted in those least happy experiences of teaching that make us wonder more seriously than usual what we're doing, how well we're doing it, and why we're so sure it's right. One story that I remember is by Elizabeth Ellsworth, and it carries the illuminating title, "Why Doesn't This Feel Empowering? Working Through the Repressive Myths of Critical Pedagogy." Too often, teachers are content to advertise their pedagogy rather than explore it. Ellsworth explores hers and that makes her, for me, a reassuring role model, especially in light of what happened in English 678.

Though I'll describe a series of classes as though it were part of one semester, the series is in fact a sampling and a composite of readings, activities, and student responses occurring over a period of three years.

Furthermore, although the story dramatizes some problems posed for both Judy and me as critical teachers, it's also *my* story, based on my reading of the experience of the course. The nature of language and the nature of learning equally ensure that Judy's story would be, must be, different. When we designed the course, Judy, who is a feminist literary critic, and I agreed that our classroom was to be a site for interrogating the sociopolitical conditions of the work of teaching writing and literature at our own institution. The emphasis was appropriate because our doctoral students teach writing and literature in our department. It also seemed proper because we knew that our students, typically returning to school after years of professional experience, would, for the most part, have recourse to values and ideas about teaching already developed over long practice. We saw ourselves as learners with our students, exchanging ideas in a place constrained, naturally, but not overwhelmed by the social and political circumstances of the graduate classroom. We hoped to make ourselves, our own practices, objects of scrutiny. Because we knew that the students might be uncomfortable exploring provocative issues of power and authority, being candid about our institutional positions as well as their own, taking stances at times opposed to ours, we decided the course would be contractually graded: that is, if the students did the assigned writing, participated in the class discussions, and completed the readings for the course, they would receive A's. At the time we were constructing the course, we re-read Freire and Shor, among other advocates of critical pedagogy, and planned our syllabus to involve students in what we believed might be problem-posing activities.

For starters, we asked students to explore in some way the material and intellectual conditions of their work as graduate teaching assistants. We suggested that they describe where their students came from (who were the students in front of them, who decided why these and not others?), or where their texts came from (what writers were they teaching, what backgrounds did the writers have, why these and not others, who decided and how were the decisions made?), or why their classroom or the building in which they taught was constructed physically in the way it was (who decided this shape rather than another and why?). The idea was for the students to keep asking the prior question, take it as far as they could go. Our students did just what we asked of them: some dug out the architectural plans from the bowels of the archives, others interviewed English editors and anthology compilers by telephone, others talked to the admission committees and examined institutional policies and regulations for ethnic, class, or other biases. The exercise made them nervous about a lot of things they had long taken for granted. But it also led them to wonder what we were up to, where we stood on the questions they were exploring, what we "expected" them to do with or about the conclusions they reached. A measure of "background" anxiety quickly started to form: these were adults and teachers elsewhere, but in this discursive setting they were students trying, like students at any level, to figure out the motives of their teachers, the (merely) local conditions of freedom and constraint, openness and guardedness, characteristic of this classroom, and of course the stakes—rewards and punishments, praise and blame, the terms of success and failure. Why should they trust us or this unnatural game in which the usual decorum of the classroom was being disrupted for reasons they couldn't discover?

In a meeting sometime later, Judy and I asked our students to read a short story aloud with us, a story that neither of us had read and that had been chosen for us by a colleague. We wanted to explore from scratch how we—all teachers of writing and literature—developed an interpretation of a story, how we made sense of the story as we read it, modifying, expanding, problematizing our readings through conversation. No one would get to play super-reader. That night in class I could again sense a collective and mounting anxiety: the story was avant-garde quasi–science fiction narrated by a lesbian. Its eccentric structure sabotaged my own, and I'm sure others', comfortable habits of fashioning coherence. I found myself reliving those uncomfortable feelings my undergraduates have when struggling to find "deep hidden meanings" in stories they don't "understand." The students foundered and so, to an extent, did we, although our plan to work together, inadequacies on the table, to "interpret" a story succeeded well enough in the strict sense: we demonstrated the fictiveness of that literary critical tranquility one sees in scholarly articles and tries to reproduce in classes. But we also disrupted another kind of tranquility, the stable relationship between teacher and student that assures orderliness amid the unsettling chaos of inquiry. Student anxiety, including a growing frustration at our methods—the apparent abdication of authority—began to signal itself in unhealthy ways. Some students, unable or unwilling to understand the fact that a lesbian relationship was being portrayed in the story, began to address the narrator as "he," leavening the atmosphere of interpretive discomfort with a dose of gender hostility, quite possibly directed in part at the two (women) teachers of the class. The evening seemed a lot longer than the three scheduled hours: things were brewing and would soon bubble over.

Judy and I decided that we'd devote the next session to posing problems about our own pedagogy—the feminist values that underlie it, the reasons for the previous week's assignment, the realities of reading we were trying to confront, the issues of power we hoped to examine while reading a story for the first time with our students, a story that left us as short of "correct" answers as everyone else. Our intent was to invite the students to join us in questioning our own values, positions, authority, praxis—to read with us the classroom that we had constructed. They joined us all right, but not from the "authoritative" subject positions we had hoped. They joined us as victims—the only role, really, that our instructional tactics had made available to them. Students complained about the games we were playing with their expectations of a responsible classroom. By asking them to question, in the first assignment about institutional practices, we were asking them to make visible the invisible, to make the "given" problematic. The result for them was a radical disorientation, which resulted in defensiveness and hostility rather than continued inquiry or any resolve to examine the potential consequences of their discoveries. In the second assignment, the story reading, we relinquished the mystique of interpretive authority, which resulted in doubts among the students about who was in charge and what sort of competence we possessed as readers. Two schools of thought emerged: some students voiced frustration that no one in the class, including the teachers, knew where all this questioning was going; others voiced indignation that what was actually happening was a tacit reconfirmation of the status quo, except that here the teachers' agendas were masked. One student that evening crystallized both positions at once: if we, "the teachers," didn't know the territory, didn't know where we wanted our students to go, then why were we there in the first place—why not have the janitor teach the course? And if we did know, why didn't we make our agendas plain so that the students could contest and resist our explicit arguments?

By attempting to convey to our students, and involve them in, a vulnerable, collaborative, nondidactic teaching practice, we had altered their habitual ways of viewing the classroom. That was the good news. But instead of coming to a more critical perspective on issues related to teacher authority, students drew back into a resentful questioning of our motives and competence—in effect accepting roles as surly student-victims rather than as active intellectual colleagues. Judy and I explained ourselves in response to students' insistent demand, made our commitments visible to their satisfaction, but the ironic consequence was that the assertive, rationalist posture they required for their own security worked against everything we were attempting to do in creating, while also investigating, the student-centered classroom. Reducing our own authoritativeness in the classroom, engaging students in institutional inquiry, inviting dialogue on teaching by opening our own practice to inspection, had not encouraged students' construction of their own stories of teaching. Rather these tactics seem to have impeded it by removing fixed reference points of classroom talk, blurring the distribution of prerogatives, expecting a kind of egalitarian venture that structures of schooling beyond (but also within) the walls of our own room have long worked effectively to deny or counteract. Our students simply didn't know how they should understand and perform within this particular instance of "school," and didn't trust us enough to believe that we would give them opportunities without penalty to find out. In retrospect, I can't think of a good reason why they should have trusted us (see Ellsworth).

It was finally easy to recreate an equilibrium for those students who had worried simply about who was minding the store. But it proved difficult for the rest of the semester to reengage students who believed that Judy and I were secretly demanding acceptance of our views as the price of "making it" in graduate school. What remained evident to them was the institutional hierarchies that render asymmetrical the positions of teacher and student, that give the teacher the power to name the world of the student in assignments, course grades, and other ways. The cruelest irony was the number of women students who saw our practices as a refusal to claim the role of intellectual authority. These women sought images of classroom presence that seemed to come easily to male colleagues but to have been denied them. Judy and I have thought often, since, about these various student reactions, about what caused the classroom to move so unproductively from communal inquiry to combative debate, sullen silence, and misunderstanding. We have fragments and glimmerings of answers, but for me they have less to do with "large" theoretical considerations (whether we did things "the right way" according to some orthodox critical praxis) than with small, local, accidental moves, class by class, moment by moment, that subtly affected relations—something said or not said in an instant when reassurance or guidance was needed, actions that signaled something other than what we had intended, responses to the little opportunities and crises that occur in the hundreds of minutes that make up a course and a conversation. Probably, we underestimated the power of conventional school reality to shape or restrict the possibilities of critical teaching. Certainly, we were naive to assume that students would be anything but suspicious and hostile, given the authority we possessed to interfere with their lives, when we attempted to alter (without, of course, really altering) power arrangements in the classroom. Possibly, we indicated in our language and actions a commitment to our own views that students found at odds with the appearance of an egalitarian community. Teachers need to keep thinking about how their institutional and intellectual positions can be used to assist students in developing a critical understanding of the world. They need to keep thinking, too, about how students' interpretive frames are enabled and constrained by hierarchical relations that inscribe us all. They need to produce narratives of failure and error and merely partial success, along with the heroic stories we all prefer to write and read, in order to help this thinking advance. But when all else has been accomplished, there will still be the little things done well or poorly, the things that make teaching artful rather than scientific, and in the end always partly insufficient. These will make the difference.

Chapter 4

Functional Literacy and the Rhetoric of Objectivism

We live among determined, well-educated, and strongly motivated competitors. We compete with them for international standing and markets, not only with products but also with the ideas of our laboratories and neighborhood workshops. . . . Knowledge, learning, information, and skilled intelligence are the new raw materials of international commerce. . . . If only to keep and improve on the slim competitive edge we still retain in world markets, we must dedicate ourselves to the reform of our educational system. . . . Learning is the indispensable investment required for success in the 'information age.'

A Nation at Risk

Literacy is an activity of great cultural, social, and economic importance that consists in the exchange of information from one person to another through the medium of written or printed materials. . . . Literacy itself then occurs when information is transferred from writers to readers via the materials, and society generally wants to maximize the volume of information exchanged in return for the resources it allocates for this matter.

John Bormuth, in
Perspectives on Literacy

The challenges of implementing a critical pedagogy, apparent in our stories from Chapter 3, largely originate from the disrupting of expectations about learning and teaching that are fundamental to the conventional classroom. Liberatory education presumes that the teacher is less dictatorial (though not less assertive) than in traditional schooling, that the student is more active, that attention is differently focused, that the very purposes of the enterprise are newly conceived. These changes bring with them predictable increases in anxiety for everyone—the anxiety of new roles and responsibilities, of not knowing the routines or consequences of performance, of having to confront questions about what usually remains tacit or understood in orthodox belief, knowledge, and activity. Critical teaching in any subject is unavoidably situated within circumstances of "normal" educational practice in American schools that are not only different from but also typically hostile to its aims and methods. Reading and writing instruction, in particular, can't be separated from the politics of literacy—the ideological conditions that determine how literacy is portrayed as a cultural value and how powerful groups define the means, ends, and measures of its attainment. Beyond doubt, currently influential representations of literacy, as well as the proper business of schools in promoting its importance, are aggressively antithetical to those implied in the critical praxis we've been describing. Necessarily, therefore, any effective effort to teach in ways that serve an ideal of "critical literacy" entails reflectiveness about those alternative, governing representations. The likelihood of success for critical teaching, whether in any one classroom or in public educational policy, depends on the fullest possible understanding and critique of what opposes it, the "common knowledge" that Americans hold concerning literacy and the purposes of schooling.

A 1991 Labor Department study, *What Work Requires of Schools*, from the Secretary's Commission on Achieving Necessary Skills (SCANS), sounds a familiar American theme in discussions about literacy: the pervasive deficiency in young people of information-processing abilities necessary if workers are to be well suited to the requirements of a high-tech economy. Some of the commission's examples about what could and should be happening in schools to address this failing lie in the area of math education, and they allow a quick, enlightening comparison between the instructional agenda of the Labor Department and that of Marilyn Frankenstein, the teacher of critical math whose work we described earlier. Recall that Frankenstein's students engaged in mathematical reasoning in order to pose problems about, and thereby gain new power to scrutinize, energy policy, or the costs of food and housing, or employment statistics among women and minorities. Mathematical competence, for Frankenstein, is not merely a technical skill useful in (and to) the marketplace; it's part of a larger capacity for critical reasoning brought to the service of responsible public conduct and the democratic negotiation of social life. The Labor Department supports an alternative notion of what it calls "math skills." One "scenario" depicted in the SCANS report to illustrate the importance of such skills involves food-service workers whose technical know-how enables them to follow inventory control techniques in order to save enough money over time to finance restaurant expansion. Another "scenario" illustrates how an emergency room admissions clerk is able to monitor diverse computerized health and financial records in an atmosphere of emotional tension. The implications of these stories concerning the importance of computational and mathematical training clearly point to a different sort of literacy agenda than that of critical math. Concern in the first Labor Department scene is the maximizing of profit through technical skill; concern in the second is maintenance of bureaucratic efficiency despite external pressures. Concern in both is for ever increasing productivity as the result of workers' enhanced functional control of the technological instruments of economic growth. Is there any chance that those food service workers might learn about Ira Shor's noxious hamburger in their schooling, its status as a cultural object, an ideological sign? Is it likely that the hospital admissions clerk would learn to read the significance of anxious patients, sometimes in pain, lining up to have their insurance policies examined before becoming eligible for treatment?

The dominant view of literacy in the United States today, whether in language or in some other medium such as mathematics, is what Hunter and Harman have called the functionalist perspective, a view so commonplace and seemingly self-evident that its ideological contours are all but invisible to the Labor Department, the Department of Education, the rest of the U.S. government, all but a handful of schooling projects, and the majority of American citizens. Hunter and Harman have offered the standard definition of functional literacy in a study titled *Adult Illiteracy in the United States*. They distinguish there between "conventional" and "functional" competencies, where the first refers to general ability to "get along within one's environment" and the second refers to a more directed capacity to perform within particular socioeconomic settings, notably work. Conventional literacy entails the fundamental ability "to read, write, and comprehend texts on familiar subjects," along with the ability to understand "signs, labels, instructions, and directions." Functional literacy, regarded as an obligatory advance upon the limited attainments of conventional literacy, is "the possession of skills *perceived as necessary by particular persons and groups* to fulfill their own self-determined objectives as family and community members, citizens, consumers, job-holders, and members of social, religious, or other associations of their choosing." Throughout their extended definition of functional literacy Hunter and Harman underline self-determination: "the ability to read and write adequately to satisfy the requirements [people] *set for themselves* as being important for their own lives." They also persistently emphasize language "skills," conceived, that is, as an instrumentality or technology: "the ability to obtain information [people] want and to use that information for their own and others' well-being; . . . the ability to deal positively with demands made on them by society; and the ability to solve the problems they face in their daily lives" (7–8; all italics in the original).

Hunter and Harman intend a richer meaning for functionalism than the Labor Department does, but their definitions nonetheless contain fascinating ambiguities that reflect certain assumptions they share with the public at large. David Livingstone offers some crucial background on those assumptions in his contribution to *Critical Pedagogy and Cultural Power*, where he details two primary beliefs that have dominated Western social thought since the later Renaissance: one is a belief in "technological rationalism" and the other a belief in "possessive individualism," both of which are regarded as "essential characteristics of the human condition." Technological rationalism assumes that human beings operate primarily on the basis of reason rather than instinct, that the exercise of reason will gradually discover the natural laws that govern existence, that the most legitimate, reliable manifestations of reason are modern science and technology, that applications of science and technology will ensure progressive social development, and that these institutions alone can guarantee human well-being. What follows is that people must attain technical skills in order to participate in, enjoy the benefits of, the world that science and technology have (already) created. Possessive individualism assumes that "what makes us human is our freedom from dependence on the wills of others and our capacity to enter into self-interested relations with other persons." Human society is a "series of market relations" between individuals "as proprietors of their own persons and capacities," rather than, say, a network of subordinations to social, political, or economic institutions. The free expression and pursuit of self-interest, in the marketplace and elsewhere, becomes in this view the guarantor of "the greatest good for the greatest number" (126). Hunter and Harman depend on these assumptions, no less than reactionaries like

D'Souza, in their arguments about literacy despite a more liberal agenda, by and large, than one finds in mainstream American educational policy.

In their emphasis on functional literacy as a matrix of reading and writing "skills" that make it possible to obtain and use information, as well as to "solve problems," Hunter and Harman reveal the influence of technological rationalism on their thinking. Literacy is an instrument for controlling one's relations to the environment (much as an ax or a rifle might have been in other times), a technical competence enabling effective participation in the forms of work and environmental management that highly technologized culture has made available. This isn't to suggest that Hunter and Harman entertain (as many do) naively confident beliefs that literacy automatically leads to personal or social improvement for the hitherto illiterate. In fact, they work to dispel the "myths" that literacy "is the primary *cause* of progress" and illiteracy "the cause of poverty and injustice" (109). They believe just the opposite, that "poverty and the power structures of society are more responsible for low levels of literacy than the reverse" (9), and that the modest attainment of reading and writing ability doesn't in itself represent social advantage. Literacy alone, conventional or even functional, separated from issues of class, race, and access to power, remains necessarily ineffectual (what good is an ax if no one lets you near the trees?). But presuming that these issues are dealt with (in a rational, indeed literate, way), the instrument will begin to pay its dividends, because "literacy is an accompaniment to," even if not "a prime cause of," social progress (108)—because reading and writing are "tools" (109), especially at the higher "functional" level, that can be "useful in the course of achieving . . . goals," such as economic security, health care, better schools, and community improvement, supposing that the possibility of socioeconomic access has been assured (108). Moreover, the higher literacy already possessed by privileged groups is the primary instrument for addressing social inequities in technologically functional ways: hence Hunter and Harman recommend setting up a "national commission" (120) to "gather data" (106) on the socially disenfranchised, to prepare "concept papers" on the social context of literacy and "inventories" of successful adult literacy programs (109), to develop "data-gathering instruments" and create "accurate data bases" related to illiteracy (114), to undertake "case studies" of particular groups (119), to establish "a number of pilot projects to test the hypotheses of this study" (119), and to create "instruments for social planning" (124). The commission, comprising highly literate scholars, politicians, and other leaders, would formulate policy proposals, write legislative recommendations, draft arguments for public funding, educate the public, and communicate experimental and research findings—all literate activities on behalf of the illiterate (who, of course, would have their input as well, but inevitably shaped and circumscribed by the limitations of their competence). Assumptions about possessive individualism are even more conspicuous in Hunter and Harman's arguments, particularly in the ambiguous relationships they imply between self-determination and the public sphere, but also in their uncritical appraisal of the character and importance of different group affiliations that affect the individual's life in society. Hunter and Harman emphasize the value of literacy for satisfying "requirements [people] set for themselves," first as "particular persons" and secondly as members of groups—"social, religious, or other associations of their choosing" (7). As autonomous individuals, their story goes, people select affiliations that, in turn, place certain constraints on them in the way of attainments required for effective participation, including equalized "one-to-one" bargaining among the singular members of any group for status and benefits. Literacy is a crucial prerequisite of success in some groups, a particular industry or profession, for instance, in which someone seeks employment. People become literate in order simultaneously to address their own needs, like earning a living, and meet the requirements of others (employers, consumers), as well as the imperatives of a hierarchical economy. So Hunter and Harman suggest, but the tensions and ambiguities in this seemingly tranquil representation are revealing. In the category of groups that people enter "of their own choosing," they indiscriminately list family and community identifications, local or national citizenship, consumer affiliations, varieties of employment, and religious persuasions. Yet one is obliged to ask whether the same kind and degree of "self-determination" is involved in each of these group choices. That is, do people choose family or community identities in the same sense or way that they choose jobs; do they choose religion in the same sense or way that they choose nationality or a city to live in? We find here an uncritical blurring of relationships between the concepts of "individual" and "group," and also of the status of one group as opposed to another, that is entirely characteristic of "possessive individualism," which celebrates self-determination in the face of such evident contrary realities as the unavoidably social circumstances into which people are born (as in family or ethnic heritage), the group impositions that plainly constrain individuality (as in, say, the military or the priesthood), the group definitions that enforce the status of individuals as either insiders or outsiders (as in national allegiance or economic class), the hierarchical arrangements within groups (leaders and followers, managers and workers), and the power differences among groups (the authority of multinational corporations as opposed to that of the Sierra Club or the Knights of Columbus).

Emphases on a radical freedom to choose one's affiliations and on a relative sameness in the varieties of affiliation (hence also the means of gaining entry to or participating in particular groups) have the effect of suppressing two important questions, the first concerning disequilibrium between individual and group interests (in favor of a belief that one set of interests is more or less equivalent to the other), and the second concerning power inequities among groups (in favor of a belief that they enjoy equivalent status). The consequence in the first case is apparent in Hunter and Harman's easy, undifferentiated reference to "skills perceived as necessary by particular persons *and* groups" (our italics), where there is no question of disparity between the interests of an organization, let's say the U.S. military and its expectation that its soldiers be skilled in the weapons of war, and the interests of an individual, some soldier who might prefer to critique the use of atomic armaments. The literacy that enables a technical proficiency in weaponry is not necessarily the same literacy that enables ethical appraisal of such weaponry. The consequence in the second case, power inequities among groups, is apparent in Hunter and Harman's equally easy correlation of "self-determined objectives" for a group like Mobil Oil or General Motors and another like the Sierra Club, with no consideration of degrees of authority, the ability of the former to enforce a widespread literacy responsive to their technological values versus the ability of the latter to promote a literacy responsive to Alaskan oil spills or the pollution of automobile exhaust. Hunter and Harman's functionalism, and indeed the functionalist argument in general, sustains conformity to existing power arrangements, the status quo, with little regard for the literacy of critique and dissent. What's good for General Motors is good for America, because General Motors is nothing more than the sum total of its individual and equal American employees.

The Bell Commission's report, *A Nation at Risk*, offers similar arguments but with further-reaching political authority. It also makes the case for functionalism far more crudely, and therefore evidently, than Hunter and Harman, whose awareness of Freirean and other ideological positions, and whose commitment to situating literacy instruction in local communities that offer the illiterate greater control of their circumstances, make them more sensitive to the government's self-serving economic agendas. There is no such reticence in the Bell report, which was issued in 1983 but which remains powerfully influential today, having set a distinctive tone for literacy debate

in the United States—a mix of jingoistic anxiety about market superiority and patriotic, often explicitly militarist, resolve to whip the
competition through improved, primarily technological, education.
To the extent that the Bell report represents conditions of social
deterioration, the loss of a former excellence, it borrows a rhetoric
that more typically serves arguments about cultural literacy, which
we'll discuss later. But its dominant theme is the need for functional
literacy, what it calls the "new basics," and a reform of slack schooling practices, in order to "reverse the current declining trend—a
trend that stems . . . from weakness of purpose, confusion of vision,
underuse of talent, and lack of leadership" (15). The National Commission on Excellence in Education that produced the report was
formed by T. H. Bell, then Secretary of Education, and included
among its members university presidents (Bartlett Giamatti of Yale,
for one), commissioners of education, school board presidents,
school superintendents, university professors, one former state governor, two school principals, the Chair of the Board of Bell Telephone
Laboratories, and a lone teacher, who had been selected National
Teacher of the Year (whatever that means) in 1981–82. No one should
mistake the authority of the Bell report to tell a story about literacy
to which Americans might give ready assent then, now, and for years
to come.

What is most intriguing about *A Nation at Risk* is not really its
recommendations, which are commonplace (a sign of their power),
but its narrative technique, specifically the bellicose representations
of economic self-interest, only occasionally relieved by flimsy, but
apparently requisite, gestures toward more philosophical, even spiritual, concerns. The report begins by warning that "our society and its
educational institutions" have "lost sight of the basic purposes of
schooling" (5). And what are those purposes? We soon learn that
"competitors" surround us, that we no longer control the world's
markets, that the Japanese and South Koreans are surpassing our
technologies, that there has been a "redistribution of trained capabil-
ity throughout the globe." We must "reform our educational system"
in order to alter this course, for "history is not kind to idlers." One
crucial purpose of schooling then is "to keep and improve on the slim
competitive edge we still retain in world markets"—in effect, to beat
the Japanese and the South Koreans. Of course, the report hastens to
add, "our concern goes well beyond matters such as industry and
commerce." Some pieties follow: "it includes the intellectual, moral,
and spiritual strengths of our people"; it includes a concern for
educating all Americans, "old and young alike, affluent and poor,
majority and minority" (latter categories apparently as settled as the
first one). But once the pieties have been duly introduced, the real

agenda resurfaces, subtly at first, with emphasis still on the spiritual: those who don't possess "the levels of skill, literacy, and training" will be disenfranchised "not simply from the material rewards that accompany competent performance" but also from "the chance to participate fully in our national life"; then with full force, as the report focuses on "indicators of the risk," poor student performance on SATs and other standardized tests "in comparison with other industrialized nations," worse performance in fact "than twenty-six years ago when Sputnik was launched," widespread "functional" illiteracy, dwindling "higher order intellectual skills," all necessary in the marketplace. The clincher, listed last and in greatest detail, is that "business and military leaders complain that they are required to spend millions of dollars on costly remedial education and training programs in such basic skills as reading, writing, spelling, and computation." All this at a time when computers, lasers, robotics, and other technologies are transforming the workplaces on which America's supremacy depends (6–9).

In this context of imperialist economic preoccupation, the report begins preparing the way for its "new basics," pausing first to chronicle America's growing frustration at "shoddiness . . . in our schools and colleges," young people coming out of high school "ready neither for college nor for work," at the very moment when "traditional jobs" are shrinking and "new jobs demand greater sophistication and preparation" (11–12). "Excellence" demands "performing on the boundary of individual ability"—"in school and in the workplace"; it demands "high expectations," "high standards rather than minimum ones," students working "to the limits of their capacities" (but with no suggestion, naturally, of "undemocratic elitism" in the fact that some have lower limits than others). This effort will be required so that "new workers entering the economy each year"—"in a world of ever-accelerating competition and change in the conditions of the workplace"—will be well suited to protecting American superiority, so that "we as a nation" can "thrive and prosper" (12–13). More requisite pieties are overlaid on the economic exhortation: education is important "not only because of what it contributes to one's career goals," but also because of what it adds "to the general quality of one's life"; people should seek "life-long learning"—because otherwise "one's skills will become rapidly dated" (14).

America is, of course, up to challenges at hand: it possesses "the essential raw materials" of reform—"the natural abilities of the young that cry out to be developed," of course, but also "the traditional belief that paying for education is an investment in . . . human resources that are more durable and flexible than capital plant and equipment," not to mention "the ingenuity of our policy makers, scientists, State and local educators [what is a State educator?], and scholars" who are so adept at "formulating solutions once problems are . . . understood" (15–16). What needs to be done, first, is to throw out the "curricular smorgasbord," where "appetizers and desserts" are mistaken for "main courses," leading students to prefer "general track courses" rather than "vocational and college preparatory programs" (18). Students must rededicate themselves "to the time, hard work, behavior, self-discipline, and motivation that are essential for high student achievement" (19). "Gifted students" deserve "enriched and accelerated" curricula, while "disadvantaged students may require special curriculum materials," but all students should put out their "best effort"—"whether destined [destined!] for college, the farm, or industry" (24). Schools must adopt "more rigorous and measurable standards" in order to "help students do their best" (27), should administer "standardized tests of achievement" in order to "certify . . . credentials," identify remedial needs, and locate those best suited for "advanced work" (28). Finally, the centerpiece of this educational Darwinism should be the new basics: English, especially functional skills of reading, writing, and speaking; mathematics; science; social studies (so that students can understand "how our economic system works" and "grasp the difference between free and oppressive societies," among other things); and computer science. It also wouldn't hurt to learn foreign languages, partly to "serve the Nation's needs in commerce, diplomacy, defense, and education," along with arts and vocational subjects (25–26). Longer school days, more homework, greater emphasis on study skills, better maintenance of discipline, more rigorous attendance policies, and more effective placement instruments complete the picture (29–30)—of a schoolroom that might, with justice, be mistaken for the sweatshop of yesteryear—a stern, no-nonsense representation of Spartan struggle for economic domination made necessary by the "shoddy and second-rate" (35) effort currently undermining the country's greatness. AMERICA CAN DO IT, the report announces (33), boldly, ominously, at its close.

The work of Hunter and Harman and *A Nation at Risk* are in some respects at opposite ends of a rhetorical spectrum, but a single spectrum: that is, both are informed by the rhetoric of objectivism. The first is more detached in its claims, observations, and recommendations, the second more overtly political in its intent, more polemical in style, less reflective and judicious. The first is intellectually subtle, aware of alternative points of view, sensitive to issues of poverty, race, and power that complicate the question of literacy. The second is a blunt instrument that might have been comic in its exaggerations of cultural jeopardy, its invocations of Ben Franklin's (or Ollie North's?) can-do zeal, were it not so damagingly influential, so likely to be supported by large numbers of people. But beneath these differences lies a fundamental trust in the core values of objectivist rhetoric, including the independent Cartesian "self" with its "instruments" of material domination, the reliability of empirical inquiry, the preeminent worth of scientific knowledge, the possibility of rationalist intellectual and therefore social progress, the specific identification of technological advance with economic prosperity and improved quality of life. Beneath them too lies a common allegiance to views of language and literacy that objectivist rhetoric characteristically advances, specifically the idea of language as tool and the equating of literacy with technical skill at encoding and decoding information for practical, in particular economic, or "functional" gain.

Objectivism, characteristically but not exclusively associated with the emergence of empirical science since the European Renaissance, holds that the "world" comprises ranges of sensory data that rigorous, dispassionate inquiry gathers, categorizes, and interrelates in meaningful (therefore practical, usable) wholes—propositions, assertions, arguments, laws, models, equations, and other forms of rational discourse (see Knoblauch, "Rhetorical Constructions"; Cassirer, *Enlightenment*). John Locke, whose 1689 *Essay Concerning Human Understanding* offers an early representation of positivist science, explains that "the senses at first let in *particular* [Locke's emphasis] ideas," furnishing the "yet empty cabinet" of memory with notions denoted by simple names. Afterwards, intellectual action "abstracts them, and by degrees learns the use of general names," so that the mind "comes to be furnished with ideas and language, the materials about which to exercise its discursive faculty" (35). The "knower" responsible for that intellective action is a sovereign subject ("cogito, ergo sum," Descartes says), an independent consciousness acting upon the sensory Other that surrounds it, heroically subordinating the material world to rational control. Scientific "method" manifests itself in the production of the discourse of science, which, according to Descartes, for instance, was best patterned on the argumentative tactics of geometry: "those long chains of reasoning, so simple and easy, which enabled the geometricians to reach the most difficult demonstrations, had made me wonder whether all things knowable . . . might not fall into a similar logical sequence" (15). In the objectivist view, empirical discourse is naturally privileged over any other because it depends, in theory, on unbiased observation and systematic argumentative procedure, thereby supposedly avoiding the beliefs, superstitions, emotional excesses, and prejudices of less disciplined, "subjective" language use.

Links between empiricism (as a philosophy of knowledge), technological achievement, and the idea of human perfectibility have been forged and strengthened through the Industrial and the Electronic revolutions, from the printing press to the computer, from the automobile to space flight, from the cotton gin to robotics. The dramatic success of objectivist rhetoric in composing the texts of modern physical science, and in reading those texts for so much conspicuous social as well as intellectual benefit, have made it a compelling force in contemporary life, a force that promotes images of social progress, of evolutionary advancement toward absolute knowledge and control of the physical world. The economic superiority currently enjoyed by the "developed" nations, which allows them to make broad claims about cultural superiority as well, is the concrete result of the success of empiricist ideology due to technological achievement. Little wonder that the dominant educational philosophy of these countries should valorize what has accounted for their standing, that the classroom should be as committed to objectivism as the rest of Western social life. Meanwhile, although philosophy of science has changed dramatically since the age of Descartes and Locke, the myths about objectivity, ultimate rational knowledge, and social progress through technological advance that emerge in their arguments, together with mechanistic, frequently positivist, assumptions about language, discourse, and hence literacy, all continue to influence, indeed govern, contemporary Western educational thinking.

Not all empirical science is positivistic, nor is all linguistic and other language theory that derives from empiricist assumptions. But the myths about science and language that have lodged in the public imagination are in the main positivistic, lending a distinctive rhetorical cast therefore to discussions of education in general and literacy in particular when constituted in the rhetoric of objectivism. Language is conceived in that imagination as a mechanism, an instrument, a tool. Its function is to label things for communicative and other practical purposes, serving as the conduit of "information" about the world. Typically, it's characterized as a container or "code" that carries information from some sender to a receiver, thereby completing a functional transaction, an exchange of material substance for pragmatic gain. The relationship between language and any speaker or hearer is that between a tool and its user. The user wields language as the lumberjack wields an ax or as the laborer operates a bulldozer. Learning to use language is conceived in similarly mechanistic ways; it's a question of mastering the technology, making the bulldozer work according to its design and intent. Students learn "encoding" and "decoding," "user skills" that can be broken into discrete subskills (on the coding side, grammar, "usage," rules of sentence and paragraph "construction"; on the decoding side, "word attack" and other comprehension abilities): each subskill is mastered individually, then put together for effective employment. Literacy is the ability to use the tool of language in order to control the world of information for personal and social advantage. The literate person is like Paul Bunyan, heroically self-reliant, an ax wielder, a clearer of forests who creates the nation's material prosperity through technical know-how, determination, and hard work.

Empiricist scholarship on language frequently supports, and sometimes directly sponsors, functionalist images of literacy. According to Leonard Bloomfield's influential *Language*, a founding document of American structural linguistics, speech situations comprise a "speaker's stimulus," an utterance proceeding from that stimulus, and a "hearer's response" (23), a stark behavioral arrangement at bottom whose variability in actual experience is due "only to the fact that the human body is a very complex system" (33). Otherwise, linguistic practices "are part of cause-and-effect sequences exactly like those which we observe . . . in the study of physics or chemistry" (33). The primary purposes of speech are, first, "to *relay* [Bloomfield's emphasis] communication" (Bloomfield's example is the "farmer or trader" who says at a town meeting or a contractor's office 'we want a bridge over this stream') and, second, to think practically in words (his example is the engineer "who plans the bridge" but doesn't have to "handle the actual beams and girders"). Language helps us "think before we act" (28–29). Even poems, he concludes, although "they do not prompt any particular immediate response," are useful because they "may make the hearer more sensitive to later stimuli" (41). "The human being," Jeremy Campbell writes in his popular book, *Grammatical Man*, "is the most complex communications network on earth, and language is a code which preserves the orderly structure of the messages of speech in ways so ingenious that they are still not fully understood" (67). The point of language is to send information-bearing messages that accomplish the world's work. Even *Finnegan's Wake* differs from other information-bearing messages primarily in its more limited "redundancy," its higher percentage of "error" or "uncertainty," the "noise" surrounding its data (71–72)—"ambiguity . . . is really a kind of noise, obscuring the sense of the message" (163). "The recently fashionable arguments in favor of 'Black English,' " Campbell observes, "are based in part on the premise that ordinary English prose can be compressed and still retain its information content" (72). Even scientists can afford to be liberals about language use as long as its mechanical efficiency is not damaged by too much noise and error, too little redundancy. Black English is all right as long as black workers can still work.

Donald MacKay, a pioneer in information theory, writes that the "meaning . . . of a message" is simply "the state of *conditional readiness* [MacKay's emphasis] for behaviour" that it creates in a hearer (23). His mechanical illustration is that of "a railway signal-box controlling a large shunting-yard." A "brain mechanism" controls the "configuration of levers" in the "signal-box" in our heads. When it receives "messages" through the instrumentality of a code like language, the result is a "change in the 'lever-settings' of the brain" (22–23). His conclusion, after suitably complicating this confessedly oversimplified metaphor, is that "the meaning of a message" is "its selective function on the range of the recipient's states of conditional readiness for goal-directed activity" (24). MacKay goes on to explain that "man as a mechanism is . . . a teleological or goal-directed system," and that "both the human organism and the human group are systems that 'run on information' " (105). He argues that "information as to the current state of (one's) environment" contributes to the "on-going selective process by which (that person's) behavior is organized." The numerous "goals of the human system" constitute a "partially ordered hierarchy, so that "many goal-settings are under the control of 'superior' sub-systems." The setting of these goals offers a "means to a . . . dominant end": his example is "a solitary man" for whom "the acquisition of a tool, or the turning of a control knob" may be "a sub-goal prescribed by superior goal-directed calculations." Now, all the complicated rank-ordering of subgoals finally depends "on current information as to the state of the field of action," which introduces the possibility that one "human system" can productively affect another by "the process we call communication," where "the individual now has the possibility of influencing his environment by way of another individual, by inducing changes in that individual's goal-complex" (105–6).

These arguments by Bloomfield, Campbell, and MacKay are not as simplistic as our presentation makes them appear: all three writers understand that they are speaking metaphorically and all three present subtle, complicated reasoning from an objectivist point of view. Our selections from their arguments are not intended to trivialize them but to draw attention to their rhetorical cast, their style of representation, because that style says so much about the functionalist habit of mind that mainly interests us, particularly its dependence on rational, specifically empirical, renderings of knowledge and its assumptions about the autonomous subject using language as a tool for acting (logically, productively) on the surrounding environment. The school world is saturated with rationalist practices of representation, as is the culture at large, sharing the same dependency on metaphors of mechanism, structure, system, algorithm, and hierarchy, the same belief in objectivity (that is, reified knowledge), the same preoccupation with efficiency and operational effectiveness, the same confidence in experiment and measurement. Not uncommonly, reflective scientists warn of the dangers of allowing the rhetoric of science and the achievements of technology to determine, in narrow, mechanical ways, the purposes and practices of schooling. Hence, Noam Chomsky points out, in *Language and Mind*, the need to resist "strong pressures" to design "curriculum and teaching methods in the light of the latest scientific advances." His concern is that "new knowledge and technique will define the nature of what is taught and how it is taught, rather than contribute to the realization of educational goals that are set on other grounds." He objects in particular to the technologizing of language instruction in the interest of "rapid and efficient inculcation of skilled behavior," including narrow drill-on-skill curricula (often aided by computer software) and "objective tests that are sure to demonstrate the effectiveness of such methods" because the methods are so starkly limited in the first place and because equally limited instructional goals are implicit in the design of the tests. Chomsky insists that what little is known about human intelligence suggests that "by diminishing the range and complexity of materials presented to the inquiring mind, by setting behavior in fixed patterns, these methods may harm and distort the normal development of creative abilities" (101). But few can hear Chomsky's cautions in a society dominated by what Henry Giroux has called "the culture of positivism" (*Ideology* 54–55).

Neither the school world nor the culture at large pays any attention to such warnings, so mesmerized are they by the magically esoteric, yet also economically and socially beneficial, knowledge that empirical thought continues to promise. Hence, in a collection of essays on reading theory published a few years after *Language and Mind*, John Guthrie exults that "in the history of reading, scientific inquiry and practices of teaching . . . have never been closer together than they are today. . . . Teachers and other practitioners are attempting to improve their programs in light of the latest research findings." To ensure an even closer relationship between research and teaching, Guthrie announces two philosophical principles underlying the essays in his collection. The first is that "perceptual, cognitive, and language processes that are important for reading comprehension should be instructional goals in educational programs"; and the second that "characteristics of effective reading programs and teachers should be interrelated and explained in theories of the development of reading comprehension" (xiii). The evident circularity of these principles is a chilling reminder of the ways in which the work of teachers is appropriated within already fixed assumptions of the research community. Several essays in the collection, as Guthrie summarizes them, argue that "a critical aspect of beginning reading programs is an emphasis on decoding printed words to oral language." One concludes on the basis of findings from "a national study" that teaching decoding was found to be a "feature of exemplary programs" (more circularity). Another provides "a detailed outline of reading instruction for decoding"; yet another offers a theoretical account of the importance of decoding; and a fourth demonstrates the value of both speed and accuracy in decoding as the foundation of "semantic processing and reading comprehension" (xiv). What is represented here is both a subordination of classroom practice to a dominating model of scientific rationality and also a technologizing of literacy that reduces it, in Giroux's view, "to the alienating rationality of the assembly line, a mastery without benefit of comprehension or political insight" (*Theory and Resistance* 206).

What is also plain here is the most serious failing of objectivist rhetoric, its persistent tendency to "forget" the human origins of knowledge by enfolding science within a mythology that celebrates the discourse of empiricism while concealing the ideologies of its storytellers and their tactics of storytelling. Objectivism lacks consciousness of its own rhetoric, even indeed consciously denying that it is rhetorical. The consequence is an elitism, plain among educational researchers, justified by appeal to the gods of the laboratory. Supporters of objectivist thinking in education will be quick to list among its achievements an "advance" in knowledge of the processes of human learning, including the development of literacy, and a newly "enlightened" willingness, of the sort Guthrie extols, to ground instruction on what can be observed about those processes rather than on unexamined commitments of liberal or conservative belief. But they will less readily confess its own ideological designs, indeed more commonly encouraging acquiescence to positivism through uncritical celebration of the glamorous arcana of scientific method. Teachers and researchers accept the least advantageous assumptions of a positivist outlook when they call for supposedly neutral "objective standards" in schools; when they trust more than scrutinize the promises, not to mention the motives, of placement and competency testing; when they want, and believe they can have, "teacher-proof" curricula; when they encourage the new knowledge of linguistics or behavioral/cognitive psychology to dictate instructional and learning agendas; and when they expect measurable consequences from rigorously schematized (typically top-down) classroom methods. Teachers and researchers who assume that students failing to thrive in scientifically refined environments are themselves responsible for the failure to reveal the ideological consequences of reifying knowledge and thereby reducing human beings or their activities to the abstract models and structures intended to "explain" them (see Knoblauch, "Rhetorical Constructions").

As *A Nation at Risk* makes plain, the momentum of functionalist views of literacy, cast in the rhetoric of objectivism and scientific rationality, is typically produced by dreams of economic and cultural domination, not only of the material environment but also of other people: workers at the bottom of the economic hierarchy who are merely "prepared" for their niches rather than educated in critical discourse; teachers who must bow before the research establishment, the testing industry, and the other managers of the school world; outsiders, especially non-Westerners, who threaten either to subvert American superiority with their outcasts (Haitians, for instance) or overtake it with their more diligent producers (for instance, the Japanese). But the motives behind educational practice and reform are never simple, and there are more progressive agendas too that borrow from similarly functional, similarly rationalist, points of view, only shorn of the cruder images of domination. A good example is Ernest Boyer's *High School: A Report on Secondary Education in America*, sponsored by the Carnegie Foundation for the Advancement of Teaching and published in 1983. The Boyer report offers a far more humane representation of the means and ends of schooling than anything found in the earlier Bell report and may be seen even as a politically effective antidote to the harm, both philosophical and programmatic, that the earlier report has so much continuing potential to do (though we'll suggest a better one in Chapter 7). Boyer offers frank images of the degrading, educationally unproductive conditions that teachers and students alike face in typical American secondary schools of the 1970s and 1980s (conditions that have changed only superficially today, as we'll show in Chapter 8). His solutions depend on a liberal rendering of technological progressivism, emphasizing, no less than the Bell report does, an equation of "cognitive skills," including literacy, with employment preparedness and the individual's hope of economic equality, but leavened with calls for better conditions, new infusions of resources (to be sponsored in part by cozy relations between schools and the business community), and an authentically broader sense of the missions of schooling than just American economic superiority.

Bowles and Gintis effectively explain the insufficiency of liberal educational reform as proposed within the discursive framework of technological progressivism—that is, Boyer's project, among others— in a study titled *Schooling in Capitalist America*. Bowles and Gintis paraphrase Marx in pointing out that "capitalism . . . is half progressive." On the one hand, it has eliminated dramatic images of "personal servitude" (the serf, the slave) at the hands of a ruling class that controls both the necessities of life and the means of acquiring them, substituting vague impressions of individualized economic potential in the "free market." On the other hand, it has even more effectively than before consolidated wealth and privilege in a single (managerial) class that monopolizes modes of production and the benefits that accrue from them. As Bowles and Gintis concretely point out, for most people "to work is to take orders in an organization over which one has no control" (viii). Schools, they go on, serve in part to sustain this arrangement through their methods of preparing the workforce—promising students that their acquisition of pertinent skills will lead to "equal opportunity" while also, from the start, quite explicitly outfitting them for particular kinds of work and social position (the practice is evident enough in distinctions between vocational and college-preparatory schools, or between universities and community colleges). The flaw of technological progressivism given this state of affairs is, according to Bowles and Gintis, its "extremely partial characterization of the capitalist system," its "overemphasis on cognitive skills as the basic requirement of job adequacy," which valorizes technical over social aspects of economic reality (47). It's insufficient, they conclude, for reformers to think simply in technical terms of "mental skills" that the school can supply to students "and for which employers pay in the labor market," without thinking also of the social structure of education, "the forms of consciousness, interpersonal behavior, and personality it fosters and reinforces in students" (9). When they focus merely on "cognitive variables," reformers can scarcely entertain the idea "that the correspondence between the social relations of production and the social relations of education ... might preclude an egalitarian or truly humanistic education" (47). Since its concern is to make local adjustments within a social structure that remains the same (by offering "skills" to those previously denied), schooling ends up enforcing some of the very conditions the reformers have sought to ameliorate, chief among them the economic pyramid that distributes rewards on the basis of sociocultural factors, including gender, race, and class, quite apart from matters of technological competence. It isn't, after all, the people who know computing or electrical maintenance, or who have clerical talents or tool press expertise, who sit atop that pyramid: rather it's the people who can pay to have such skills put to use on their behalf. Meanwhile, the school's own top-down bureaucratic framework replicates similar structures elsewhere in society. Bowles and Gintis couldn't find a better illustration of their point than Boyer.

The Boyer report lists four "essential goals" to educational reform: (1) schools should help students "develop the capacity to think critically and communicate effectively through a mastery of language;" (2) they should help students "learn about themselves, the human heritage, and the interdependent world in which they live through a core curriculum based upon consequential human experiences common to all people"; (3) they should prepare all students "for work and further education through . . . electives that develop individual aptitudes and interests"; and (4) they should help students "fulfill their social and civic obligations through school and community service" (66–67). In Boyer, plainly, one finds neither the aggressive militarist language nor the blatant economic self-interest that pervades the Bell report. Instead, one finds sympathy for richer, if vaguer, values—"the human heritage," "individual interests," "consequential human experiences." He notes in his Foreword that school reform is only partly about new "standards," that it is most crucially about "the quality of the relationship between teachers and students." In his view "schools have less to do with 'standards' than with people" (xiii). But past the liberal sentiments, one also finds a preoccupation with "skill" development, with a strong emphasis on remediation for those who lack requisite skills (needed in particular for the world of work). Literacy is characterized as "the essential tool" (85), mastery of which serves as basis for the rest of learning. Accordingly, language development "should be carefully monitored," records of "proficiency" in the use of "oral and written English" should be "maintained . . . from grade to grade," and remedial programs should be available at every stage to ensure steady progress (87). This elaborate technological training and management is to go on, meanwhile, in school settings that continue to support all the customary economic and other social arrangements of American life, with little consciousness that those arrangements are directly relevant to the failures or frustrations of many students, the depressed conditions of teachers, and ultimately the problems of schools that have created a need for reform in the first place.

Nothing speaks more eloquently to the central thrust, as well as difficulty, of Boyer's recommendations than his enthusiasm for, and extended account of, new forms of cooperation between "classrooms and corporations," where marketplace values, together with an attendant functionalist conception of learning, can be explicitly affirmed in school under the name of resource development. Boyer lists five advantages to this comfortable arrangement, which he regards as a hopeful development under way all around the country: businesses can work with students who are educationally disadvantaged (271); they can help "gifted" students "especially in science and mathematics, and the new technologies" (272); they can provide teachers with new forms of information (the latest in computers, for instance), give them experience in different kinds of work, offer grants, and provide "teacher excellence awards" (273); they can help students "take the step from school to work" (275); and they can serve as administrative advisers, evaluators, or "trouble shooters" (277). Simply going down the list of these proposals for cooperative ventures between schools and industry, one finds a detailed illustration of the point that Bowles and Gintis want to make. Under the first proposal, for instance, Boyer gives an interesting example of helping "needy" students. A Chicago candy manufacturer, he writes, has developed a "creative project" for one hundred local high school students in need of remedial help (remediation is a recurring theme throughout the report). The students were organized "into small competitive teams that were challenged to produce a new candy and market it to fellow students." The teams were responsible for every step of the process "from market research to design, production, advertising, and evaluation" (271). We can't help but notice the task-oriented, "hardball" rhetoric of the business world: the sorts of human relations implied, for instance, in words like "team," "competitive," "challenged," and "market." But more than that we notice the assumptions about literacy, not to mention other social values, implicit in an exercise aimed at persuading "fellow students" that what the world currently needs is yet another candy bar.

The benefit for the candy manufacturer in this arrangement is plain enough: an opportunity (further) to inculcate market values in "the needy," who may or may not wind up with jobs as a result of the exercise but who will certainly receive a new infusion of enthusiasm for such compelling values as profit, indiscriminate consumption, audience manipulation for personal gain, beating the competition, and creating demand for superfluous products in the interest of economic "growth." As though to reinforce these values, Boyer gives more than one example of the same kind of "cooperation," seemingly oblivious to their underlying significance. In another instance, he cites a large high school class in remedial mathematics that has been visited by a bottling company. Three executives from the company break the students into three groups ("Sunkist, Dr. Pepper, and Hawaiian Punch"), giving each company "mock grocery chain accounts." One group discusses "ways of conducting product-demand surveys"; another looks at "various types of packaging that could be used for their product"; the third tries to figure out "unit pricing formulas." Boyer records the teacher commenting that these students have "never before found basic math so relevant or understandable" (268). Now, this is a high school class in remedial math. How many students, one wonders, will leave the room or the school for management jobs in this bottling company or in other businesses that feature not merely sophisticated math "skills" (which these students certainly aren't getting from high school basic math in any case) but also an applicant pool for such jobs that depends on far different racial, gender, and class configurations than those one might safely predict for this group of students? We would be dubious about the value of this instruction even if there were some broad economic payoff at the end of it. But we're more dubious because of the manifest likelihood that there will be no such payoff, that the main value is further indoctrination to economic practices (for instance, using marketing strategies to sustain fictions of The Good Life) that serve more to oppress than to enfranchise. In any case, Boyer's idea of reform here is to make mathematics more interesting by appeal to practical uses that simulate the socioeconomic conditions responsible in the first place for distinctions between the managerial class and the "needy." The fox cleans up the chicken coop, but by eating the chickens.

Boyer's intent, plainly, is more "liberal" than that: he sees opportunity for making math more palatable to those who are failing at it; he sees further opportunity for the development of workplace "skills" through direct contact with the business and industrial settings that require them; and he sees the possibility that "remedial" students might gain some educational, hence ultimately economic and other social advantage from such contact. All well and good to a point. What he doesn't apparently see is the replication of hierarchical economic values among those who have historically profited from them the least and who, presently, have every chance of remaining as subordinate as they have always been, their brush with white-collar reality notwithstanding. And there's something more. It isn't strictly true, of course, that no one ever makes it out of depressed social circumstances through skill acquisition in school, eventually grabbing the brass ring as a result of hard work and determination. It's only true that *most* don't. There is misguided, if not misleading, advertising here, although "well meant," as there is in the dreams held out to ghetto children of eventually making it in professional sports if they practice hard enough on the local court or ball field. A few will do it, true enough, and thousands upon thousands will fail to do it. Yet the faith of most Americans in concepts of individualism, personal initiative, and equality of opportunity remains so strong that they will continue to preserve rather than critique a system that abuses and betrays the many by appeal to the attainments of a handful. If one student from the remedial classroom makes it in the business world as a result of Boyer's program, everyone will say "better the one than nobody at all," instead of wondering what's wrong with a program that makes such idle promises to large numbers of students on the strength of so minimal a success rate. Still less will anyone wonder what kinds of social myths are being sustained, to the benefit of the advantaged rather than the disadvantaged, by having schools provide so much free advertising of the values of the economic status quo.

The other proposals in Boyer's argument about ties to business and industry are similarly alarming for their complicity in circumstances of social life that he takes altogether for granted in the process of advocating school reform. His examples under "enrichment for the gifted" mainly entail the rich getting richer: Shell Development and IBM go into schools to provide advanced study for "promising students," offer "awards" to students "who demonstrate outstanding leadership," and incidentally scout out possible recruits for their businesses (272–73). His examples under "helping teachers" mainly assume the traditional position of teacher as apprentice knower, needing still more infusions of skill, except that in this scheme university in-service is replaced by corporate in-service (273–75). His examples under "connections to work" emphasize the relationships between "entry-level work requirements" and students' school "preparation," making the clear point that, elective opportunities notwithstanding, the important curriculum is the vocational curriculum, the acquisition of "skills" (275–76). Finally, his examples under "school management and leadership" mainly illustrate how managerial hierarchies already firmly in place not just in the school world but also beyond it can be successfully maintained: for instance, corporate executives "aiding principals in their capacity as both manager and leader" (277–78). Our point here is not that there is utterly no value in any of these proposals. It's that these proposals represent exactly the difficulty Bowles and Gintis point out in underscoring technical skills while ignoring the social realities that surround them. Teachers who learn more about computers have acquired a new classroom "skill," but their subordinate position in a hierarchy of knowledge and authority remains unchanged. "Needy" students learn about business without becoming conspicuously more eligible for the jobs their classwork has simulated (jobs that those IBM and Shell representatives have already offered to "gifted and talented" students, who usually come from more privileged socioeconomic groups).

Little wonder that the Boyer report, for all of its authentically liberal sentiment, should nonetheless retain, here and there, the same reflexes found in other, less progressive functionalist arguments. Recall, for instance, Livingstone's concept of possessive individualism, a corollary of which might be the view that we are all alike in our essential subjectivities, that we all begin with the same rights and entitlements, then wend our individual ways toward personal prosperity. For Boyer, since all Americans are equal and basically identical to other Americans, differing only in the degrees to which they possess serviceable skills, it follows that all students should experience a common core curriculum, so that everyone might sprint for the American Dream from the same educational starting line. That core should emphasize ideas and traditions "common to all of us by virtue of our membership in the human family at a particular moment in history." Specifically, he notes "our use of symbols, our sense of history, our membership in groups and institutions, our relationship to nature, our need for well-being, and our growing dependence on technology." But who's the "we" implied in all those "our"s? The question is intriguing given the subtle shift of plural pronoun at other points in this passage, as when he asks, "what, then, do we see as the basic curriculum for all students?" Or later, when he says that the core is, "we believe, appropriate for every student" (95). A quick scan of the trustees of the Carnegie Foundation for the Advancement of Teaching (xv) reveals university presidents and chancellors, corporate CEO's, school superintendents and principals—all the usual members of such groups—but no teachers or students, no "needy" people, no representatives from working-class America (except a union president or two). It's true, albeit somewhat trivial, that the Appalachian coal miner and the CEO of First Boston Corporation are equally members of "the human family at a particular moment in history." But it's surely a less than self-evident claim that the only thing differentiating the two is unequal development of cognitive capacity, or that the core curriculum Boyer has in mind is equally pertinent to both, or that exposure to that core is somehow the principal alchemical influence for someday making one into the other.

Recall, too, Livingstone's concept of technological rationalism, a corollary of which might be that there is nothing more logical or efficient than top-down organization of a process of school reform, where the most highly trained, the most literate, the most technologically informed, the most highly credentialed, give direction to everyone else. Boyer is intriguingly conflicted about who ought to be in charge. He straightforwardly observes that "if the quality of American education is to improve, top-down planning will not do. Teachers and administrators in the public schools must be full partners in the process" (266). But then, one wonders, what's the status of his report? Who has written its recommendations, who's endorsing it, who's the 'we' it keeps talking about? Granting the fact that there might be endless conversation about possible details of its implementation, if the Department of Education were to say, "let's do things Boyer's way," how much negotiating room would the average teacher have? Later in the report, in a section on "clarifying goals," Boyer offers two principles: "we recommend," first, that every school should have "clearly stated goals—purposes that are widely shared by teachers, students, administrators and parents"; second, that "school goals should focus on the mastery of language, on a core of common learning, on preparation for work and further education, and on community and civic service" (301). As we read these principles, two effectively repudiates one. The first gives lip service to enfranchising teachers and others in the process of determining goals while the second represents, at least in broad strokes, what the goals are supposed to be. Suppose teachers wanted to recommend a focus on diversity or multicultural instruction alongside (or in place of) Boyer's "core," whose references to "our common literary heritage" (96), for instance, make it sound a lot like E. D. Hirsch's core, as we'll suggest in the next chapter? Would the Boyer Commission dutifully carry that recommendation to the Department of Education (which might listen to Boyer but certainly not to a local group of teachers)?

The Boyer report is finally a better, if not necessarily a clearer, illustration of functionalist arguments than the Bell report, because it's subtler, more generous, broader in its understanding and aspiration. We're not suggesting that Boyer's arguments should be repudiated: they may be the best the country can get from an educational and political establishment generally bent on a course of economic imperialism. Better Boyer's relatively enthusiastic (albeit misled) classes of aspiring advertisers and executives than Bell's sweatshop. Nor do we imply that education should not aim to prepare students for the workplace or for other productive capacities in American life. We're arguing instead that literacy ought to offer *more* than training for work, that educational practice should situate the concern for work within a fuller set of expectations about what constitutes an informed, critical citizenry, whose reading and writing abilities enable them to address inequities and renegotiate the terms of their lives. We're suggesting the limitations of functionalism, its idolizing of objectivist rhetoric, its narrow equation of technological superiority and social "development," its tendency to restrict the possibilities of literacy instruction to vocational ends (touched up just a little by vague references to spiritual growth), and its preference for existing social norms and institutional hierarchies (where the rich stay that way but spend some of their money showing the less rich how to work—for them—more productively). Functionalist educational practice is an instrument of domination claiming to be an instrument of liberation, a means of distributing skills to outsiders according to terms set by insiders—according to the economic ambitions of advantaged groups. The country as a whole, not just its outsiders, deserves a more ennobling sign of its prosperity than that.

Chapter 5

Literacy and the Politics of Nostalgia

Our nation is at risk. Our once unchallenged preeminence in commerce, industry, science, and technological innovation is being overtaken by competitors throughout the world. . . . The educational foundations of our society are presently being eroded by a rising tide of mediocrity that threatens our very future as a Nation and a people. . . . Our society and its educational institutions seem to have lost sight of the basic purposes of schooling.

A Nation at Risk

Now flamed the Dog Star's unpropitious ray,
Smote every Brain, and withered every Bay;. . . .
Then rose the Seed of Chaos, and of Night,
To blot out Order, and extinguish Light
Of dull and venal a new World to Mold,
And bring Saturnian days of Lead and Gold.

Alexander Pope,
The Dunciad

I want a poet who can write! *Some are no more, and they that live are base.*

Aristophanes, *The Frogs*

The lamentation is a familiar one these days, echoing through the current national debate about levels of literacy, the quality of schooling, and the country's future vitality. One hears it not only from educational commissions of the sort that produced *A Nation at Risk* in 1983, but also from such popular prophets of cultural decline as Allan Bloom and E. D. Hirsch. It's the melancholy song of the conservative imagination, which conceives of history in tragic terms, as a record of eroded standards, depleted capacities, lost states of high attainment. America once was strong but is growing weak, once was educated but is becoming illiterate. Cultural elegies and a nostalgia for lost worlds, lost eras, are of course perennial. And nothing stands to be gained from inquiring whether American culture, in this case, is "really" in the peril that *A Nation at Risk* proclaims: as with belief in goblins or flying saucers, conviction precedes demonstration. One either believes or not; but presuming belief, the signs of peril lie everywhere. What's interesting is the frame of mind, the ideological disposition, that has led to the composing of such mournful stories of cultural jeopardy and decline through the centuries. To be sure, the stories often respond to conditions of authentic social disequilibrium, the impending defeat of Athens in Aristophanes' time, the rise of the merchant class in Pope's era, the uncomfortable reality, for Hirsch, of pluralistic culture in contemporary America, the uncomfortable reality, for Bloom, of recent ethnic and gender militancy, open enrollment and other equalizing opportunities in schools. The stories have "real" causes, but they also reflect particular habits of mind reacting to the facts of cultural change.

Beyond the concrete social circumstances of their emergence, the stories' common preoccupation with the decay of High Culture testifies to the enduring allure of an ancient Western myth, the Fall from Grace, an ages-old expression of the fear of change that haunts the conservative temper, for which all change (other than "going back") invariably means degeneration from a once glorious, reverently (if dimly) recalled Golden Age. The perennial fear is that some hallowed array of values and traditions, some settled distribution of power and entitlement, some privileged canon of knowledge, some range of tastes, some favored memory of the past, some ideal form or practice of language, is now besieged by forces, construed to be alien and barbarous, that threaten the established, hence rightful, order of things. Any such tampering with absolute and timeless meanings is a descent from coherence into chaos. In *The Frogs* Dionysus journeys to Hades to bring back Euripides (who had recently died) because there are no good writers left in spiritually bankrupt Athens. In the competition staged there between Euripides and Aeschylus (who had died some fifty years earlier), the still higher literacy, hence greater wisdom, of the latter (and older) wins out, with the finding that Euripides is, by comparison, prosaic and commonplace, lacking in the grand style of tragedy, and therefore somewhat less suited to Athens' public need. By the conclusion, however, it's clear that even the dead Euripides would be preferable to any live modern, whose incapacities are far more serious. The general rule of corruption theories is, the later the generation, the more advanced the decay. Pope's *Dunciad* laments the coming of the "Smithfield Muses," representing a new middle-class taste in art and literature that threatened the "neoclassical" aesthetic of the privileged class of early-eighteenth-century English society. For Pope, newly developing preferences for the novel and other "domestic" prose vehicles over the specialized, typically poetic, classically allusive literary forms of High Culture seriously threatened the spiritual life of the country, not to mention the prestige of those "correctly" educated, generally well-to-do artists who maintained the traditional literary values. Hence, *The Dunciad* mourns the descent of cultural night: "Nor public Flame, nor private, dares to shine;/ Nor human Spark is left, nor Glimpse divine!/ Lo! thy dread Empire, Chaos! is restored;/ Light dies before thy uncreating word;/ Thy hand, great Anarch! lets the curtain fall;/ And universal Darkness buries All" (IV, 651–55).

The contemporary American cultural jeopardy is variously characterized, although, as in the past, it always involves language, literature, and literacy to some important degree. It can be external and economic in nature, as in the Bell Commission's claim that as a result of their superior education the Japanese are making better automobiles and the South Koreans better steel mills, thereby compromising America's dominance of international markets. It can be internal and moral or intellectual in character, as in Bloom's conviction that the philosophical barrenness of the 1960s has led to the collapse of American learning and civility. The threat can be concrete and immediate, a "formalist" curricular proposal, for instance, that compromises the rigor of "content." It is often framed in the rhetoric of objectivity, a "drop" in test scores or in somebody's head count of literate people. It can also be vaguer, more conjectural, as in Hirsch's fear of the nation's loss of a common core of knowledge. It can be the consequence of sin or intrinsic evil, unavoidable imperfection, the aggression of "outsiders," corruption, softness, or just lack of diligence. It can be inevitable, like dialect variation, where the commitment must then be to retard it as much as possible; or remediable, like feminism (according to Bloom), where the objective is to extinguish it before too much harm is done. But whatever its nature and origins, it embodies the fearful spectre of change, whose coming, like a fifth horseman of the Apocalypse, is to be dreaded, lamented and, to the extent possible, resisted with desperate heroism.

Let's be clear, however, about the difference between legitimate concerns for stability and cohesiveness, on the one hand, and harmful myths about cultural decay, on the other. It would be foolish to deny the importance and value of tradition, the need to maintain and nurture cultural memory, in education and elsewhere, the authentic relationship between institutional coherence and quality of life. The project of binding present to past belongs to the larger quest for social survival and perpetuation that properly distinguishes any healthy culture. There are legitimate issues to be addressed in this domain: the ways in which pluralistic culture can discern its own themes and develop them, through ceaseless negotiation, in the service of social justice; the ways educational practice can define and pass to students the (manifold) forms of public identity that can promote a conscientious, productive citizenry. But we have something else in mind here, a story about culture that is consciously and systematically designed to create anxiety, unreflective reverence for an Eden-like past, and fidelity to a single (usually implicit) set of values in the service of reactionary political agendas that are tailored to maintaining social privilege. We're concerned with a neurotic sense of loss and with attendant arguments about redemption used to manipulate the public imagination in ways that protect given distributions of entitlement. People need stories about their past, their kinship, their interrelatedness. But the stories about "cultural literacy" that we propose to critique here are not finally about interrelatedness; they are "explanations" of the superiority of some groups of people and the inferiority of others, energized by a nostalgia for the simplicities of absolutism.

Golden ages of literacy (there have been many) are perfected conditions, cultural Edens, in which values that are now decaying once shone with brilliance and purity. Necessarily, the time of perfection lies at least within the distant memory of the elder generation: if everyone had forgotten it, after all, there would be no energy left for lamentation. In *Cultural Literacy* Hirsch remembers his father's ability to quote Shakespeare to his business colleagues. "In his day," Hirsch writes, with the mix of fondness and melancholy characteristic of these recollections, "business people could make such allusions with every expectation of being understood" (9). Men were men: they could make a profit and be cultivated at the same time. Indeed, they could turn their cultivation *toward* a profit, the best of two worlds. Humility prevents Hirsch from claiming for people of his generation the same heroic stature as their fathers, but he implies that their cultural memory is at least good enough to reverence and imitate the paternal ideal. It's the younger generation (as always, it seems, when old men compare the present with the past) that has sunk to the threshold of barbarism: "young men and women now in their twenties and thirties" are substantially illiterate (8); their children, in schools now dominated by "the content-neutral ideas of Rousseau and Dewey," are in still worse shape. Hirsch can date explicitly the last stage of the Fall: "During the period 1970–1985, the amount of shared knowledge that we have been able to take for granted in communicating with our fellow citizens has . . . been declining" (5). Bloom's *The Closing of the American Mind* disagrees slightly about the dates but not about the reality of the Fall: as late as 1965 "good undergraduates" were still in stock (49), but by the second half of the decade student souls had become "exhausted and flaccid," the culture approaching "spiritual entropy" (50–51).

The latest Golden Age of literacy—let's call it a time prior to 1968, but more likely (depending on one's calculation of the heyday of Hirsch's father) sometime between Teapot Dome and Joe McCarthy—featured, by contrast to these tawdry times, a fixed galaxy of ideals. Bloom agrees with Hirsch that men were men. More important for Bloom, women were women, properly mindful of Plato's view that "the female bears and the male begets" (*Republic* 454e). Because in the Golden Age females were still "modest," they both knew their own place and allowed men to occupy theirs; "female modesty extends sexual differentiation from the sexual act to the whole of life. It makes men and women always men and women" (102). No feminism—that "latest enemy of the vitality of classic texts" (65)—existed when men were men and women were modest. The patriarchs of Bloom's Golden Age lived life by the Book, specifically the Bible, but by extension the no less sacred books of "great scholars and thinkers who dealt with the same material." They knew that "life based on the Book is closer to the truth," providing access to "the real nature of things." Bookless moderns speak only in "cliches and superficialities"; they are "narrow and flat"; they lack "refinement" and "real taste" because the existence of such qualities is "impossible without the assistance of literature in the grand style" (61). The Golden Age knew quality and wasn't afraid to say so: since Good and Bad were absolute distinctions, good students were really good, bad students were really bad, and "select" (51) students, those in the Ivy League (except Brown, which "dismantled liberal education in the sixties" [84]), and, of course, at Chicago, where Bloom professed, were the best of all. Today, affirmative action and other such irrational institutions deny true quality and merit, even in the "best" places: "everybody knows" that "the average black student's achievements do not equal those of the average white student in the good universities" (96), but silly liberals wish to pretend otherwise—to the detriment of black and white alike, Bloom insists. The Golden Age is anti-relativist, justly confident of its claims to "intellectual imperialism" because of its possession of "the rational principles of natural right." The United States, in particular, represents a supreme achievement of "the rational quest for the good life according to nature" (39). Hence, the Golden Age is specifically situated within Western tradition, and the American experience in particular. Of course, Bloom means Old America, the land Hirsch also has in mind when he speaks of "the Founding Fathers' idea of a literate and informed citizenry" (108). Fathers get a lot of credit in the Golden Age.

Evidently, much of the lament for a lost Golden Age of literacy in Bloom and Hirsch involves specific correlations between language use, sacred books, and culture. We will use the term "cultural literacy," therefore, to designate a story about literacy that presumes a certain kind of connection between language and culture, where the purpose of language use is, ultimately, the preservation of fixed ideals of heritage and civility, where, as for Aristophanes or Pope, any corruption in the standards of "correct" talking, reading, and writing implies a corresponding cultural jeopardy. This definition is broader than the one Hirsch has offered in his popular arguments. For him the concept means specifically "the background knowledge necessary for functional literacy and effective national communication" (xi). Hirsch shrewdly incorporates notions of pragmatic social gain available from a functionalist perspective with notions of shared understanding and tradition associated with the cultural perspective. By this tactic, he gains the political advantages, so clearly recognized by *A Nation at Risk*, of appealing to American economic, no less than chauvinist, preoccupations. At the same time, his concern is clearly for reconstituting a cultural consensus, rooted in the values he shares with others in his privileged class, that has been lost in recent times through "a gradual disintegration of cultural memory" (113). Like Bloom, his instincts lie with the rather morose, traditional humanists of the university establishment, his colleagues who sulk about assaults on the literary canon and about students' dwindling enthusiasm for Wyatt and Surrey. But he is savvy enough to know that a rationalist argument about America's inability to compete with Japan will carry more weight in the corridors of real power than precious fussing over low enrollment in Juvenalian Satire or even neurotic attacks against feminism.

As Harvey Daniels has shown in amusing detail in *Famous Last Words*, conservative laments about degenerative language practice, and about the decline of language itself, resound through history, suggesting, illustrating, embodying forms of cultural decline. In Western tradition, aware from ancient times of the variety of speech and the reality of linguistic change, language has nearly always been portrayed as corrupted with respect to some earlier, pristine condition—the language of Adam, the *Ursprache*, a primordial tongue that maintained a perfect one-to-one relationship between words and things. The Book of Genesis says that God created the birds and animals of the world and then brought them before Adam (Eve was still just a rib at the time) "to see what he would call them; and whatever the man called every living creature, that was its name" (2:18). Hence, in the beginning, "the whole earth had one language and few words" (11:1). Later, however, as God, a jealous patriarch, watched construction of the Tower of Babel and noticed the unseemly power available to human beings in the ability to name and communicate, He decided that ejecting them from Paradise had not sufficiently cured them of their pride, and He scrambled their speech for good measure: " 'let us go down, and there confuse their language, that they may not understand one another's speech' " (11:7). Language has been in a state of disrepair ever since, a babel, only grudgingly responsive to the valiant efforts of grammarians, etymologists, lexicographers, and other guardians of usage through the centuries to halt its continuing slide into barbarism. Measured against the original power of the Ursprache, present-day language can only be regarded as enfeebled and vulgar, fallen from grace. Further decline is inevitable, a consequence of human depravity, but the moral obligation of the truly literate (one of God's purgatorial challenges) is to resist further corruption through ennobling struggle, the equivalent in philological heroism of Roland's stand at the bridge.

Because the stakes are high, military metaphors are in fact not uncommon. *A Nation at Risk* maintains that, had an "unfriendly foreign power" attempted to cause America's present mediocrity, "we might well have viewed it as an act of war" (5). As it is, Americans have committed "unilateral educational disarmament" (5); Roland would be appalled. The retrieving of literacy (among other educational attainments) is a matter of plain patriotism, since "citizens know intuitively" that their "material well-being," and their "safety," depend on protecting "the Nation's intellectual capital" (17). Culture itself is at stake, since "the intellectual, moral, and spiritual strengths of our people," which "knit together the very fabric of our society," depend on literacy for their expression and preservation (7). George Orwell had concluded as much in 1945, in "Politics and the English Language," when he observed that "the present political chaos is connected with the decay of language," and that "one can probably bring about some improvement by starting at the verbal end." The condition of language and of language users, the quality of speech, the level of reading and writing ability, the state of literature, are all central to the health of Culture, which is dependent upon language for articulating The Old Values and perpetuating the way of life they serve to rationalize. Language is a vessel, a chalice, containing the wine of Culture. Sacred Books are the cellars in which the cultural vintage resides, where young and old can sample the variously delectable grapes of their (presumably) common heritage. To drink is to prosper.

Cultural literacy, then, means speaking and writing correctly, reading the proper books, knowing the right knowledge, making sure that others do these things as well, and protecting children from those who don't. "Literature," Ernest Boyer assures Americans in his Carnegie report on the troubled state of secondary education, offers "perspective on historical events," tells people "what matters," transmits "enduring spiritual and ethical values," illustrates "moral behavior," and speaks "to all people" (97). Truly literate citizens are obliged therefore to safeguard the canon of Sacred Books, where Culture is inscribed, introducing them in school so that the moral lessons they convey, the cultural ideals they represent, will ensure the right-mindedness of coming generations. Moreover, as William Strunk and E. B. White explain, every language user has a solemn responsibility to cherish and safeguard heritage by protecting the chalice of language, as Saint Stephen did the chalice of the true Church, from the onslaughts of barbarism represented by dialect pluralism, vulgar usage, the intrusion of other languages, mediocre or immoral writing, and any violation of the standards of Clarity and Grace. *The Elements of Style* confidently, if vaguely, commands writers to "choose a suitable design and hold to it," communicating values of order, purposefulness, self-control, steadfastness, and etiquette. "Write in a way that comes naturally," it says, "place yourself in the background," "do not overwrite," "do not overstate," "avoid the use of qualifiers," "do not affect a breezy manner," "do not explain too much," "avoid fancy words," "be clear," "do not inject opinion," "use figures of speech sparingly," "do not take shortcuts at the cost of clarity." None of these injunctions is itself "clarified" for practical application because the intent is not to produce a handbook for writers but rather a catechism of the values of High Literacy. What emerges, then, and what is intended to emerge, is an image of linguistic good breeding, including beliefs about rationality and objectivity, about what it is to be natural, modest, and plainspoken, about the properly austere communicative function of discourse, about the inappropriateness of personalized, expressive, or imaginative writing in daily affairs. By telling people about language Strunk and White tell them what sort of people they should wish to be.

Inevitably, this view of literacy—an amalgam of privileged cultural inheritance and verbal decorum, colored with ever present threats to its well-being—also stipulates quite clearly what people should not wish to be. It offers a portrait of insiders—the culturally literate—and therefore, by implication at least, a portrait of outsiders as well. The portrait is filled with images of competition between cultures (*A Nation at Risk* speaks often of "determined, well-educated, and strongly motivated competitors" [6], frequently of Asian origin), of civility as opposed to barbarism (Orwell's rule of rules is never to "say anything outright barbarous"), of linguistic jingoism (the variety that the English First movement practices, for instance), of "standard" dialects of English and nonstandard ones, of "national" culture and merely local culture, of "Honors" tracks in school and "remedial" ones, of central curricula like the Great Books (Bloom's "good old Great Books approach" [344]) and "alternate" curricula like African American Studies. The differentiations, often presented by appeal to the *topos* of "separate but equal" (the kind of argument that the more equal frequently mount when addressing the less equal), invariably betray a hierarchical arrangement of social values rooted in class, ethnicity, and gender. If the political program is not always explicit in the reasoning, it's always given away in the language. Consider a few more of Strunk and White's commandments: "do not use dialect unless your ear is good," "prefer the standard to the offbeat," "avoid foreign languages," and "use orthodox spelling." Consider Boyer's examples of the capacity of great literature to represent moral behavior through specific characters—"Job, Odysseus, Oedipus, Hamlet, Billy Budd, Captain Queeg," all standard male heroes and antiheroes of the Western, white, middle-class literary experience. Consider Bloom's language at those moments when his melancholy turns ugly, as it too often does: his smug allusions to the "best" and the "brightest"; his reference to Black Studies programs as "this little black empire" (95); his unabashed misogyny; his flaunting of the male pronoun as a pugnacious call to the Grand Old Days before sensitivity to the politics of language had become such a nuisance for gentlemen scholars.

Cultural literacy derives its energy from fear of the outsider, the alien, the barbarian, whose culture is exotic and threatening in its difference, hence viewed as no culture at all. The fear is that the outsider might contest the inside, might alter the status quo, which could only result in degenerative change. Cultural literacy arguments plead, accordingly, for the absolute, the timeless, the ontological nature of the values they commend, along with the genteel necessity of decorous language practice, which keeps the insider clearly separate from the outsider, and the special place of Sacred Books as the repositories of "our" heritage. Those outsiders who desire to give up barbarism, to "be like" insiders, are encouraged to try (a variant of "the white man's burden"), provided they accept the instruction of the insiders. The rest lie quite beyond help in any case. Plato makes the point clearly in *The Republic*, which is, Bloom writes revealingly, "for me *the* book on education, because it really explains to me what I experience as a man and a teacher" (381). According to Bloom's reading, *The Republic* describes "the real community of man," made up exclusively "of those who seek the truth." The community doesn't admit just anybody: it "includes only a few, the true friends, as Plato was to Aristotle." The community of the "philosopher kings" is where real literacy resides: "they have a true community that is exemplary for all other communities," one in which the knowledge of truth and the love of wisdom distinguish insiders from lesser "men" (381–82). Bloom speaks often of the select group he has in mind for the reeducation project that will be necessary to recover some fragment of the Golden Age. He proposes to "intervene most vigorously in the education of those few who come to the university with a strong urge for *un je ne sais qua*." We are, he proclaims, "long past the age when a whole tradition could be stored up in all students, to be fruitfully used later by some." It's hopeless to "attempt universal reform," hopeless to inspire the rabble. Only the "best" are now "fit for a bookish adventure" (64–65). Bloom speaks warmly of "freedom and equality" when celebrating the virtues of American civilization, but Plato is always in his heart—the Plato who despises democracy, who believes that "philosophy is impossible among the common people," who compares ordinary folk to "a large and powerful animal," that must be "handled" in its many moods, that must be controlled, not given control (493b). Bloom imagines himself a philosopher-ruler and wishes to speak only to others of similar breeding.

The fact that Bloom's culture hero is Plato is far from coincidental. It isn't coincidental, either, that Hirsch should extol "Ciceronian literacy" (109). And it's no accident that Bloom should speak so often and so approvingly of Aristotle: "certainly all the philosophers, the proponents of reason, have something in common, and more or less directly reach back to Aristotle" (310). Bloom's claims, and to a lesser extent Hirsch's, about self-evident values, more or less absolute cultural ideals, correct practices of language, and Sacred Books are importantly grounded in what we would label the "ontological" rhetorical perspective (Knoblauch, "Rhetorical Constructions"), which is well represented by the dominant tradition of classical rhetoric, including Aristotle and Cicero. (Arguably, Hirsch also owes much to "objectivist" rhetoric, although mainly for the veneer of empirical chic it offers to an otherwise traditionalist agenda.) In the ontological view, an emphasis on formal propriety in discourse reflects assumptions about the nature of language as a "dress" of thought, where the clothing of words should suit the particular speaker and occasion of speech, where the jewelry of metaphor should aim at a tastefully glamorous effect, where acts of language are a measure of one's background and prestige, intellectual capacity, moral sense, and civic responsibility. Philosophically, the ontological argument presumes an absolute distinction between the concept of "language" and the concept of "reality," the second prior to the first and denoting an intrinsically coherent metaphysical order on which language is based and to which language "makes reference" when it is properly used to speak the truth. Languages differ and degenerate, but reality is a constant. Writing and speech, Aristotle says in *On Interpretation*, are "not the same for all races of men. But the mental affections themselves, of which these words are primarily signs, are the same for the whole of mankind, as are also the objects of which those affections are representations or likenesses, images, copies" (115). In this view, language use is largely irrelevant to the substance of knowledge but crucial for its transmission. As Cicero writes in *De oratore*, the graceful and harmonious style of the orator "must inevitably be of no account if the underlying subject matter be not comprehended and mastered by the speaker." Assuming this independent understanding, however, "whatever the theme, from whatever art or whatever branch of knowledge it be taken, the orator ... will state it better and more gracefully than the actual discoverer and the specialist" (I, xii, 51–52). The underlying "substance" of discourse is one thing, its surface characteristics another. The literate person certainly knows the medium of expression; but a correct knowledge of "things" is prior, the true measure of literacy.

This knowledge from which the forms of language arise and to which they refer is not, in its fundamentals, subject to growth or change. The ten Aristotelian "categories" (substance, quality, quantity, relation, and so forth) produce fixed grammatical forms, giving language its "parts" of speech to rule over the diversity of usage. Such metaphysical constructs as "being" and "becoming," "cause" and "effect," "substance" and "accident," such ethical constructs as "good" and "evil," or the "mean between extremes," such logical constructs as the law of contrariety, such political constructs as hierarchical class structure (Plato's Rulers, Bureaucrats, and Property Owners) based on intrinsic or god-given merit, are essentially static, "underlying" and giving meaning to the flux of the phenomenal world. Aristotle's *Rhetoric* offers fascinating insights into this metaphysical order, where reason reigns supreme, where a teleological design enables clear, rational understanding of human motives and practices, where truth can be distinguished from falsity on logical grounds and through oratorical skill. For Aristotle, "truth and justice are by nature more powerful than their opposites"; moreover, "what is true and preferable is by nature always easier to prove, and more convincing"; hence, "human nature . . . has aptitude enough for discerning what is true, and men in most cases do arrive at the truth" (5–6). This air of intellectual confidence, born of a sense of the stability of the metaphysical order, its a priori and self-evident rightness, runs through the *Rhetoric*, enabling absolute judgments about the way things are or ought to be. Specific events in the world can be referred to metaphysical realities as the means of evaluating them. People can be judged, sorted, by appeal to abstractions that account for the possibilities of character and action.

For instance, Aristotle asks at one point, "What makes men choose to do harmful and evil acts contrary to law?" His answer may seem a curious one: "The causes are vice and moral weakness; for if people have bad qualities, one or more, then whatever the point of their failing, there is the point at which they will do wrong." He gives some examples: "the illiberal man will do wrong with regard to money; the incontinent man with regard to bodily pleasure; . . . the coward with regard to dangers" (55). Now, an empiricist could readily follow this reasoning if it were *reversed*—if the person who had run from the enemy were to be called a coward; if the person who had refused money to the needy were called miserly. An observed behavior then would give rise to a customary name for it (although not necessarily to a "cause" for the action). But Aristotle reasons in what appears a circular manner. To illustrate: imagine a woman who kills the husband who has been beating her for years. When an empiricist is asked why this woman killed her husband, the answer might be "because he beat her," or "because she had a lover," or even "who knows?" But Aristotle's answer is: "because she is a murderer." For Aristotle, an intrinsic fact of the woman's character, her murderous disposition, accounts for her specific crime; for him, metaphysical constants regulate and explain the world of ordinary life, so that his reasoning is not circular—it truly attributes an experiential effect to its abstract cause.

Other constants underlie other aspects of life in similar ways, for instance "natural" orders of merit and superiority among people or groups of people. For Aristotle, "the virtues, and corresponding works, of a class that is naturally higher are more noble; those of a man, for example, are nobler than those of a woman" (49). For

Aristotle, when an "average" person "gains an advantage that does not befit him," it is "a case for indignation," as it is also when "a worse man . . . enters into rivalry with a better." In fact, even when two people are not better and worse with respect to the same pursuit, "we are indignant with one who is inferior in any way, when he sets himself up against his superior" (125–26). For Aristotle, it's a cause of shame for one not to join in "the honorable things in which all men, or all or most persons like ourselves, participate." The people he has in mind are "those of the same race, or city, or age, or kin, or, in general terms, those who are on our own level." As an instance, presuming a certain "level," it "makes us ashamed not to be as well educated . . . as the rest are." Moreover, "the shame is greater if the fault appears to lie with the individual himself, for then the deficiency will have proceeded rather from inward badness" (113). The importance of scrutinizing the rhetoric of Aristotle's *Rhetoric* for understanding a contemporary such as Allan Bloom should be growing clearer. Even Saul Bellow, who generally approves Bloom's arguments, feels compelled to note in his Foreword that "a style of this sort will seem to modern readers marred by classical stiffness— "Truth," "Knowers," "the Good," "Man" (12). But it isn't just the style that "mars"; it's the style of thought. Both Aristotle and Bloom reason from absolute premises, themselves beyond the range of scrutiny, fixed in a world of icy metaphysical tranquility. Imagine the alarm if the sociocultural assumptions that Aristotle catalogues in the *Rhetoric* (and elsewhere in his work) were to be challenged by a "relativist" attempting to alter the status of women, or members of another "race," or people not "on our own level." An entire worldview stands to come crashing down, not merely some local entitlement. No wonder Bloom has composed an elegy for High Culture.

For Aristotle, the Sacred Books comprise the works of the poets and tragedians, the historians, the philosophers, of his culture, from whom he regularly quotes and from whom he derives much of the substance of the *topoi*, those "places" of argument in his system of oratory that offer knowledge and formal alternatives, stored in memory, for the producing of new statements. The Sacred Books store the unassailable wisdom of the past: when read correctly they offer wisdom to the present and enable the preserving of the truths of cultural tradition. The Sacred Books are ultimate sources of learning, their pages endlessly perused for their secret meanings. Interestingly, when Descartes challenges the intellectual absolutism of the classical world, he does so by attacking the Books and substituting direct sensory perception as the starting point of knowledge. Where Aristotle commends "books of travel" to political scientists who wish to learn of other forms of government, "since from them one may learn the laws and customs of foreign nations" (23), Descartes, in the *Discourse on Method*, laments the fact that "from my childhood I lived in a world of books," which had left him "in the ranks of the learned" but "saddled with so many doubts and errors that I seemed to have gained nothing in trying to educate myself." He resolves henceforth to "seek no other knowledge than that which I might find within myself, or perhaps in the great book of nature" (5–8). What's involved in this disagreement is not a contest of preferences, either for reading or for a more active life, but rather a profound change of attitude about the reliability of the meanings that reside in the Sacred Books. For Aristotle they are to be believed and cherished; for Descartes they are to be scrutinized, reappraised, even altered or done away with, as external, empirical tests of validity require.

Saint Augustine provides a sustained defense of the truthfulness of the Sacred Book—which is for him, as for Bloom, primarily the Bible—in *On Christian Doctrine*, a treatise that may be read for the ontological perspective as constituted within Judeo-Christian rhetoric. Augustine also explains, in fascinating detail, the hermeneutic—the theory of reading—that derives from belief in the Book, a theory that remains powerfully influential among contemporary advocates of cultural literacy. For Augustine, no less than for Aristotle, metaphysics (in this case, the "revealed" truths of Christian theology) underlies discourse and is both the source and test of the reliability of statements. Knowledge is separate from and prior to its representation in texts, as it was for Cicero, but it receives textual form through the vehicle of divinely inspired writers. "The truth of propositions is a matter to be discovered in the sacred books of the Church," which contain that truth as a vessel contains liquid. It is discovered by close and attentive reading, in the context of certain belief that "the truth of valid inference was not instituted by men," but is instead "perpetually instituted by God in the reasonable order of things" (68). To be sure, the true meanings of a text are not always apparent. The Bible contains "obscurities and ambiguities," passages covered with "a most dense mist." The faithful reader encounters difficulty in seeking correct understanding because human pride, at Babel, has led to corrupted language. "This situation was provided by God to conquer pride by work and to combat disdain in our minds, to which those things which are easily discovered seem frequently to become worthless" (36–37). Diligent reading, assisted by divine grace, always arrives at the truth.

The Sacred Book cannot lie but it can be wrongly read. "Anyone who understands in the Scriptures something other than that intended by them is deceived, although they do not lie" (31). For Augustine, unlike some modern, "relativistic" readers, the concept of "intention" is unproblematic. The Church already knows what the truth is, what God meant to say, so that the process of reading Scripture is one of referring statements to an external theological standard for their meaningfulness. Augustine exemplifies the point with reference to a distinction between literal and figurative usage. The "rule" is "that what is read should be subjected to diligent scrutiny until an interpretation contributing to the reign of charity is produced." In short, a cynic might say, one is to read a passage until it can be brought into line with established Church teaching: if that can be done easily, the passage is "literal"; if not, it is "figurative" and requires more "study." If, for instance, "a locution is admonitory, condemning either vice or crime or commending either utility or beneficence, it is not figurative." On the other hand, when a statement, such as "Except you eat the flesh of the Son of Man . . . ," does appear to recommend something evil, "it is therefore a figure" (93). The "therefore" is a remarkable word choice: it makes explicit the contention that a statement that does not immediately conform to an established, "canonical," view is necessarily figurative and must be read "more deeply" until its meaning falls into line. This view remains commonplace today among conservative readers, including, for instance, traditionalist historians of rhetoric, for whom Aristotle and Cicero are now sacred texts, whose meanings are literal when they make sense to the modern reader and figurative (rather than wrongheaded), hence needing "scholarly" study to arrive at the correct reading, when they don't. The Book, whichever one it is, remains always current, always the wellspring of knowledge and virtue, always a Father of the Culture.

The larger point here, in summoning the spirits of Aristotle and Augustine, is that the ontological perspective in rhetoric serves effectively to rationalize the habits of mind that we've been sketching in connection with cultural literacy: its metaphysical appeals to the uncontestable rightness of its values and assumptions, a concern for canons of linguistic and literary good breeding, a belief in the Fall from Grace and the need to retard further degeneration, a conviction that nothing less than Pope's Universal Darkness lies on the horizon if a conservative political and educational agenda is not immediately adopted. Mortimer Adler proposes just such an agenda (indeed, it has been attempted in the Chicago school system) in *The Paideia Proposal: An Educational Manifesto*, the language of which harkens back to Aristotelian metaphysics, albeit "reread" in the context of contemporary American life. Adler's "paideia," not unlike Hirsch's specific definition of "cultural literacy," signifies "the general learning that should be the possession of all human beings" (Dedication page). Adler submits his program of "general learning" to all Americans who believe "that the decline [there's that word again] in the quality of public schooling is damaging the futures of their children" (xi). The program, in a nutshell, entails a mandatory core curriculum through the twelve years of public education and the elimination of all "sidetracks," including "specialized" and "elective" courses (21). It also entails the inclusion and repetition of three "modes" of teaching and learning: first, the "acquisition of organized knowledge," by "didactic" instruction, chiefly textbooks and lecture; second, the development of "learning skills," through coaching and imitating; third, the "enlargement of understanding," by "Socratic instruction," which for Adler means "active participation" of students—he specifies that "it must be the Socratic mode of teaching" (22–32). In case this plan doesn't strike the reader as conspicuously democratic, Adler assures everyone that his recommendations are "not a monolithic program to be adopted uniformly everywhere" (34). Only the "core" is required; local communities are free to differ in the details.

If all of this, so far, sounds perfectly reasonable, that isn't surprising: it's intended to sound that way. Ontological rhetoric is nothing if not confident of its own programs. But the language is revealing. First, there's the odd sound of certain general assertions that underlie Adler's proposals. "We are politically a classless society. Our citizenry as a whole is our ruling class" (5). "It is natural for children to rise to meet higher expectations" (35). "Children are all the same in their human nature" (42). These propositions aren't argued in the text; they are merely intoned here and there, as bits of sacred wisdom not requiring defense or clarification. They are the stuff of ancient syllogistic reasoning, major premises that anchor lines of thought. They share the self-evident authority that Aristotle intended for similar assertions: "What makes men choose to do harmful and evil acts contrary to law? The causes are vice and moral weakness." Is it true, though, other than in American governmental mythology, that our citizenry *as a whole* is our ruling class? What does "nature" mean, when one speaks of what children "naturally" do? Are children who fail to rise to meet higher expectation going against Nature? What does "human nature," that pious abstraction that conceals so much difference beneath a mantle of reassuring sameness, really mean? One need not argue that such statements are false in order to suggest that they are not self-evidently true. It's enough to say that, for many people, if not for Aristotle and Adler, they belong *inside* an argument, not standing aloofly beyond its reach. Yet Adler unselfconsciously proceeds from metaphysical absolutes, step by step according to the system of classical dialectic, to necessary conclusions about education. ALL PEOPLE POSSESS THE SAME HUMAN

NATURE. Therefore, ALL PEOPLE ARE EQUAL. Therefore, ALL DESERVE THE SAME SCHOOL PREPARATION. Therefore, Adler's core curriculum is preferable to other, less centralized forms of curriculum. Therefore, those who challenge Adler's particular beliefs and concerns about the nature and present condition of American education "have little or no reason to feel a passionate commitment to reforms that will improve the quality of the schooling we give the children of this country" (78).

Naturally, the core of Adler's core, the substance of his third and highest level of learning, "enlargement of the understanding," is the Sacred Book. He has in mind many different "products of human artistry," from science to history to poetry, even from print to cinema to music and dance. His only proviso is that the texts to be studied are "works of merit" and that the discussion about them emphasize "the ideas, the values, and the forms embodied in such products of human art." The words "merit" and "embodied" are noteworthy. He doesn't need to say what merit means; texts that have it are readily distinguished from those that don't. Books of merit are those that "embody" ideas, values, and forms, delivering correct knowledge to learners. In particular, "discussion" of the Sacred Book "introduces students to the fundamental ideas in the basic subject matters" of "organized knowledge" (Adler's first stage of learning), "and especially the ideas underlying our form of government and the institutions of our society." Hence, the Sacred Book *contains* a truthfulness that students must be led to discover through close reading. That reading, Adler insists significantly, is to be carried out in the context of "Socratic discussion." What Adler doesn't point out about Socratic dialogue is that the sides aren't equal: the questioner leads, the answerer follows. The questioner (in this case a teacher) has all the rhetorical advantage because she gets to determine the ground of discussion, the questions to be asked, and the significance of the answers for the posing of new questions. How often did Socrates lose his Socratic arguments? How often did he even have worthy opponents? (Occasionally, he did, but more often he didn't.) Socratic dialogue is manipulative: it isn't dishonest but it does maintain firm control of its outcomes. Legal adversaries in a court proceeding engage in a species of Socratic dialogue with witnesses: they ask all the questions and they only ask those for which they already have answers. The point of controlled questioning of Adler's Sacred Book is to lead students to the "right" answers. The aim is to "help" students "raise their minds up from a state of understanding or appreciating less to a state of understanding or appreciating more." There is a difference, of course, between notions of "understanding" and "appreciating," on the one hand, which imply veneration and passivity before acknowledged truths, and notions of "critique" or "scrutiny," on the other, which imply active evaluation and reconsideration. Adler carefully avoids this trouble-making alternative category of literate activity, focusing exclusively on the "enhancement" of students' "appreciation of cultural objects" (28–31).

All of this teaching and learning activity is ostensibly democratic, but, as in the case of Bloom's democracy, one must look more closely. Adler celebrates "the democratic promise of equal educational opportunity" (5). He uses this "promise" to insist on the importance of providing exactly the same *kind* of education to all students, regardless of background. "There are no unteachable children," he solemnly intones (8). Hence, all students "deserve" the same "quality" of education, the same standards, the same books, the same three levels of learning. It's the democratic way, the way that ensures "an adequate preparation for discharging the duties and responsibilities of citizenship" (17). Since all people are "equal," Adler can speak confidently of his program's suitability for providing all children "with indispensable knowledge about nature and culture, the world in which *we* live, *our* social institutions, and *ourselves*" (24). But there are, finally, some difficulties. We've italicized three words in the last passage in order to suggest one of them. Who are the "we" here? Adler doesn't have to ask such questions because "we" are all philosophically equal. But does the poor Hispanic mother, living in the barrio and raising her children on food stamps, really inhabit the same world, really share the same culture, the same opportunities, the same understanding of social institutions, really have the same sense of self, as the white, male, chief executive of a Fortune 500 company, living in Westchester? Who are "we" in Adler's tranquil metaphysical universe?

Another problem: Adler eventually concedes that, although all "children are educable," they are educable only "in varying degrees." Among the things that are "natural" to human nature, then, he cheerfully lists different degrees of merit. When he then quickly adds that "the variation in degree must [nonetheless] be of the same kind and quality of education," his agenda finally becomes plain. He's insisting, in the name of democratic values, that what America really needs in order to remediate its fall from grace, and what uniform schooling will reliably ensure, is a meritocracy, just like Bloom's, where the best "naturally" rise to the top through intrinsic competence (their "educability") and hard work. It may be "natural for children to rise to meet higher expectations," but in Adler's world it's also natural for some to rise higher than others. Students who fail to thrive from reading the Sacred Book, students from Harlem and the barrio, female students who don't see much of themselves re-

flected in the heroism of Achilles, students whose backgrounds reflect alternative cultures, traditions, values, or include less privileged
home and school lives, are "naturally" less gifted, hence naturally
better suited to lower positions in the meritocracy. They can vote—
that's the American way; but they can't be president of the country
(except in meaningless theory) and can't run General Motors because
their education has proven what was, in fact, natural to begin with—
the limits of their ability. There are some questions, meanwhile, that
Adler doesn't invite us to ask. Granting that people are, after all,
"different," who gets to create the scale, the standard, by which merit
is evaluated? Who gets to decide which books, which curricula,
represent "our" heritage? Who gets to decide the reasons for failure
and the remedial steps to be taken? When Adler speaks urgently of
"a democratic society intervening" to "remedy the cultural inequality
of homes and environments" (39), who belongs to that interventionist
group? Clearly, Adler is included, a white, upper-class male from an
elite university. Clearly, the twenty-two members of the "Paideia
Group" are included, nineteen of whom are men, all of whom are
presidents, directors, chairs, heads, fellows, principals, and otherwise designated philosopher-rulers. No plain old teachers are included, however, certainly no students, and certainly not the mother
from the barrio.

Hirsch's and Bloom's conservative agendas are not sufficiently
different from Adler's to require exhaustive comparison. In any case,
the detailed substance of their designs on American education matters less here than the rhetoric in which they are constituted. Bloom
is more morose than Adler, more persuaded perhaps by John Calvin's
view of the world than by Benjamin Franklin's. Hirsch is less dog-
matically rationalist than either Bloom or Adler, more concerned to
plead an empirically neutral case for the necessity of his program.
But they argue from similar premises, the state of educational decline, particularly in literacy, the need for a renewed, culturally
preservative curriculum, rooted in the Sacred Book, the always un-
spoken understanding that the ruling elite must take rightful responsibility for ensuring that the meritocracy remains in place, ensuring
that the best and brightest get even better and even brighter. (To be
fair, it would also be all right with the three of them if the poorer and
dimmer got a little less poor and dim, provided that standards are not
"compromised"—meaning, changed in any way that would accommodate natural outsiders.) Bloom's case for the Sacred Book is,
however, far more conscious, more direct, than Hirsch's or even
Adler's and therefore deserves a comment. And Hirsch's objectivism
introduces a rhetorical change of pace not found so evidently in
Adler or Bloom, so it requires some mention as well.

First, Bloom. He leaves no doubt about the library of the Book: his own text contains many of the favored titles. Generally speaking, the "great books" are by men and for men: they are the reading material of a gentleman's club. "Men may live more truly and fully in reading Plato and Shakespeare than at any other time, because then they are participating in essential being and are forgetting their accidental lives" (380). Essential being is at the club; accidental life is at home with the little woman. By our count only thirteen women are mentioned in a book of some four hundred pages, liberally salted with names of the great and famous. They include Margaret Dumont for her ridiculous "displays of coquettish chasteness" (70), Brigitte Bardot for her inexplicable award of "one of France's highest honors" (77), Lotte Lenya and Marlene Dietrich for their singing, specifically their ability to symbolize "charming, neurotic, sexy, decadent long-ing" (151), Elaine May for her routines of "obsessive prattle" (125), Erica Jong for the debased therapeutic value of *Fear of Flying* (229), Virginia Johnson for her debased "orgasmic" therapy, Margaret Mead for her debased "sexual adventurism" (33) and her "unsophisticated" but popular legitimizing of "repressed sexual desires" (367), Yoko Ono for the wealth she has accumulated from sleazy popular culture, Ayn Rand for *The Fountainhead*, which is "hardly literature" (62), Hannah Arendt for her ignorance of history (152), and the author of *Pride and Prejudice* (375), who is, however, not named. Let no one doubt by whom and for whom the Great Books were written. For Bloom, great cheer is available from the triumphant, if still slightly melancholy, remembrance that "the books in their objective beauty are still there, and we must help protect and cultivate the delicate tendrils reaching out toward them through the unfriendly soil of students' souls" (380).

Hirsch's *Cultural Literacy* stirs together ontological and objec-tivist rhetoric in a potent mix of metaphysical necessity and scientific proof. He deploys a heady array of "facts" about test scores, the 1978 NAEP report showing a drop in students' knowledge of civics "be-tween 1969 and 1976" (7), the College Board's report that "56% more students scored above 600 in 1972 than did so in 1984" (5). He appeals to abstruse bodies of scientific knowledge, including schema theory, language acquisition, historical linguistics, information the-ory, and psycholinguistics. He insists that "the content of cultural literacy changes over the years," to reflect new knowledge, new events, alterations of taste, thereby establishing a parallel between a scientific conception of culture and a similar conception of language, both massively resistant to change but both nonetheless changing over time. He distances himself from charges of elitism or other unscientific bias by claiming merely to be reporting on the world as it is: the priority of some kinds of knowledge over other kinds "has nothing to do with intrinsic merit, only with the accidents of culture" (26). But this objectivism is more a matter of convenience, a plea for special authority, than it is a constituting medium for Hirsch's central claims and judgments. Much of the science is, in fact, irrelevant to those claims and judgments, though Hirsch implies that it's crucial. Schema theory, for instance, an explanation of which takes up almost a third of the text, establishes little more than a *non sequitur* in Hirsch's reasoning: people understand each other by appealing to shared, orderly patterns of prior knowledge, stored in memory; therefore, American education needs Hirsch's specific "content" curriculum, needs a tidy display of selected bits of information, a list of what "everybody knows," if America is not to collapse into an anarchy of cacophonous voices and meaningless sounds. Playing with degrees of generality and specificity to suit his purposes is Hirsch's favorite tactic: offer a specific fact about test scores, followed by a general conclusion about cultural decay; then offer a large, scientific generalization about mind or language, followed by a specific agenda for schooling and the retrieval of lost literacy. The response is the same to each of these versions of the non sequitur: one does not have to dispute the scientific research involved (though one often could) in order to dispute the conclusions Hirsch draws from it and the recommendations he calls on it to validate. Hirsch's science is finally, in its applications, little more than pseudoscience.

Meanwhile, the ideal of cultural literacy is pure metaphysics, however dressed out in analogies to scientific views of mind and language. For Hirsch, "national culture" is a standardized central stock of knowledge that existed in the past, has disintegrated in the present, and stands to be resurrected through a "content" curriculum of the near future. The images of decline and potential rejuvenation make plain the fact that this culture is an Object, an Aristotelian Substance, a fixed Essence. It is High Culture, an abstraction, not something related to the variegated, ongoing, changing life of a people. Otherwise, how could anyone recognize its deterioration? If culture is, as Hirsch insists, "always changing," then how is anybody to know when the change is degenerative? Only when one holds a view of culture as metaphysical object is it possible to assume that literacy has decayed merely because middle management business executives no longer quote Shakespeare. Even if Americans don't share the knowledge of *Julius Caesar* any longer, they continue, it appears, to work productively—the GNP and the Dow Jones averages are no less robust than they were when Hirsch's father dressed their production in literary allusions. Americans communicate among themselves, watch the same television shows, figure out public transportation schedules, fly to the moon, go to church, even go to school in growing numbers. They don't always whip the Japanese, but sometimes they do, supposing that's a "cultural value." Large numbers of them maintain, by their own reckoning, reasonably happy lives. They read (in fact they've made Hirsch and Bloom best-selling authors, right along with Michener, Erica Jong, and D'Souza). When it becomes crucially important for them to refresh their memories about Tom Sawyer or the Torah, they know some ways to do it. They can always ask Hirsch. In any case, they must share *some* kind of culture.

Are they, and are their children, "still" cultivated? Are they decorous? Such questions continue to presume a metaphysical constant. Who gets to say what "cultivated" means? In what nontrivial way was Hirsch's Golden Age more "cultivated" than the present? Were the robber barons more cultivated than recent corporate raiders and junk bond dealers? Was the country more humane in its dealings with American Indians than in its dealings with contemporary Mexicans and Asians? Were fewer wars fought in the Golden Age? Were the working classes less exploited? Were the poor less forgotten? It seems as though "standards," whether of civility or of barbarism, have remained essentially intact with and without the Great Books. Hirsch is right, of course, about change. Cultures do that. If he were content to be "scientific," to chronicle "the way things are," he would note certainly some alterations in the content of "cultural literacy," a growing dependence on electronic media for "shared knowledge," an alteration of school curricula in response to current social conditions—the reality of pluralistic culture, for instance. But he wouldn't, couldn't find, as "scientist," a degeneration of culture itself. People produce and reproduce culture in the process of living, whether they want to or not; they couldn't make culture "decay" even if they tried, any more than they could make language decay, let's say by resolving to speak only slang. Their slang would *become* "the language"; their altered practices would *become* "the culture." Only Hirsch, the metaphysician, can answer the question, when does a cultural change represent something more insidious than just a new wrinkle in the fabric of "our" heritage? When is it a descent from some condition of high estate? His answer is, when there is a deviation from the norms of High Culture. But a more skeptical answer is, when someone who has a strong preference for the status quo, and who has the power to complain about changes in it, steps forward to say so and to do something about it.

Hirsch's plea for cultural literacy, no less than Bloom's or Adler's, is more about power, about who has it and who should get to keep it, than about saving an imperilled republic. It's another instance of latter-day philosopher-rulers noting some potential for disobedience among the populace, even perhaps an assault—by outsiders—against their mountain top. Hirsch's rulers are only slightly more difficult to identify than Bloom's. He argues that "a random group of literate Americans" ought to get together to compile a list of the core contents of cultural literacy (overlooking the question of how many might still be literate enough to do the job in these decadent times). Two sentences later he announces that he and two colleagues from the University of Virginia (whose gender and heritage we leave to readers to guess) have begun the compilation. Strictly speaking, this is indeed a large enough number to constitute a "group," and one certainly wishes to believe Hirsch's claim that they were "randomly" chosen. But the choice also appears to have been made with unseemly haste; and it appears to be more restricted than even the depleted condition of American culture would necessitate (135). Later he proposes to build curricula on the basis of his list by convening "a distinguished group of educators and public leaders" (no undistinguished followers need apply). And of course there must be tests, to be devised by "an independent group of scholars, educators, and concerned citizens" (141), also no doubt chosen at random. Finally, it isn't all that hard to tell the rulers from the rabble.

And that's our principal point in bringing all the rhetorical scrutiny of the preceding pages before an audience that we hope comprises largely teachers and students. The evident fact is that most teachers and students are not included in the sociopolitical category of philosopher-rulers. A small number of university scholars belong, of course, though not the majority of college-level practitioners. Administrators, bureaucrats, and politicians belong. But teachers and students are conceived as workers, not thinkers; doers, not planners; objects of other people's wisdom, not speaking subjects legitimately responsible for transforming educational life. Hirsch makes the case explicitly, arguing that it belongs to "cultural politics" to change "the content and values of culture," while it is the restricted aim of schooling "to promote literacy as an enabling competence" (137). In other words, the rulers get to make fundamental decisions about the list, while teachers and students busy themselves with a passive replication of whatever cultural values the list promotes. All three of the books we've examined here incorporate curricular agendas that remain in the control of the philosopher-rulers and are intended to be implemented by the "work" of teachers and students. Their rhetoric, specifically their contemporary rendering of traditional Western metaphysics, assists in the realizing of their ends. They are not intended as academic exercises, any more than our reading of them has been intended as an academic exercise in response. What's at stake is precisely the freedom of people who inhabit the school world, "workers" whose interests are not always well served by the philosopher-rulers who seek to maintain control of that world. These books have designs on people's lives, the lives of parents, teachers, and students. Their urgent, apocalyptic rhetoric is a way of insisting on those designs, a way of concealing their lack of necessity. To the extent that teachers remain uncritical of the rhetoric of conservatism (and that of the left as well), they stand to be enveloped by it, presuming that what is powerfully said must be as true as it is powerful.

Those who inhabit the educational world as workers rather than rulers may well sympathize, nonetheless, with some or all of the agendas that cultural literacy advances. A conserving impulse lives in all of us, as teachers, parents, citizens, human beings. If it didn't, there could be no sustained coherence to the realities, educational and otherwise, that we compose for ourselves. Even the most radical educator seeks the validation of history, wishes the perpetuation of favored values, sees in the present a failure to honor some of the meanings of the past. Moreover, that impulse lives in all times and places, though always distinctively shaped by local circumstances. It isn't conservatism as such that is potentially harmful, but conservatism unmodulated by other values, specifically values of change and accommodation necessary to ensuring the freedom of people who have not prospered historically from the world as it has been. Since we've presented the conservative agendas of cultural literacy advocates in an unflattering light, some may well find our own implicit designs even less palatable than theirs. Well and good. Teachers and students should read Bloom, Hirsch, and Adler, let them argue their own cases from their own points of view. We have, and we neither sympathize with them nor feel apologetic here about the transparency of our disagreement. Choices must be made. We continue to make ours in the educational world and submit them to public scrutiny; others are obliged to do the same—evaluating *our* claims with the same distanced critical attention they bring to the claims of others. Disagreement and active assent are equally preferable to passivity.

Chapter 6

Expressivism
Literacy for Personal Growth

*Writing must be motivated, and . . . the best writing is
deeply motivated; therefore, any attempt to induce writing
must begin by tapping feelings—desire, pain, ambition,
curiosity, and many more. . . . Once the motivation is stimu-
lated, it will in turn tap language resources dammed up
inside every human being; language will rush forth when
the need and desire are genuine. . . . Language must serve
the individual, in a fundamental way, in the exploration
and discovery of himself [sic] and his world; and it must
also serve the individual by relating and connecting him to
others, in dialogue, discussion, and communication.*

James E. Miller,
Word, Self, Reality

*In a sense I have nothing to offer but two metaphors:
growing and cooking. They are my model for the writing
process.*

Peter Elbow,
Writing Without Teachers

There is little doubt that functionalist and monoculturalist representations of literacy will continue in the foreseeable future to rationalize "normal" practices of reading and writing instruction. The

123

principal business of schooling will continue to be the reproduction
of dominant social relations, specifically the hierarchical and meritocratic organization of the country's economic life. Schools will go
on "explaining" to students, especially through skills teaching and
testing, that these arrangements are inevitable, exhorting them to fit
themselves for service as managers and workers, but above all as
consumers, within the "free enterprise" system. Adding special impetus to this economically grounded reality is the unhappy fact that
Americans these days are in an ugly mood, pressured by growing
influxes of "aliens," especially Hispanics and Asians, anxious about
their seeming inferiority in the world market, and supported in latent
jingoistic and homophobic attitudes by an increasingly reactionary
federal government. Clarence Thomas has come to the Supreme
Court trailing suspicions of sexual harassment; David Duke, a political opportunist with roots in American Naziism and the Ku Klux
Klan, proved himself, however temporarily, a sufficient national
presence to be able to spread his brand of blow-dried racism via a
1992 presidential campaign; the membership of Congress, Democrats
no less than Republicans, is all but monolithic in gender and heritage, if not also in its zeal to support the interests of rich over poor,
white over black and brown, men over women, management over
labor, and American military/industrial dominance over "the global
village"; the country, in 1993, continues in recession; Japan, meanwhile, is beating us at our own economic game. These local circumstances will pass, but the rhetoric of fear and crisis promoting
right-wing literacy agendas at this moment is merely the flip side of
a rhetoric of cultural, specifically technological superiority that af-
flicts American society in happier times. For that reason, conservative agendas have a momentum and durability that are likely to
outlast any particular set of detrimental economic circumstances.

It's no less true, however, that American schools also remain sites
of cultural conflict and struggle, despite the often crudely oppressive
aspirations of curriculum, testing, and educational management.
Schools tell a variety of stories about literacy, not just the two dominant stories we've read so far. Liberal and even radical representations vie for authority as well, albeit from marginal positions,
and offer possibilities for creative intervention. Dramatically changing demographic trends partly ensure this continuing struggle, as
African, Hispanic, and Asian Americans begin to outnumber those of
European background in some of the nation's larger cities and therefore many of its school districts. These people deserve and will come
to expect improved attention to their cultural histories and achievements, their languages, their past contributions to American civilization, and their present as well as future entitlements as productive

citizens. Assuming that their political awareness grows along with their numbers, they need not wait forever on well-intentioned European Americans for social justice, nor need they indefinitely tolerate its withholding by the less well intentioned. Meanwhile, the altered consciousness of women in education, teachers and administrators as well as students, will ensure that schools become gradually more aware of patriarchal domination in their managerial as well as curricular practices. And finally, the altered grounds of disciplinary knowledge, the emergence of nonpositivist epistemologies in feminist, Marxist, and postmodern theory will continue to unsettle traditional concepts of teaching, learning, and scholarship, including the contested terms of reading and writing instruction. The ongoing transformation of English studies—from custodian of the British/ American literary canon to advocate for fuller values of literacy through textual and cultural critique—represents one mark of that destabilization, assisted by the decay of classical humanist ideology and the methods of New Criticism. The dominance of prevailing arrangements notwithstanding, schools are a fertile ground for negotiating social change through the mediation of altered educational practice.

Several "liberal" or progressive representations of literacy, for instance, have emerged during the past thirty years and have enjoyed enough success in schools to legitimate and dramatize the possibility of directed educational change. These include the "whole language" movement associated with Kenneth Goodman, the British program of "expressive writing" (popularly named after the central category in James Britton's taxonomy of "utterance functions" [81ff.]), and John Dixon's "growth model" of English education with its attendant "process pedagogy," dating conventionally from the Dartmouth Conference of 1966 and subsequently associated with a number of theorists including Britton, James Moffett, Ken Macrorie, Janet Emig, Donald Graves, Peter Elbow, and others. We'll refer to these stories under the general heading of "expressivism," a perspective strongly indebted to neo-Kantian philosophy, in particular the thought of Ernst Cassirer and Susanne Langer, to the linguistic theories of Edward Sapir and Roman Jakobson, and to the psychological theories of George Kelly, Jerome Bruner, and Lev Vygotsky. Expressivism encompasses a group of arguments emphasizing in common (1) an active, unified, "organic" human consciousness, distinguished from the passive mind of classical metaphysics or the reactive mind of Lockean positivism, and regarded as the source of "expression"; (2) the power of human consciousness or "imagination" to constitute and order experience by recourse to diverse modes of symbolic action; and (3) the creative potential of all forms of discourse and of all individual language users. Sometimes a fourth emphasis is included as well: the "natural," distinctive quality of "personal voice" and "style." These arguments together encourage a preoccupation with *how* instead of merely *what* readers read and writers compose—the "process" as well as the "product"—and find instructional realization in such practices as "open classrooms," which acknowledge the messiness and serendipity of the human search for meaning; "collaborative learning," which allows for dynamic interactions and mutual support among language learners; "whole" experiences of reading and writing as opposed to mechanical drills and acontextual exercises on supposed "parts"; "facilitative" rather than "directive" responses to student work (emphasizing new opportunities to read and write rather than sterile correction of past performance); and attention to the individual learner through tutorial and small group arrangements. Implicit in these practices is not just an acknowledgment of but a fundamental regard for the creative abilities of all students, including those who are socially and therefore educationally disenfranchised.

Expressivism has posed by far the most popular and successful challenge to conservative educational arrangements over the past quarter century. Yet it has also come under frequent attack, not just from the right (which has, for obvious reasons, always opposed it) but also, especially lately, from advocates of more radical social visions, including many proponents of critical teaching (see Aronowitz and Giroux; Bowles and Gintis). This liberal-bashing on the left is unfortunate, in our opinion, given its capacity to distract progressive educators from their common purposes, and it requires some discussion if only because our own professional biographies oblige us to conceive our present in terms of what remains for us, at the least, an honorable past. We would contend that the pedagogies of expressivism are the precursors of critical teaching, despite the fact that they don't, for the most part, derive from the customary sources of liberatory praxis—Marxism, feminism, postmodernism—and despite the fact that advocates of these latter, now flourishing arguments frequently, and properly, note the limitations of neo-Kantian idealism. Those who dispute our view are too often satisfied to dismiss expressivism as romantic, solipsistic, naive, ineffectual, politically disengaged, and finally complicit in the very structures of oppression that its practices have sought to subvert. We reject the dismissal, even though we're sympathetic to certain of the charges, sharing with others a frustration, born of our own experience, at the idealized revolutionary ambitions of expressivist teaching. We will grant, for instance, its arguably myopic focus on the single student, the single teacher, the single classroom, without regard for their situatedness within larger school and other social realities. We also concede its tendency to emphasize the power of the free individual to change society through sheer force of moral vision or imaginative insight without considering the extent to which society constitutes, defines, and limits notions of "individuality" and "freedom." Finally, we acknowledge its tendency to mislead well-intentioned teachers about its practical ability to affect settled conditions of the school world. We've seen the damaging cynicism of teachers and students whose faith in overglamorized concepts of "consciousness," "imagination," "style," "creativity," and "individual voice" has collapsed in the face of political interests that are at once hostile to these notions, more powerful in their representational authority, and vengeful toward those who have tried to promote liberalizing practices. Instead of taking canny, tactically subtle advantage of the conflicts and struggles inherent in school reality, expressivist pedagogies have too often failed to study or even acknowledge the dynamics of institutional power, resulting in their continued marginality within substantially unaffected curricular and instructional programs.

At the same time, however, we resist the self-interested revisionism of contemporary theorists whose preferred intellectual commitments have led them to patronize the social agenda, along with the conceptual limitations, of expressivism. Their scholarly righteousness suggests to us a struggle for prestige within the academy as much as any significant rededication to educational reform. It's a distortion of history to deny the aspirations for change at the heart of expressivist pedagogy, and more so to deny its concrete effectiveness in schools. No reflective English teacher who has come of age during the past thirty years can fail to have encountered whole language curricula or process pedagogy, can be unaware of the effects of the Dartmouth Conference, the National Writing Project, or "Hooked on Books," can be altogether unacquainted with the work of those like Goodman and Britton who have changed the ways in which schools approach language instruction. The changes have been international in scope, not merely local, and durable, not ephemeral. Two generations of teachers have worked to make schools more creative, more humane, and more productive places for readers and writers than they used to be, permanently reconceiving literacy instruction along the way. In reading classrooms today, entertaining books, suited to gender and heritage as well as age and interest, now compel attention as much as basal readers; normal reading activities now compete legitimately with phonics exercises and spelling drills; interpretation is (almost) as valuable a concept as comprehension. In writing classes, narrative now complements analytic discourse, free writing exists alongside the term paper, response and revision have become richer activities than they were when associated with grammar and logic "errors," small-group work now often replaces lecture and isolated practice, writing centers and cross-disciplinary writing programs have replaced (or at least challenged the centrality of) the ghetto of traditional English Composition. Whole language programs have also had modest success in resisting conventional assessment practices (substituting "portfolios" for example) and the preference for tracking (or "streaming") that characterize functionalist approaches to literacy. These administrative, curricular, and instructional changes not only have much in common with the aspirations of critical pedagogy but they also deserve credit for giving those aspirations a material foundation in contemporary educational reality.

The undisputable limitation of this effective work is that the achievements of expressivism have resulted from practices that for the most part neither presumed nor entailed any broader awareness, let alone reconstituting, of school life in the context of other social formations. On the contrary, its successes have been possible primarily because they could be envisioned without serious challenge to underlying political conditions. The Darwinian rationales behind sweatshop education remain alive and well, despite superficial gestures of liberation in "discoveries" of "personal" voice or freedom within supposedly "open" classrooms. Prejudice and unfairness, homophobia and xenophobia, brute competitiveness and vulgar consumerism, continue to thrive. Suburban children attend comfortable and well-equipped schools supported by the greater tax revenues of their middle-class parents while inner-city children struggle in the shabby conditions that have always been their lot. Sadly, there's greater likelihood that whole language curricula will be found in wealthy schools than in poor ones. At the same time, however, it's worth recalling that the origins of expressivist pedagogy lie not in comfortable suburban locales but in the working-class neighborhoods of London, the open enrollment colleges of CUNY, where Mina Shaughnessy did her pioneering work, and the reformatories of Michigan, where Dan Fader first developed the "Hooked on Books" program that later spread to public schools (see Applebee 225ff.). One impulse from the beginning was to honor the linguistic resources of the individual child, regardless of native language or dialect or "skill level" or socioeconomic status, affirming that child's entitlement to speak by first celebrating the "natural" ability to speak. Another was to enfranchise marginalized populations of students through a pedagogy that values difference and begins with what historically oppressed learners already know, instead of presuming that the purpose of schooling is to force such students into the mold of the dominant culture while "explaining" their (likely) failure by appeal to intellectual inadequacy or laziness. These are revolutionary ambitions. If it's true to say that they haven't been realized, it's also true to say that no other contemporary project of school reform has done as much, notwithstanding the impatient condescension of more contemporary arguments sporting expanded liberatory agendas. It's hardly surprising that schools, along with the corporate and legislative establishments that govern them, have taken all available measures to limit the success of progressive alternatives—including testing apparatuses that compel mechanistic teaching, textbook acquisitions that mandate traditional curricula, teacher evaluation practices (intrusive classroom visitations among them) that ensure the orthodoxy of the classroom, and top-down school management models that serve primarily bureaucratic rather than educational interests. These effective defense measures await new challenges from proposed models of critical pedagogy that have persuasively critiqued the power arrangements of schooling but have not yet authoritatively engaged them in the world beyond theory.

Limitations aside, in other words, expressivism has made a difference, albeit by couching its reforms within acceptable, classically American rationales, including romantic conceptions of the individual and attendant arguments about self-determination, freedom of speech, fair play, and the possibility of enlightened, if also minor and gradual, social change. The burden to demonstrate concrete usefulness beyond or in opposition to expressivism rests now on currently developing theories of pedagogy that are staking their prestige on a far more ambitious, although not always clearly specified, program of social as well as intellectual reconstruction. The burden is also on Marxist, postmodern, and feminist critics to elaborate a classroom practice materially related to their theoretical visions. There is, to be sure, already a more overtly political content to critical teaching than there is in expressivist practices, a commitment to cultural critique that distinctively influences the kinds of talk, writing, and reading one can expect in the classroom. But from a methodological standpoint, arguments for critical teaching have tended largely to reiterate the tactics of whole language and writing process classrooms—the "open," participatory arrangements that disrupt authoritarianism, the small-group formats that encourage collaborative concepts of knowledge, the emphasis on "dialogue," the uses of narrative and other nonanalytic forms of writing. Depending on one's point of view, the similarity may suggest that new theories are largely going to validate old practices within an altered intellectual framework (in the way that relativity physics validates Newtonian mechanics with

some highly specialized exceptions), or it may only suggest that the
new theories, whatever their aspirations, have simply lacked the
teacherly imagination, so far, to conceive a practice pragmatically
matched to their conceptual and political daring. In any case, the
continuing imitation of expressivist teaching, despite the fanfare of
new conceptual starting points, shows the extent to which critical
pedagogy still depends on its educational precursors, theoretically
no less than practically, for its inspiration.

Sharon Crowley's recent *A Teacher's Introduction to Deconstruction* illustrates our point. The book aims to present an explanation of primarily Derridean postmodernism for the benefit of
teachers, hoping presumably to inspire a more radical pedagogy
than expressivism has offered. The book introduces some familiar
Derridean concepts—"the metaphysics of presence," "inscription
and signification," *"différance,"* "supplementation," "absence," the
"plenitude" of interpretation—and readers can judge for themselves
the adequacy of Crowley's descriptions. We would observe in
passing that the crisp definitions of Derrida's vocabulary implicate
Crowley, perhaps inevitably, in the very "analytic" tradition she
aims to critique in her privileging of "deconstructive reading" (6).
But never mind: we're not implying that we could contrive a better
theoretical introduction. What's significant instead is her story of
the possibility and substance of "deconstructive pedagogy," where
two themes stand out: her consistent muting of any political designs
in deconstruction and her extensive reliance on the teaching practices of expressivism when describing the instructional implications
of Derridean postmodernity. Either she's suppressing the true potential of deconstruction to rewrite the prose of the school (by
directing its irreverent gaze toward the Pledge of Allegiance, for
instance, or the principal's memos) out of tacit recognition that
radical social projects are fundamentally implausible, or she really
believes that deconstruction simply shares the modest reconstructive goals that expressivism has already envisioned. Either she has
not yet been able to imagine a deconstructive pedagogy beyond
what expressivism has already conceived or she really believes that
deconstruction is chiefly a conceptual adjustment with limited,
even if theoretically important, instructional consequences.

We find it particularly noteworthy that she talks around more
than about the social project that might be associated with deconstruction. In the absence of such a project, deconstruction remains
the plaything of the scholarly elite, a diversion from the tedious
clarities of New Criticism, a self-important intellectual pirouette
lacking the ethical bearings or social commitment or explicit educational focus that have distinguished expressivism despite its limits.

Yet the social theme emerges only here and there, tantalizingly, and then disappears in favor of a generally philosophical and apolitical account. Crowley offers it most plainly when suggesting that a deconstructive pedagogy might "engage students with issues that concern them . . . socially and politically, and would direct the resulting discourses into the communities where such things matter" (38). But the theme isn't pursued or clarified: it merely ends a section concerned with the question of how to motivate writers. Political implications are repeatedly dodged in this way. Later, for instance, she recalls a literary scholar who once argued in her presence that the aim of any pedagogy should be to politicize students, making them aware that "they and their culture subscribe to a number of constraining ideologies regarding class, sex, and race." She observes, parenthetically but we assume pointedly, that she is "in sympathy with his proposal." We're prepared to learn the connection between Derrida, teaching, and politics. It turns out, however, that she offers the anecdote not because she wants to explore the potential for critique in deconstruction but only in order to complain about a bifurcation between scholarship and teaching in English studies. This critic, she says, didn't really want to address questions of pedagogy, even though she managed to pull an insight out of him, because, in her view, literary scholars in general don't take teaching seriously (25). We accept her observation, and we understand that she wants to bring together interests in deconstructive theory and practical pedagogy. But a substantive issue that she introduces only obliquely is the potential for cultural critique in deconstruction. Given her confessed sympathy for projects of social change, why dance away from the question?

The swerve around political issues is repeated elsewhere and often. For instance, Crowley cites some composition theorists, notably Susan Miller, who rely on deconstruction to challenge traditional writing instruction (see *Rescuing the Subject*), but only to survey the range of views about it among writing teachers, not to pursue any suggestion that such a challenge entails broader cultural scrutiny (23). She says that teachers should "sensitize their students to the institutional realities in which they write" but only to make them aware of the "special brand of writing," namely academic discourse, that they are expected to learn (47). She says in the Preface that her own work in poststructuralism has taught her to deconstruct "the academic ideology that governs a good deal of literacy instruction in American schools" (xvi), and she is surely aware of the relationship between this critique and the social designs of a liberatory pedagogy. But again the observation ends instead of begins a paragraph; there's no follow-through, no clarification. Her political commitments remain tacit, obliquely proposed, unspecific, merely potential, as though she felt that teachers might refuse her project altogether if she were to be more explicit (as well they might!). She notes ambiguously that the "clamor" surrounding deconstruction often results from "simple or willful misunderstanding . . . of its pedagogical and political potential" (25). But what kind of misunderstanding? A belief that it has such potential when in fact it really doesn't? A belief that it doesn't when in fact it does? A belief that it's more radical than it really is? Perhaps Crowley is attempting to domesticate deconstruction so that people will find it palatable. In any case, the "glissage" in her remarks leaves us wondering what she thinks deconstruction really has to offer. Is she concealing its revolutionary potential fearing that teachers would refuse its arguments if she were frank? If so, she isn't playing fair with unprotected, nonuniversity colleagues who would be taking the risks of implementing a practice whose potentially unsettling consequences any astute administrator would recognize quickly enough. Or does she secretly suspect that radical pedagogy is politically unrealistic, a titillating theory without practical consequence? Or does she in fact reject aspirations of revolutionary change in deconstruction, seeing it as essentially a theoretical amendment to expressivism that shares the same modest aspirations for social change? If so, the conceptual alteration is minor from a teacher's point of view and of far greater significance to university scholars who measure their standing to an important degree by the authority they can claim for their scholarly investments.

Her notions of the actual makeup of a deconstructive pedagogy are similarly ambivalent, implying substantial satisfaction with the basic features of expressivist practice. She concedes that the critique of more traditional pedagogies "may be as far as deconstruction will take us," adding that "I am not sure that a deconstructive pedagogy can be realized—the term is itself an oxymoron" (45). If she really believes this conclusion, then what is the intent of her book? Critique, after all, is empty in the absence of a transformative vision. Here there is no vision. The book invites teachers to learn a new theory (as scholars are always asking them to do) the use of which is chiefly to remedy lack of conceptual sophistication, not to propose much of an alternative in their teaching or their aspirations. We don't challenge the intellectual interest of the postmodern critique of logocentrism and the Cartesian unified subject. But by Crowley's account, once the noise subsides the "new" for the most part merely fine-tunes the old: "reassuringly enough, a deconstructive reading of writing pedagogy underscores the appropriateness of much of the lore connected with process pedagogy" (31). Consequently, her text emphasizes the importance of "collaboration" (37) and rewriting (40); the rejection of formulas, empty "generic categories," artificial subskills, and mechanical notions of intention (41); and the need for teachers to write along with their students (46) while resisting traditional classroom power arrangements (45). Above all, a deconstructive pedagogy "would reinforce the notion . . . that writing is a process," although the concept of "process" would be interpreted "more profoundly" as "differentiation"—the endless play of signification—not "repetition of the same"—the imitation of stable forms and rearticulation of prior texts (46). In short, similar activities would go on but their rationale would be altered. The rationale would be "more profound."

There are differences to be sure, and they may matter. The "author centeredness" (32) of process pedagogy is discarded, according to Crowley, in favor of a preoccupation with discursive practice as an enveloping reality that constitutes the writer-as- subject. The focus in class, then, is not on "discovering" personal (in the sense of "unique" or even "solitary") voice but on learning the features of some community's writing in order to acquire position to speak. The knowledge that discourse articulates is similarly impersonal in character, not the result of a private journey of discovery but instead collective and public, constraining the knower by its substance and decorum even as the knower "contributes" to its abundance. The payoff of these theoretical adjustments *could* be a more critical, perhaps more empowering, awareness, for teachers and students alike, of their situatedness, their "subject positions," within the webs of signification, including their inscription within institutions (like school) that language enacts. There could be a payoff, that is, provided that the social project of deconstructive teaching, in its differences from the modest ambitions of expressivism, were made fully manifest to teachers so that their work could be purposeful, not just accidentally mischievous. But Crowley's rhetorical emphasis is otherwise, restricting the significance of the theoretical adjustments to a modifying of the pedagogy of expressivism. In the absence of any explicit, developed sociopolitical program that might underwrite an altered educational praxis, the argument remains an academic exercise, vacillating between abstruse intellectualism, surely more appealing to the scholar than the teacher, and instructional recommendations that expressivism has, to its credit, long ago rendered commonplace. If the various postmodernisms, feminisms, and Marxisms now competing for philosophical attention in the academy are to fulfill their promises of reconceiving educational life beyond it, promises they seem to imply in their critiques of the political no less than intellectual "naiveté" of expressivism, they're going to have to do better than that.

By contrast, the story that proponents tell about literacy for personal growth is appealing to Americans, including teachers, for all the reasons that make postmodernism, among other radical ideologies, unappealing: it defends more than critiques myths of freedom, individualism, self-reliance, and tolerance that have traditionally framed the American historical experience. Its effectiveness lies in its evoking of these myths in the service of a more humane educational practice. It can be frank about its social ambitions because it aims, in the changes it promotes, to realize values that most Americans want to believe they share. John Dixon's *Growth Through English*, which reports on the central issues and arguments of the Dartmouth seminar of 1966, offers a good example of the rhetoric of expressivism, suggesting the appeal of its liberal commitments to seminar delegates, from Great Britain as well as the United States, who had been steeped, as we all are, in the tradition of European romanticism. The conference, Dixon writes, "proposed a new interest in the learner," in the individual child's language development, and in "the processes of using language to learn" (112), echoing deeply ingrained European philosophical sentiments of individualism and organicism. He concedes immediately that this focus, formed in 1966, turned out to be somewhat narrower than it should have been, narrower than a follow-up meeting at York (England) in 1971 could still accept, because it invited participants "to focus on the learner in abstraction from [her] social relationship with the teacher," and by extension the public circumstances of educational life. But his text implies that participants recognized the social, and also the reconstructive, dimension of their work from the start in their emphasis on creating community in the classroom, even while focusing on the learner's distinctive needs. Concentrating on a child's language development is "just one microcosm of a far wider struggle," which has to do with "teacher and learner, parent and child, manager and worker," along with "the dilemmas of coercive authority and inescapable subordination" in contemporary society (111). The school world becomes a "microcosm" of the larger circumstances of social life: teacher and students become "a language community, in which all are learning together as they develop a classroom dialogue that in part can be internalized by each pupil." They use language, talk, reading, and writing to "explore their common universe, each one "taking up from the discussion of experience what will make sense of [her] own world." To write, for example, is "to move from the social and shared work" of preceding conversation "to an opportunity for private and individual work" (44).

There's a philosophical premise in this depiction of the separate but related spheres of private and social reality that goes to the heart of expressivist ideology: an assumption that individual, autonomous consciousness is the source of that collective meaningfulness that comprises social and cultural experience. The traces of this emphasis are everywhere in Dixon. Schools should offer "language knowledge that helps the pupil perceive himself, and for that matter Man, as in some sense the organizer of his experience" (11). The pupil's inner world comes first and the outer second; the individual knower casts a sovereign eye upon herself and upon humankind. Expressivism does not accept a notion of the isolated self, as some reductive critics have charged, nor is it insensitive to the social dimension of language. According to Wilhelm von Humboldt, a prominent nineteenth-century Kantian linguist, "language develops only in social intercourse, and humans understand themselves only by having tested the comprehensibility of their words on others" (36). Ernst Cassirer, foremost of the modern neo-Kantians, insists in *The Philosophy of Symbolic Forms* that, if the linguistic sign "had merely expressed an individual representation produced in the individual consciousness, it would have remained imprisoned in the individual consciousness, without power to pass beyond it." On the contrary, he concludes, "since language arises not in isolated but in communal action, it possesses from the very start a truly common, 'universal' sense" (286). At the same time, however, the tendency of expressivism, from such British romantics as Coleridge to contemporary advocates of "personal voice," has been to privilege imaginative consciousness apart from any explicitly social shaping of its character and also, at the extreme, to individualize (but *not* to isolate) that consciousness in order to dramatize the creativity of personal utterance. Von Humboldt argues, for instance, that speech "proceeds from the interior of a living creature, consists of the articulated sound of a thinking person, and is received as an unarticulated one by a sensitive fellow human being" (34). Hence, if objectivism is liable to err in finding language a mechanical system of rules precisely constraining individual speakers, expressivism is liable to err in offering the particular speaker a more or less radical freedom to mean in personal terms—to recreate language as a personal instrument (Knoblauch, "Rhetorical Constructions," 133).

This habitual philosophic orientation has consequences for both the educational and the larger social projects that expressivism has undertaken. It directs attention to the "personal growth" of the individual learner and it presumes that the source of social change is the fully matured independent subjectivity newly willing to share with others, and actively promote, the satisfactions of developed understanding. What it tends to miss is the situatedness of the individual in social orders that constitute her independence, that constrain it in the service of encompassing designs (economic and otherwise) that take precedence over personal interest, and that actively, purposefully resist local challenges to its privileged arrangements. James Britton and James Squire, both delegates to the Dartmouth seminar, address these issues in an illuminating way in their Preface to the third edition of Dixon's *Growth Through English*. They concede the failure of Dartmouth to "relate the teaching of English to the sociopolitical contexts in which young people live today," pointing specifically to the desegregation controversies of the era, the "crisis in values" prompted by the Vietnam War as well as the revolts on college campuses, and the American economic crisis that resulted not only in surpluses of teachers but also in "staggering rates of unemployment" among school and college graduates (xi). They concede that any dissatisfaction in recent times with traditional schooling practices has probably resulted "from social and economic forces not envisaged at Dartmouth" (xv)—that "idyllic and isolated discussion in the White Mountains of New Hampshire" (xi). But characteristically they see the successes of Dartmouth, notwithstanding these limitations, from the vantage point of their still strong expressivist commitments. They grant that dreams of national and indeed international reform were dashed despite five years of "teacher institutes and of Project English research" because they couldn't convince "a sufficiently large body of school and public supporters" that their program was worth continuing in a time when "the crisis in urban education" was forcing "transfer of federal and foundation funds to new priorities" (ix). They then suggest that the impact of the conference's discussions should not be sought "in new and widespread curriculum designs" (x). Instead "the Dartmouth ideal" lives principally "in the enterprise of individuals" (x). They are convinced, they say, that effective curriculum change "begins with a teacher reflecting upon his own experience . . . , thereafter modifying classroom behaviour (vii)" and presumably offering a good enough example to colleagues as to have a suasory effect on their own change. Whether or not this is a sufficient account of how educational change takes place—and one must wonder, given Britton and Squire's concessions about overriding socioeconomic realities that finally terminated much of their work—there is little doubt of an intellectual congruence between their views of such change and their views of literacy instruction: everything begins from the individual, teacher or student, and flows outward toward social interactions.

Be this as it may, their claims to success have merit: they point to the "intense interest in self-discovery through language and in self-expression, with writing to realize oneself" that now powerfully occupies the attention of many teachers. They point also to "assaults on traditional patterns of schooling," including the open classroom, as evidence of a more institutional kind of change. Dartmouth set out to challenge two dominant models of English teaching, the "skills" approach (functionalism) and the emphasis on "cultural heritage" (essentially "great books"), and to recommend an alternative that Dixon refers to as a model of "personal growth" (1). It challenged the adequacy of skill arguments by appealing to their uncontextual nature, their ignorance of the "broader processes that prompt a child to use language in the first place" (2), and it challenged "cultural heritage" arguments by pointing out the reified, static concept of "culture" that underlies them, a concept that ignores culture as a process—a "network of attitudes to experience and personal evaluations" that people develop "in a living response to . . . family and neighbourhood" (3). By contrast, an educational program emphasizing relationships between language and personal growth accepts "a central paradox about language": it "belongs to the public world" of human converse but it also allows "each individual" to "take what he can from the shared store of experience and build it into a world of his own" (6–7). The educational idea is to view language activity as a "process" of constructing and construing experience and to offer students, "as they develop," multiple opportunities to "explore their power" as makers of meaning "to bring a new, simplifying order to the complexity of life" (25–26). The teacher begins, according to Dixon, with "a respect for each pupil" as that person is, "and that means for what expresses [her] identity, notably [her] language" (30). Teaching and learning begin with each child's expressive resources: dialect, for instance, "is personal and valuable, not an incorrect version of standard," and a good starting point for classroom language activities such as oral narrative; learning standard dialect is associated "with pleasure rather than with drudgery or uncertainty"; the teacher draws attention "to the human purposes in language" (17), not to artificial decorums reflecting sociopolitical judgments about the prestige or importance of the language of some dominant group. "When a pupil is steeped in language in operation we expect, as he matures, a conceptualizing of his earlier awareness of language, and with this perhaps new insight into himself (as creator of his own world)" (13).

The challenge to traditional classroom arrangements, but also to the social realities that promote them, is apparent, albeit couched in the congenial language of Anglo-American individualism. Dixon advocates, for instance, the use of "free forms" in writing instruction rather than practicing "topic sentence" paragraphs and fixed poetic stanzas. He cites the "common experience" that children "enjoy free forms" and points out that artificial constraints are "more likely to

prevent their having something to say than assist it." Students need
freedom to "choose the form that suits them," a need that "springs
from a natural variety in mood, intention and level of insight, and
often reveals an intuitive sensitivity in the choice of an appropriate
form." The reason that Dixon gives for this instructional flexibility is
noteworthy: it's to help students "reach their own decisions in writing rather than take ready-made those of society" (46). The critique
of unimaginative conformity here, which surely challenges the dominant intent of schooling to mass-produce workers for the economy,
is framed in a language of personal initiative and romantic rebellious-
ness that Americans find appealing in mythic terms even if finally
unacceptable in light of pragmatic social interests. As a result of this
persistent tapping of American mythic images—specifically the free
individual exploring the mysteries of experience through personally
evolved formal experiments in order to "create" her "own" world,
Dixon is able to make plausible assaults on school practices that
thwart hallowed individualism even as they achieve the "real" purposes of schooling.

Hence, he can believably critique "skills" instruction, even though
it effectively prepares the work force, in favor of "personal growth,"
which might well have just the opposite effect—a work force no longer
satisfied with the levels of self-fulfillment available in routine, alienated labor. He can challenge the privileged authority of the teacher,
which replicates and supports the top-down structures of authority
that control economic life, in favor of a "dialogic" model of teaching
(34), which subverts capitalist notions of ownership and control
(whether of knowledge or some other commodity), by appealing to an
authentic capacity in the free individual to govern herself and contribute her own intelligence to democratic negotiation of social reality. He
can challenge tracking (100–101), which rationalizes the distribution
of workers through the economy on the basis of "skill level" or other
competence, in favor of "individual progress in a heterogenous class"
by appealing to the "fact" that "creativity and imagination are not the
exclusive province of academically bright children" (103), pointing
out the contradiction in American educational policy that schools
"nominally" offer "the same education for all" yet begin tracking—
"open or concealed"—right from the "beginning of the elementary
school" (101). And he can challenge assessment on similar grounds
(92ff.) as a "weird kind of game" that distracts teachers and students
alike from "the natural uses of language to shape and order experience," right in the face of an entrenched educational commitment to
reproduce existing socioeconomic hierarchies through the abstract
quantitative norms that assessment creates. All in all, this rhetoric
could be considered skillful manipulation of mythic values that retain

some force in American life despite social realities that contradict them. However, it might be more skillful, ultimately even more successful, if it were more conscious of the fact that it *is* manipulative, that it *is* designed to confront realities that actively oppose the values it seeks to affirm, and that it *isn't* a "natural" tapping of the nation's basically sympathetic disposition toward democracy, fair play, and human rights. The vulnerability to manipulation-in-reverse that persistently threatens expressivism lies not in its use of these mythic values but in its own uncritical acceptance of them.

The expressivist tendencies in Kenneth Goodman's work entail similar aspirations of social change matched to similar conceptual and pedagogical means of pursuing them—with similar consequences in the widespread success of whole language curricula yet persistent marginalizing of their ambitions within essentially unchanged school and other social realities. In *Reading: Process and Program*, a book that Goodman coauthored with Olive Niles, the parallels to Dixon and the Dartmouth seminar are apparent. The goal of reading, they assert, is not the mastery of a skill for its own sake, but rather the production of meaning, the discovery of "new knowledge" that leads to "a desire for more knowledge." Meaning is "the constant goal of the proficient reader," who "continually tests his choices against the developing meaning by asking himself if what he is reading makes sense." Reading is an "active," not a "passive" process, an "interaction of language and thought" in which the reader is "involved in cycles of reading, reflective thinking, flights of fancy and then more reading." The process is never pursued in isolation from purposes and needs, a fact that remains as true "in the stages in which reading is being acquired as it is in the stages of proficient reading." Materials used in reading instruction "must necessarily be meaningful," so that children "with different purposes and interests" require "a variety of materials to keep them reading." The "development of competence," they conclude, is "best achieved when the learner's focus is on the content of materials and not on reading itself" (20–21). These assumptions constitute the essential argument of whole language, with its emphasis on the fullest exercise of readers' "competence," as opposed to the practice of isolated skills (like "word attack"), through repeated opportunities to engage personally meaningful subjects. "Reading to learn may well stimulate learning to read" (23).

This emphasis on "the full language situation" (18) is accompanied by a concern for individual learners, their innate capacities as language users, and their different starting points as readers. Drawing on Chomsky, Goodman and Niles distinguish between "competence," a native ability to be nurtured in the classroom, and "performance," the "uttering of words," which ends up a restrictive, behaviorist preoccupation when it becomes too much the focus of teacherly correction. Everyone, even though "a beginner as far as literacy is concerned," brings to "the task of learning to read the sum total of [her] life's experiences and the language competence [she] has already acquired." This fact remains true regardless of "what rung on the socioeconomic ladder [her] dialect occupies." Learners only become disadvantaged when schools "reject [their] experiences as unsuitable to build learnings on while accepting those of other children." At the same time, "language difference is not a disadvantage unless the school rejects certain dialects and insists that a child must speak and read in a dialect in which he is not competent." In a move that plainly signals the social critique at the heart of whole language pedagogy, Goodman and Niles point out that remedial reading classes "invariably have more boys than girls, more blacks than whites, more minority group youngsters than is proportional in the population these programs serve." The reason is to be found, they insist, less in "real weakness" within these groups than in "the failure of school reading programs to adequately reach them." Too much institutional time goes toward "trying to find weaknesses and deficiencies in children," time better spent developing curricula that would "capitalize on the strengths of children of both sexes and of all shapes, sizes, colors, ethnic and cultural backgrounds, dispositions, energy levels, and physical attributes" (28). What is revealing, however, as it is also in Dixon, is the lack of follow-through in locating the specific socioeconomic as well as other cultural commitments that account for the uses of institutional time and effort. There's no suspicion in the text that the emphasis on finding weakness instead of building on strength might be something more than an accidental misdirection of public and instructional energy, that it might purposefully serve the interests of a prevailing social order.

The argument that Goodman and Niles advance regarding effective reading curricula contains frequent—but persistently implicit and uncritical—challenges to existing school as well as larger societal arrangements. It begins, for instance, with the illusory value of skill sequencing, pointing out that the reading process "requires that a multitude of skills be used simultaneously," and of course also in context. As a result, "any sequence will necessarily be arbitrary." But instead of inquiring into the reasons for the continuing popularity of skills instruction, despite what seems to them a demonstrable truth about reading, Goodman and Niles are satisfied to mention, as though it were simply a correctable matter of misguided understanding, that sequenced instruction "has often been strongly advocated by publishers and curriculum workers" (34). Indeed. But in the absence of inquiry into the deeper (and darker) rationality that pervades this apparent curricular irrationality, only puzzlement can attend the fact of its continuing popularity, not a sustained effort to subvert it by opening up the foundations upon which it rests. The argument proceeds to consideration of the "affective climate" that must be created before any kind of instruction can be responsive to student needs, including "feelings of security and success," and a belief that learning to read is important, worthwhile, and enjoyable. Invoking the organic metaphor characteristic of expressivist ideology, they suggest that "the climate in which a reading program is developed has as much effect upon its success as the weather has on the growth of a plant" (42–43). They criticize the "unfavorable" climate of many secondary schools, pointing to several reasons: teachers who believe that there is "something wrong with the student" who doesn't read at the expected level or else with the elementary program that was "supposed" to take care of such "skills"; the bare walls, poor facilities, and absence of book collections that are too common in reading classrooms and centers; the lack of friendly, busy, well-stocked, supportive central libraries and other reading spaces in schools (43–47). They go as far as to suggest the correlation between school climate and "a corresponding climate in the community" (47). It's "ridiculous," they say, that Americans can voyage to the moon but can't wipe out illiteracy, and they suggest the possibility of universal literacy "if enough people decide it is the thing to do and will support it." They exhort the nation, in the name of what's right and just, to "support such a task," mentioning by the way that it will require "vast sums of money" and "the commitment of a tremendous amount of professional energy" (47–48). But moral sincerity and scholarly insight notwithstanding, they concede that eliminating illiteracy is a distant dream as of the date of their book. Indeed, it remains a distant dream today, twenty years later. And nothing in the argument suggests that the authors know why more hasn't been accomplished. They simply express frustrated incredulity that moon landings have received priority.

The rhetoric of moral sincerity carries over into the curricular recommendations that Goodman and Niles eventually offer. First, such a program should attend, not just to competence and contextualized skill development, but also to "the affective aspects of the process." Second, it should "respect all groups of students: the handicapped, the gifted, the ethnically or socially different." Third, it should be also "a respecter of individuals," providing for "their needs and interests so far as it is possible to do so." Fourth, it should be "continuous and sequential through the entire range of a school system's responsibility." Fifth, it should be "relevant" to "conditions in a school and a community." Sixth, it should be implemented "by the entire professional staff," in light of "the best available theory and practice." Seventh, it should exist "in an atmosphere of expected success on the part of both teachers and students." Eighth, it should be "supported by a community which willingly supplies the funds for adequate staffing and materials." Finally, it should be evaluated and changed as shortcomings become apparent (71–72). These are worthy sentiments and we share them. If the American public were to accept and implement them, the consequences would be as revolutionary as anything envisioned in more radical arguments of social reconstruction. But the public hasn't accepted them, as the text itself concedes: "it hasn't been done in the past for lack of determination and dedication" (47). Unfortunately,the future holds no more promise than the past if no strategy of implementation can be envisioned beyond appeal to the taxpayer's, the politician's, the court judge's, or the school administrator's better nature.

It's interesting—and also ironic, given the tendency of Goodman and Niles to avoid scrutiny of the sociopolitical conditions conspicuously thwarting their work—that they should approach the very threshold of critical pedagogy in observing that an ultimate intent of reading instruction should be development of the "critical sense." They note that "to read critically is to read skeptically," suggesting that three kinds of awareness are important to "critical reading competence." The first is a knowledge of criteria for determining "plausibility, credibility, ulterior motives of the writer or publisher, and so forth." The second is a recognition that acquiring critical competence is both possible and necessary. The third is a familiarity with "the devices which writers use to appeal emotionally and subtly" to readers in an effort to influence them. With what seems to be an innocence that calls into question their own "critical sense" Goodman and Niles write in italics that "*much of the reading required of children in school deters rather than promotes critical reading.*" How, they ask, can schools expect students to view essays in their reading texts critically when they aren't expected to scrutinize other texts, when they're asked to believe that "there is always one right answer to a question," or that "books are never wrong," or that they aren't competent "to judge the merits of their social studies or science books"? What seems not to occur to them is that school curricula might be *designed* to mystify, to domesticate, to promote obedience and docility rather than challenge or dissent. They conclude that "the strategies required to read critically must be developed for all reading tasks and not just for special ones designed for instruction" because "one either reads critically or one does not." And as evidence of the need for such essentially political vigilance, they mention the marketing tactics of advertising agencies, which can be as effectively employed in selling political candidates, for instance, as (other) commercial products. But this sensible insistence on skepticism is belied by the argument's own rhetoric, which depends on moral earnestness, on appeals to "common sense," on beliefs regarding public benevolence and a persistent commitment to "do the right thing" or at least to do what "the best available theory" advises, for the force and effectiveness of its recommendations. The will to change current social inequities exists, yes, in Goodman and Niles, but in the context of an assumption that powerful people surely desire such change and will encourage it when the means are available. Unfortunately, this isn't a critically perceptive judgment. And without a clear recognition of the purposefulness of the school arrangements that they desire to challenge, there's little wonder that their tactics proceed only as far as exhortation.

What we've said about Dixon and Goodman, however, we must say also, in conclusion, about ourselves. That is, we mustn't exempt our own previous work, in particular *Rhetorical Traditions and the Teaching of Writing*, from the critique of liberalism that we've directed here at arguments we've admired in the past and continue to value. Our work has in fact been critiqued along similar lines and in ways that have enabled our continued learning—by John Schilb, Steve North, Pat Bizzell, and Jim Berlin, among others. We need to acknowledge those useful criticisms, not as a *mea culpa* but as a gesture of self-awareness and—dare we say it?—personal growth. Of course, criticisms of *Rhetorical Traditions* have come from various alternative positions, not all of which merit the same attention. Comically ferocious challenges from the special interest group of traditional historians of rhetoric have commanded more attention than they're worth, given a conspicuous relationship between their overheated defense of classical theory as a Sacred Text, the Father of composition studies, and their awareness of the priestly status at stake for those who now search its rich recesses. This teapot tempest has raged far from our point, which had less to do with the history of rhetoric than with more and less humane practices of writing instruction. To the extent that we framed our position as a latter-day Battle of the Books, we've certainly brought the silliness on ourselves. But that doesn't make it anything better than silly.

A serious criticism, however, is the unself-consciousness of our storytelling, the insufficiency of the intellectual-historical romance we constructed to carry our argument, where for all our dramatic villainizing of classicism, the only thing we managed to do is substitute one master narrative for another, a group of slightly more contemporary male European literary figures for a slightly less contemporary group, and one totalizing philosophical scheme in place of another, all in the service of bewitching and/or browbeating teachers. A second justifiable criticism is our dependence on modernist conceptions of the autonomous self, the "progress" of knowledge, the "growth" of mind, and the interiority of writing. While our arguments aren't cognitivist in nature, they do presume, much as Cassirer does, the existence of a sovereign imaginative capacity composing the world through its own instrumentalities. A third criticism, related to the second, is our failure to situate writing theory and practice within the politics of education, so that the energy of our instructional commitments could be conceptually refined and tactically channeled through an awareness of the power arrangements inscribed in discourse, including the prose of the school. We have been somewhat effective, as others have, in persuading teachers of the merits of whole language and writing process pedagogy, but ineffective in helping teachers understand and anticipate the institutional opposition they inevitably face in implementing those practices. More than that, we've represented the ends of writing instruction—as a kind of personal empowerment—in terms that render the practice necessarily nearsighted, naive about the sociopolitical character of discourse and power, and worst of all, fraught with peril for the unwary who may have taken us at our word.

The limitation of "personal growth" arguments, our own included, has been precisely their personalizing of circumstances that are profoundly social and political in character. The single whole language or process teacher struggles heroically to do what's right for the individual student in an atmosphere of trust, support, and hopefulness. But dedication notwithstanding, everything that happens outside that classroom (and much that intrudes within it—the testing, the textbooks, the regimented quality of educational time and space) works toward the satisfaction of goals that are antithetical. The teacher next door believes the same things but is similarly isolated. Or—just as likely—he believes that more traditional curricula are proper and that no one should make waves. Or—just as likely—she has burned out long ago because the lack of caring, the discipline problems, the frustrations of disaffected learners, the hauteur of overbearing superiors, have extinguished earlier commitment and high expectations. The principal wants efficiency and productivity, measured in high test scores, teachers and students who punch the clock when they're supposed to, and a silence through the building (apart from the drone of instructional voices) that demonstrates iron discipline or dutifulness to task or both. The district and the local and state governments want these things as well, at as little cost as possible and with as great a return as possible in the way of productive workers for the economy. American society wants all of this plus assurances that "outsiders' children" won't get the perks of socioeconomic privilege before the insiders' do (because the former are alien or ignorant or lazy or all of these together). And they want schools to prove to them that their country can still whip the Iraqis at war, the Japanese at commerce, and the rest of the world at patriotism, sports, and religiosity. The sweatshop of *A Nation at Risk* is a more efficient place than the open classroom in which to provide these signs of educational "success." The usefulness of the open classroom in such a setting lies only in the strategic release of pent-up pressure it can provide from the stresses and the alienation that are by-products of the sweatshop. Hence, free writing interrupts the sober, tedious, but more important business of the term paper, while an amiable group discussion of *The Color Purple* offers brief diversion from the more "rigorous," useful, and "value-neutral" work of classes in engineering or industrial management. The lonely process teacher is playing to a stacked deck.

Meanwhile, according to our local newspaper (the Albany *Times Union*) of 9 January, 1992, almost thirty years after Dartmouth, a study released by the National School Boards Association shows that schools across the country are resegregating—going back to the dual system of the 1950s in which the white population attended one group of schools while blacks attended another. In the Northeast specifically, the newspaper reports, half of the region's black children attend schools with fewer than 10 percent whites, while one in three go to schools that are 99 or more percent minority. Hispanic children are even less likely than African American to share classrooms with whites. Since 1974, three years after the publication of Goodman and Niles, the Supreme Court has presided over the legalizing of this trend toward resegregation. It has ruled, in Milliken vs. Bradley (418 US 717 [1974]), that busing between cities and suburbs is only required when proof can be provided that the suburbs were "responsible" for the city's segregation. It has also ruled, in Board of Education of Oklahoma City vs. Dowell (498 US 112 [1991]), that school districts can be released from judicial oversight once they have eliminated past segregative practices even if their current practices maintain the same inequities in a new guise. Rulings soon to come from the current Court promise further diluting of the ethical and legal standards established by the different caliber Court that decided Brown vs. Board of Education (349 US 294 [1954]). According to the 1990 census, the article concludes, most major cities are as racially divided as they were thirty years ago. But the scope and significance of segregation in the 1990s is greater than it was in the 1950s, it adds ominously, because one student in three today is from a minority group while only one in ten had been nonwhite in 1954. We find it difficult to read such reports, indeed to witness what is passing before our eyes, and still believe that free writing is a key to educational change.

Chapter Seven

Critical Literacy
Language and Power

Transformative intellectuals make the pedagogical more political and the political more pedagogical. . . . This means inserting education directly into the political sphere by arguing that schooling represents both a struggle for meaning and a struggle over power relations. . . . Within this view of schooling, critical reflection and action become part of a fundamental social project to help students develop a deep and abiding faith in the struggle to overcome injustices and to change themselves. . . . Transformative intellectuals take seriously the need to give students an active voice in their learning experiences. . . . [However] the starting point pedagogically for such intellectuals is not with the isolated student but with collective actors in their various cultural, class, racial, historical, and gendered settings, along with the particularity of their diverse problems, hopes, and dreams.

Aronowitz and Giroux,
Education Under Siege

In problem-posing education, [people] develop their power to perceive critically the way they exist in the world with which and in which they find themselves; they come to see the world not as a static reality, but as a reality in process, in transformation.

Paulo Freire,
Pedagogy of the Oppressed

147

Since the beginning of the twentieth century the International Ladies Garment Workers Union has looked to the education of workers and their families, many of whom are newly arrived immigrants to the United States, as an essential aspect of its responsibility to the people it serves. In 1985, the ILGWU joined six other unions in establishing the Consortium for Worker Education in New York City and it has subsequently developed the Worker-Family Education Program under the auspices of the consortium. The ILGWU program, largest in the consortium, includes seventy classes distributed in various factory and other sites throughout the boroughs of New York and adjacent counties. The program emphasizes instruction in English as a Second Language, given the fact that the majority of students have come recently from China, Latin America, and the Caribbean. Some of these students have extensive educational backgrounds in their countries of origin, while others have only elementary preparation; but most of them have had little experience of English in their own home and work settings. The focus of instruction, however, is neither on the acontextual technical skills of school-based functional literacy programs nor on the narrow job preparation of functionalist workplace programs. Instead, it locates speaking and listening, reading and writing in the framework of comprehensive socioeconomic needs: hence, at some sites language teaching goes on together with the learning of garment skills such as pattern making or the use of sewing machines; at others, it's associated with citizenship classes; at still others with health and safety workshops, union and labor history workshops, bilingual (specifically Spanish) classes, and in some cases classes for laid off workers in skills of alternative employment. Neither is the program concerned with the implicit indoctrination of cultural literacy agendas: indeed its curriculum guide stresses the importance of developing "an awareness of the cultural differences between yourself and your students," fostering "a mutual respect." The curriculum developers, Deidre Freeman and Maureen LaMar, make a point of noting that "people have emigrated here for a variety of reasons and it should never be assumed that anyone is forsaking their culture to embrace your own" (n.p.).

In the summer of 1991, LaMar and Emily Schnee developed an ESL workshop for the program entitled "The Global Factory," intended, they explain, "to explore an economic trend whereby transnational corporations send production and assembly operations to the Third World in search of cheap labor" (n.p.). This practice has obvious implications for the quality of life of U.S. garment workers, but it has implications as well for the continuing exploitation of workers around the world within the power arrangements of late capitalism. The activities of LaMar and Schnee's curriculum are evidently patterned on the instructional practices of the Brazilian educator, Paulo Freire, and as such constitute an effectively practical representation of critical literacy. In the first "lesson" of the curriculum students are invited to introduce themselves to one another through an activity designed to exercise English language abilities while also illustrating "the pervasiveness of the global factory." Each student is asked to write responses to five questions on an index card, and then to wear the card while circulating through the classroom and conversing with other students about the information on the card. The questions are (1) what is your name? (2) where do you work? (3) what do you do? (4) where was your shirt made? and (5) who made your shirt? After conversation, students take their seats and, in turn, read their answers to questions 4 and 5. Then the activity "coordinator" introduces the theme of "the global factory," focusing on where the shirts were made and who made them. The answers are revealing: Gap shirts, for instance, are made in Malaysia, Bonjour in India, Touagle in Taiwan, Fantanic in Pakistan. It's a safe bet the designers and their marketing agents live elsewhere.

In the second activity, students discuss and compare working conditions for garment workers in different countries, cooperating in small groups of three and four, always of course in English. Each group receives a photograph of a garment worker in a particular country as well as a list of six questions asking where she works, how many hours a week, what her hourly wage is, whether she belongs to a union, who she works for, and what her working and living conditions are like. Sharing their background knowledge of the garment industry, group members respond to the questions, with one member writing down answers; then they designate someone to present the group's findings orally to the class. The coordinator then offers additional information about each situation. Sample answers in the curriculum guide include: (1) "Mexico; 48 hours a week; 34 cents; no union; Kimberly-Clark factory; no ventilation, no exhaust fans, lots of dust causing headaches, sore throats, and eye infections. Lives in cardboard shack with a corrugated tin roof. No running water or sewage." (2) "USA; 11-1/2 hours a day; $3.50 an hour; no union; Singer factory; machines that burn, sewing machines that can cause injuries, a lot of caustic chemicals and potential dangers such as open elevator shafts. Lives with a family of five in a one-bedroom apartment in Brooklyn." In subsequent activities, students read descriptions of the global factory system and discuss what they've read in the context of their own experience; they find out about the geography of the global factory through maps that track the stages of garment production from America and Europe to the third world and back again; they sing and learn the lyrics of a song titled "Are My

Hands Clean" by the group Sweet Honey in the Rock: "I wear gar-
ments touched by hands from all over the world / 35 percent cotton,
65 percent polyester, the journey begins in Central America / In the
cotton fields of El Salvador / In a province soaked in blood, pesti-
cide-sprayed workers toil in a broiling sun / Pulling cotton for two
dollars a day. . . . / This third world sister / And I go to the Sears
department store where I buy my blouse / On sale for 20 percent
discount / Are my hands clean?" (Lyrics and music by Bernice
Johnson Reagon, Songtalk Publishing, 1985). Eventually, participants
begin, with help from lectures, reading, and other research, to identify the international structure of the garment industry and to discuss
how it has changed throughout the twentieth century. (The above
discussion of the global factory workshop is based on LaMar and
Schnee).

Students and teachers participate as equals in these workshops,
teachers serving in appropriate roles as facilitative "authorities" but
not in the authoritarian postures of more traditional instruction.
Indeed, students are as instrumental in the design of workshops as
they are active in their roles as learners. At the conclusion of one
workshop, students together produced a magazine, titled *Our Mural
of Cultures* (Acevedo et al.), which had the multiple benefits of
validating students' work by rendering it in published form, encouraging a critically grounded literacy by writing for self-directed, frequently political purposes, and evaluating students' acquisition of
reading and writing abilities as manifested in the stories, letters, and
other materials in the magazine. A student-organized "Magazine
Committee" read and reviewed manuscript submissions and handled
the editorial work of production. The writing is organized by themes
that emphasize and integrate forms of personal and social knowledge: "Guess What Happens in Our Second Home"; "How Can I
Forget My Friend?"; "Dreams and Realities"; "Problems in the
World"; "Our Loving Caribbean Countries." The articles in the magazine range from short personal narratives: "The job is very hard. He
works all day. The boss's shouts are very bad. The payment is very
cheap. The place doesn't have good air conditioning." (Luis Rodriguez's story as written by Morelia Arias); to a series of letters
written to "Paul Douglas and the Pittston Company" regarding the
unacceptable working conditions faced by Pittston coal mine workers in Appalachia. The stories and letters are reflective, moving, often
politically engaged, sometimes angry; the writers have learned, as
Freire puts it, to use words "to denounce the world." One student
editor, Fernando Guerra, writes: "Sharing experience is sharing life.
This is the way I have felt during the days that we have spent
organizing the magazine. All of us have told part of our lives in the

articles. This is the best way to know our feelings and aspirations." Another, Gladys Loaiza, writes: "This was my first time that I participated in preparing the magazine of the English classes. It was a good experience because I learned how to put together a magazine. I hope to do it again. I also learned to read a little more English."

The principles at work here are evident enough to anyone familiar with Freirean pedagogy. Jonathan Kozol has offered similar illustrations from the community-based literacy workshops he describes in *Illiterate America*. He speaks of a "freedom school," for instance, that held literacy classes in the basement of a church, attracting "two hundred persons nightly" and finally overflowing "into a network of apartments" rented "in the many semivacant buildings of the neighborhood" (44). The curriculum of the workshop aimed to "take action on the words we learned" and on the "world of anguish and injustice which those words revealed" (45). He points to a session that evolved around the words "tenant," "landlord," "lease," "eviction," "rat," and "roach," which "led to one of the first rent strikes in our city." He describes the study of words "connected to the world" which led to a repainted apartment building, to the reconstruction of a rotting fire escape, and to the replacement of illegal exits that could only be opened from outside. His workshop was a "collective action-center structured upon words that can denounce the world" (45). Both the ILGWU workshops and the community programs that Kozol discusses articulate in their practice the central principles—reflection and action—of Freire's representation of "critical literacy": (1) "through generative words and themes"—the workshop's "global factory," Kozol's "landlord" and "roach"—instruction "proposes to learners a critical reflection of the concrete contexts of national reality, a process that requires reflection on the present moment of reconstruction, along with challenges and difficulties to be overcome"; (2) instruction aims to be "in the service of the nation's reconstruction and contributes to the people so that by taking more and more history into their own hands, they can shape their history" (Freire and Macedo, 65).

It's important to notice here, in the context of defining "critical literacy" in its instructional dimension, that both of these examples derive from the world outside schools, suggesting a need to contextualize the nature and possibilities of "schooling" by appeal to an oppositional construction of the idea of "education." Of the four broad representations of literacy we've discussed, only critical literacy is framed as a sociopolitical "educational" commitment that may well strive to incorporate the school but that is not limited in focus or aspiration to the narrow project of schooling, with its implicit and massively resistant devotion to reproducing capitalist socioeconomic life. Aronowitz and Giroux pursue this theme at length in *Education Under Siege*, because it's the logical foundation for any project of critical literacy that might eventually take hold within institutional school settings. Schooling, they explain, occurs within institutions that are "directly or indirectly linked to the State through public funding or state certification requirements" (131). As such, they serve the interests of the state, embodying "the legitimating ideologies of the dominant society." Possibilities exist within schools for the emergence of a critical pedagogy, but invariably under constraining circumstances that limit its scope and prospects, leading to the difficulties and failures we discussed in Chapter 3. Education, on the other hand, is a broader concept, and, as Aronowitz and Giroux employ it, an oppositional practice occurring necessarily beyond as well as within the institutional boundaries of schooling. For them, the concept refers in its radical sense to "a collectively produced set of experiences organized around issues and concerns that allow for a critical understanding of everyday oppression as well as the dynamics involved in constructing alternative political cultures" (132): in short, precisely the activity of the ILGWU Worker-Family Education Program, whose participants are working-class immigrants faced with oppression along axes of gender, race, class, and ethnicity as a daily fact of life. The point of educational praxis, quite distant from the conventional purpose of "schooling" in American life, is to eliminate these forms of oppression by pursuing the notion of an "active citizenry based on the self-dedication of a group to forms of education that promote models of learning and social interaction that have a fundamental connection to the idea of human emancipation" (132).

Critical literacy, the intent of a critical reading and writing pedagogy, entails an understanding of the relationships between language and power together with a practical knowledge of how to use language for self-realization, social critique, and cultural transformation. As Aronowitz and Giroux explain, critical literacy is "linked to notions of self- and social empowerment as well as to the processes of democratization" (132). It emerges from an interrogation of the interestedness of existing social arrangements, the extent to which they have been constituted by and work to serve dominant groups. It depends on a connection between language learning and critical consciousness, where the forms of knowledge and institutional reality that language enables are recognized as objective but not as eternal or ontological in character, are recognized as powerful but not as monolithic or even particularly stable, and are therefore understood to be in process, changeable. It functions "to help students and others understand what this society has made of them . . . and what it is they no longer want to be, as well as what it is they need to appropriate critically in order to become knowledgeable about the world in which they live" (132). Freire's own colorful metaphor (though in his own experience it hasn't always been just a metaphor) is that people first must eat—then must fight. They eat first because if they're hungry they can't fight. English reading and writing skills are necessary in this culture if people are going to eat. But they eat so that they'll be able to fight: they learn the skills that enable their participation in economic life so that they can apply those skills toward relieving oppressive conditions. Hence, the garment worker, newly literate in English, applies her reading and writing abilities not only to the enhancing of her employment prospects (albeit a primary goal), but also to learning about, and ultimately critiquing, unfair, unsafe, and unacceptable circumstances of her working and living. She assumes new control of her life by coming to understand her position as a historical subject and no longer an object (see Freire, *Pedagogy*).

This utopian program of language learning in the interest of democratic living can be most readily sustained among groups who recognize the extent to which their own interests depend on its realization. Hence, the relative plausibility of the ILGWU efforts and those of community literacy projects among the adult urban poor. But if a similar project is to be sustained among teachers and within the circumstances of school life, where dominant culture actively resists modification, it will have to search out group affiliations that relate schooling to what Aronowitz and Giroux call "oppositional social spheres" beyond it. A practice that aims narrowly to "empower" students within the restrictive circumstances of school reality, even when the population to be served is marginal with respect to the dominant culture, is at once poorly theorized and doomed to failure, as liberal arguments for reform have demonstrated. The activist teacher must work, not only with other teachers in a spirit of solidarity, but also with activist parent associations, activist school board members, supportive state education officials, supportive funding agencies, local churches and community groups, union educators, the local gay rights or feminist organization, the activist publisher, like-minded public policy advocacy groups, and other sympathetic citizens. The intellectual representation of "critical literacy" presumes a dialectic between the individual and the communal, the local and the general. Similarly, its practical realization necessitates the same dialectical activity. Aronowitz and Giroux emphasize how important it is for critical teachers to see themselves not only as filling larger public roles than their daily classroom practice requires, but also as involved within and related to collective enterprises that

protect and nurture them while also making their labor more meaningful in the context of collaborative struggle. Efforts within schools
must be "linked to alliances and social formations which can affect
policy decisions over the control and content of schooling." The
struggle must be carried to sites "other than those influenced and
controlled by the State." These oppositional sites, the union meeting,
the church gathering, the community workshop, the parent association, offer "the possibility for using collective aspirations and criticisms in the development of alternative cultures" (134). This doesn't
mean that academics and teachers claim authority in these other
spheres. Part of the goal must be "to debunk the idea that expertise
and academic credentials are the distinguishing marks of the intellectual." Oppositional groups form their own leadership, their own
intellectuals, "rooted in and committed to the history, experience,
and set of goals they share with the people such intellectuals represent" (135). The aim is to forge alliances, not struggle internally for
ownership of other people's lives.

Predictably enough, most academic sponsors of critical literacy
languish in their university enclaves, supporting themselves through
articles and books trumpeting theoretical revolutions. If anything,
they're more isolated than process and whole language teachers are,
because, apart from their journals, they lack even the organizational
identities, including the National Writing Project for instance, that
have become available for liberal practitioners. Moreover, they continue to face both theoretical and pedagogical identity crises as
Marxist, feminist, and postmodern conceptual alternatives vie with
each other for intellectual authority while posing their own distinctive problems for the concrete development of critical praxis. (More
of that in a moment.) There have, however, been a significant number
of organized, pragmatic challenges to dominant educational realities
of state schooling on the part of action groups with members simultaneously within and outside state-sponsored institutions and with
sympathies corresponding to the broad tenets of critical literacy.
Some academic programs, Women's Studies, African American and
other ethnic studies, with roots in the communities they serve outside academe, occasionally represent such challenges, although these
are typically co-opted by institutional structures that hold them to
standards of academic knowledge and inquiry that they might initially have intended to resist. New associations and conferences are
emerging within the academy—for instance, OpenMind: The Association for the Achievement of Cultural Diversity in Higher Education, which aims to enhance the status of non-European and
nonmasculinist modes of knowing and forms of knowledge in college
and university curricula as well as faculty profiles. Alternative

schools, formed through the efforts of radical parent associations, have sought to redefine schooling in terms of local community and liberatory values. These are for the most part new, fragile, and frequently imperiled undertakings, rendered more so in present circumstances of budgetary crisis and widely encouraged right-wing political bluster.

A notable instance of organization across disparate communities in the service of a critical ideal of schooling is the National Coalition of Advocates for Students, a network of organizations committed to public education, equal access, and responsive curricula for all students and committed also to local and national advocacy as a means to effect constructive educational change. It includes such diverse groups as the Children's Defense Fund in Washington D.C., the Coalition for Quality Education in Toledo, Ohio, the Parents Union for Public Schools in Philadelphia, the Arkansas Advocates for Children and Families, and the Center for Law and Education in Washington D.C. During the early 1980s, the National Coalition of Advocates for Students gathered substantial funding from foundations and other nongovernmental sources to mount a "board of inquiry" into the state of the nation's schools. The board included well-known public figures such as Harold Howe, Marian Wright Edelman, and Vito Perrone, along with (among others) Martin Carnoy of Stanford, a university educator, Carol Ouimette, a public school teacher from Minneapolis, Sam Meyer, an official of the UAW, Jose Cardenas of San Antonio, a former school superintendent, Angela Brown of Detroit, an inner-city youth worker, Robert Clark of Mississippi, a state representative, Gumecindo Salas, president of the Michigan state board of education, and Linda Martin, a parent activist from Griffithsville, West Virginia. The board accumulated more than one hundred hours of oral testimony, and additional written responses, from public hearings in ten cities. Witnesses included parents and students, teachers, social service representatives, community organizers, union officials, academic researchers, economic analysts, and others, all engaged in communal dialogue about the current conditions and future imperatives of American schooling. In 1985 the Board of Inquiry Project produced a report, titled *Barriers to Excellence: Our Children at Risk*, that offered a nationally based antidote to the poison of *A Nation at Risk*. Purists can argue whether the intellectual commitments and practical agendas of the National Coalition point toward a radical pedagogy or a critical conception of literacy, but we would suggest that, from the standpoint of organized resistance to prevailing structures of schooling, few other groups have taken the battle so far out of theoretical camps in universities and so far into the political arenas of American educational life. We would also suggest that the rhetoric of the report well illustrates critical literacy in action in its subtle reading of the prose of the school and its unveiling of the sources of educational inequality. The report is a thoroughgoing critique of that inequality, detailing discrimination and differential treatment along lines of gender, race, class, and culture, together with a sad catalogue of barriers to "children at risk," including inflexible school structures, tracking, testing abuse, narrowness of curriculum and teaching practice, lack of support services, lack of early childhood programs, and lack of democratic governance. From its opening pages, the report boldly affirms the premise that schools actively impede the educational progress of certain groups of students, children from poor families, children from minority and immigrant groups "who face discriminatory policies and practices," many girls and young women "who miss out on education opportunities routinely afforded males," and children with special needs who are poorly facilitated because of physical or learning difficulties. The development of these students "is hampered by schools that do not serve them adequately; by expectations on the part of educators that they will not or cannot succeed; by denial of access to special needs programs; by fiscal policies that limit educational services; and by inattention to the difficulties young people face in moving from school to work" (Introductory Message). There is moral indignation in this rhetoric reminiscent of expressivist criticism. But it's complemented by a sharper awareness of social, political, and economic realities that account for the enumerated grievances, and by a correspondingly shrewder sense of how to challenge and subvert these realities in the interest of social justice.

Because the report aims to have a concrete public impact, it refrains from the abstract, intellectualized, and inevitably alienating critique of socioeconomic structures that a radical academic theorist, for instance, might offer as the means of explaining the sorry conditions of schools. It allows very little ambiguity, however, in its conclusion that schools are what they are not merely because of local ignorance, well-intentioned blundering, accidental prejudice, unfortunate economic timing, or poor on-site administration, but because the corporate, governing, legislative, and judicial institutions of the country speak in massive accord, through their deployment of wealth, property, services, and opportunities, for the privileging of some groups over others in the maintenance of a hierarchic scale of socioeconomic well-being. The root issue of the report is nothing less than "which children matter . . . and to whom?" and the report's principal conclusion is "that large numbers of children do not matter enough to many of those who set the education and economic policies of this nation and its states and localities." More specifically, "minority children do not matter as much as non-minority children do to some school officials, judging by the disproportionate numbers of such children who are excluded and underserved by the schools" (viii).

The report systematically implicates structures of government from the local district to the federal bench in a program of discriminatory practices reflecting the nation's core social and economic assumptions. It shows how these practices are subtly normalized within individual schools. And it reveals the mystifications within public rationales for the ways in which schools are funded, organized, and linked to the economy.

The funding of schools, for instance, effectively dramatizes the systematic, government-sponsored nature of educational inequality, because it depends on a legislatively determined and legally protected relationship between school resources and the value of property, both within and across districts, in effect mandating that economically privileged communities will enjoy better opportunities for quality schooling than those that aren't. The report shows the role of the Supreme Court in maintaining this inequity, when for example it ruled favorably, in San Antonio School District vs. Rodriguez (411 US 1 [1973]), on the constitutionality of school financing based on the prosperity of a community. Thurgood Marshall is quoted as writing in his dissent that the ruling makes it lawful for a state "to vary the quality of education which it offers its children in accordance with the amount of taxable wealth located in the school districts within which they reside" (76). The report also shows how state policies for supplementing local funds end up supporting inequities even as they claim to relieve them—by including provisions that ensure equal shares of revenue across districts or that distribute on an "equal per pupil basis." According to the report, several states continue to depend on "inequitable distribution formulas . . . which provide more to the rich than the poor" (77). The report documents, at the same time, how income level remains "a major determinant of the quality and quantity of education" that different children receive (5), showing that the purposeful legislative relationship between wealth and the availability of quality schooling results predictably in a relationship between wealth and the actual enjoyment of educational services among different groups of citizens.

Individual schools organize themselves in ways that recognize and maintain this disparity, through placement and tracking, through programming, through assessment, and through structures of governance. The report documents gender, class, and racial discrimination in the assumptions underlying each of these practices. It points, for instance, to the fact that black students are "more than three times as likely to be in a class for the educable mentally retarded" as white students, but only "half as likely to be in a class for the gifted and talented" (10). It points out that "teachers of low-income children tend to emphasize rote learning and minimize discussion and interaction on cognitive issues," while teachers of middle-class children take their questions more seriously and provide opportunities for active learning (7). It points to the fact that norm-referenced, standardized testing more often serves "political than educational purposes," emphasizing the ranks of students and schools in order to create a top and a bottom, rather than determining individual student strengths and needs: "our hearings gathered enough testimony about who generally wins and who loses to know that it is likely to be low-income, minority and handicapped students who find themselves on the bottom of the curve" (45–46). Finally, it points to school governance practices that place control and discipline, particularly in the case of minority students, ahead of responsive teaching or purposeful learning, with unsurprising results in "apathy, alienation, and dropouts" (61–62). And it points to top-down administrative arrangements as well as implicitly hostile bureaucratic procedures that "fail to draw on the resources of students, parents, and teachers in the immediate school community or of citizens in the larger community" (61), thereby effectively sealing off the governance of schools from nearly everyone who has a legitimate stake in it. Each of these practices plays its part in an educational self-fulfilling prophecy about who will do well and who poorly, even as government and school officials reiterate pieties about democracy, equal opportunity, and a connection between hard work and success.

The report is subtlest in its deconstruction of the rationales that are constructed to account for the ways in which schools are organized and also for the directions of state-sponsored school reform. Official rhetoric typically relates success in school, as cause, to social and economic success, as effect, maintaining an assumption that everyone starts equal with respect to a set of neutral academic standards, then over time meets those standards to a greater or lesser degree, eventually "earning" an appropriate spot in the economy. The report documents how this reasoning has things exactly backward: socioeconomic success, measured in income and property, leads to school success; standards favor certain groups and discriminate against others, predicting in advance for the most part that desirable employment and other success after school will fall to those who belong to the right groups. Official calls for school reform entail reiterating the rationale that hard work in school leads to The Good Life, only repeating it more aggressively by insisting on *harder* work while dangling illusory economic carrots to make it appealing. Stick and carrot: the report notes that, one year after publication of *A Nation at Risk*, the Department of Education released a survey identifying five areas of reform—thirty-five states had enacted stiffer high school graduation requirements; twenty-nine had enacted statewide testing policies, most of them tied to "minimum competency" criteria; twenty-two had introduced statewide curriculum guides to increase the standardization of the curriculum; eighteen had implemented "instructional time requirements"; twenty-nine had established "academic enrichment programs," including "intensive summer study" (presumably for remedial students) and "year-round programs for gifted students" (51–52). That's the stick. The carrot is the abundance of highly skilled jobs promised implicitly in arguments that better schooling is needed in order to prepare people for the fast-paced technological world they live in. In fact, the report documents, "only seven of every hundred new jobs are related to high technology occupations . . . and most of those are low-skilled jobs" (87). The carrot, in short, is illusory: a young person interested in computers is more likely "to work as a $4.00 per hour key punch operator than as a $25,000 per year programmer or repair person" (87). The point of the phony carrot is to mystify existing economic arrangements; the point of the stick is to show how earnestly those arrangements will be maintained. The report notes, with well concealed irony, that it's "almost as if the discussion of the economy, and the discussion of educational reforms tailored to certain definitions of the needs of the economy, were going on in two quite separate worlds" (84).

The point of this critical scrutiny is not, however, to push American noses ever deeper into their own nefarious motives either as a scorched earth exercise in castigation or in search of some purgative effect. Critical engagement with social reality entails something more than cynical rereadings of rationales, promises, and practices, the gleeful but pointless baiting that's available from any newspaper. The report aims to prompt creative intervention in the circumstances of schooling by representing American self-interest from an altered perspective. It insists repeatedly that what's at stake is not merely the aspirations and prospects of minority students, but in fact the future of all the nation's children, and therefore the future of the nation. When it rejects the implication "that excellence in education for some children can be made available only at the expense of other children," it does so by affirming a belief that "excellence without equity is both impractical and incompatible with the goals of a democratic society" (xi). When it critiques lockstep, rote, unimaginative curricula for students at risk, it affirms the value of creative, individualized learning for all students: "even in the 'best' schools and the highest tracks, schools often teach in ways that constrict rather than broaden students' minds" (50). When it protests the harm that standardized assessment has done to those children, it affirms the fact that "all children also suffer when testing narrows the content of curriculum and promotes teaching to the test" (47). Why, the report asks, "should we bother to invest public resources in programs for poor and minority children?" The answer is twofold: first, it's the only ethically responsible thing to do; second, the "long-term benefits" are in the national interest. The report argues, for instance, that a "push to equalize educational opportunity" for black students alone, who constitute only a third of all poor children, would result in completely eliminating shortages of engineers, computer programmers, and health professionals by the year 2015. Moreover, "we could stop worrying about funding social security, since the extra taxes on additional income produced by that new generation of . . . workers would total more than $20 billion a year in today's dollars." The nation would also "reap the benefits of eight million more 24- to 30-year-old Americans who have completed high school and some college with academic success, who have not been labeled handicapped or retarded, who have not been arrested, and who could be described . . . as 'socially competent' " (ix–x). This is constructive reflection, not sour grapes or rabble-rousing.

The report's recommendations for fair and effective schooling, once adjusted for scope, share much in common with those of Goodman and Niles, differing substantively only in their greater attention to political and economic realities that constitute the conditions of schools. They include (1) minimizing class bias by supporting programs that serve poor children; (2) eliminating racial discrimination by altering the programs and practices that sustain it; (3) minimizing discrimination against students from language minorities by supporting bilingualism and bilingual programs; (4) ending sex discrimination through appropriate programming; (5) improving special education for the moderately and severely challenged, while mainstreaming children with milder learning difficulties; (6) eliminating tracking, realizing that it works against able and vulnerable students alike; (7) eliminating excessive and inappropriate standardized testing; (8) broadening curriculum and teaching practices to suit diverse student populations; (9) moving vocational programs away from a narrow, acontextual focus on job skills; (10) assuring democratic governance of schools by giving parents and students decision-making authority and by recognizing the professionalism of teachers; (11) supporting high-quality early childhood education and child care programs as a means of preventing school failure later; (12) creating additional programs to respond to the personal and social problems of the increasing numbers of children who leave school because of inadequate support; (13) creating more equitable systems for financing schools, so that the opportunity for quality education doesn't depend on where a child lives; and (14) providing a comprehensive school-to-work transition program for all youth (108–23). Obviously, the reasoning supporting these recommendations can be rejected, just as expressivist arguments have been, because of the very self-interestedness that the critical inquiry has exposed. Obviously it *has* been largely rejected by the Reagan and Bush administrations of the eighties and early nineties. But its oppositional representation of the school world can also open eyes that expressivist ethical appeals tend to leave (guiltily or confusedly) closed, and the proposals that follow from it await only a sufficient number of newly activist, critically conscious students, parents, teachers, and other citizens for their implementation.

The practical problems of implementing such proposals, and also more specifically developing programs of critical literacy in schools, are of course plain. If social reality is always in process of forming, it's also always strongly resistant to specific, purposeful interventions. Those with the most to gain from things as they are will be least cooperative in changing them; those who have power can powerfully oppose those who seek to alter its distributions; inertia conspires with dedication to sustain the status quo. There are, accordingly, complex strategic and tactical considerations to be addressed only in specific social, historical, and institutional circumstances that can't be anticipated here. We want to turn instead to another set of problems, no less awkward, no less intractable, that precede questions of implementation. For the fact is, the conceptual sources of critical literacy pose serious difficulties of their own, born of the very reflectiveness, the resistance to metaphysical absolutes, and the commitment to fairness and equal access that have characterized their difference from other philosophical points of view. We're obliged to explore these problems because no advocate for a critical literacy can escape casting the same cold eye upon that project that is cast so ruthlessly on others except at cost of contradicting the assumptions and values that animate it. The sources of critical literacy and pedagogy are to be found in an assortment of Marxist, feminist, and postmodern intellectual positions (none of these is a unified theory), each of which contributes characteristic focuses of attention while pursuing certain common purposes, and each of which presents conceptual difficulties that make the theorizing of critical praxis every bit as daunting as its realization in concrete school as well as other settings.

Marxist arguments for critical praxis, including Freire's and Giroux's, although these two differ in their specific genealogies (Giroux,

Theory and Resistance), all begin from a "sociological" vantage point that puts them clearly into opposition with both the metaphysical tendencies of classical humanism and also the expressivist concentration on individual, autonomous consciousness. In Marxist thought, the concept of "society" and the concept of "individual" stand in dialectical relationship to each other. Society is, to be sure, a human construct, but the individual is also a social construct: one's sense of "self" is made possible through the essentially social identifications—family, home, country, culture, religion, gender, ethnicity—in terms of which selfhood defines itself. "Individual consciousness," writes V. N. Volosinov, a prominent member of the Bakhtin Circle, "is not the architect of the ideological superstructure, but only a tenant lodging in the social edifice of ideological signs" (13). In the same way, the concept of language—a social practice that serves importantly to objectify the world—stands in dialectical relationship with the concept of language user, each conditioning the other within the contexts of material social reality and historical change. As social practice, language is neither an abstracted system of unchanging rules nor a merely individual medium of expression. The life of language, including its normative appearance at a given moment, is a function of its users, yet the users are themselves constituted by the processes of language (Volosinov's "stream of speech") as well as by the other material, historical realities that language objectifies. People are born into languages that they don't themselves create, and they learn, even as they use those languages, the attendant values, world assumptions, images of self and other— all the social realities that particular languages convey. "Signs," according to Raymond Williams, the prominent British Marxist and literary critic, "can exist only when this active social relationship is posited. . . . The real communicative 'products' which are usable signs are . . . living evidence of a continuing social process, into which individuals are born and within which they are shaped, but to which they then also actively contribute, in a continuing process. This is at once their socialization and their individuation" (37). The world that language presents to its users as an objectified condition both appears to be and is profoundly actual, immediate, material, and enveloping. Yet it's also wholly historical and dynamic, a human product upon which human beings daily make their impact.

The phenomenal world, then, the "world of everyday life," is a material and historical reality—not less real because it's a product of human energies and therefore subject to continuous change, but also not less capable of alteration because it's an objective social fact. This is the starting point for Freirean and other arguments for critical reconstruction. Marxist or, more broadly, sociological rhetoric shares

with expressivism a liberationist concern for people facing the dominating conditions of social life. Domination is taken as a constant,
since any social formation entails power arrangements, not unhealthy in themselves—in fact necessary to organized living—but
continually tending to suspend the struggle for democracy. Change,
however, remains a constant as well, as groups of people ceaselessly
renegotiate the terms of their relationships with other groups (class
struggle, in traditional Marxism). Faced with domination, sociological rhetoric doesn't propose the romantic gesture of liberalism, the
individual engaged in heroic defiance of institutions as though only
arbitrarily or contingently related to social orders. It proposes, instead, a collective consciousness of being (variously) situated within
those orders and a collaborative critique of their tendency to "forget"
their origins in human activity, their historicity, thereby monumen-
talizing themselves at cost to the quality of human life. The motive
for liberation is always to be found in a perceived jeopardizing of that
quality, which depends upon the dialogic interaction of human beings working endlessly toward the realization of their freedom. Ideally, language acts are dedicated to that end; ideally the social
realities that derive from those acts work to serve that end. But in
practice, people forget the nature of their participation in life, seeking
to perpetuate themselves and prevail as the evolved conclusion of a
process that anticipated them from the beginning. Whence the emergence of ideology, an "explanation" of the rightness of things as they
are that conceals its interestedness within an assertion of necessary
superiority. Groups seek positions of domination from which to
coerce anyone whose difference from themselves threatens their
hegemony. Oppression, therefore, in the service of privilege is a
persistent social condition, which critical consciousness aims to
expose and relieve (Knoblauch, "Rhetorical Constructions," 134–36).

    While this argument offers a strong general rationale for a strug-
gle against dominating conditions and explains the inevitability of
class as well as other group conflict, along with the nature of critical
inquiry and the imperatives of activist intervention, it runs up against
its own assumptions when it seeks to justify specific intervention by
proclaiming the material fact of oppression at a given historical
moment. What the argument supposes to be true about dominant
ideology—that it's a concealment of interestedness within an assertion of superiority—it must also either concede about itself or else
suspend on its own behalf by appeal to a transcendent rationality. If
it implicates itself in the interestedness of all claims to knowledge
and insight, it stands to lose ethical clarity and the vigor of commitment. If it doesn't, then it becomes its own best example of how
ideology works to naturalize privilege. Consider the first possibility,

self-incrimination (as in Gramsci's view of the necessarily ideological character of all social interaction). The critical agent is no less constructed by language, by ideology, and by the ceaseless conflicts of social life than those whom the agent "recognizes" as rulers and oppressed. Indeed, the representation of social relations as patterns of oppression and liberation is itself an interested, ideological position. If the agent has no appeal to a *dis*interested location outside the realities to be critiqued—a transcendent vision born either of metaphysical certainty, as ontological rhetoric enjoys, or of empirical certainty, as objectivist rhetoric enjoys—then the claim to have revealed the conditions that require liberatory action is in principle a troubled one. Freire may well avoid the difficulty in practice when working with the grossly impoverished and disenfranchised peasants of northeast Brazil, but the critical teacher working in an American school, or even in a community workshop, may feel the difficulty more acutely. Why is that teacher privileged to name the oppressor, the oppressed, and the conditions of domination? How are the critic's own interests bound up in this naming? What are the critic's claims to trustworthiness, to believability, if the critic has already conceded the ideological character of any argument or commitment? How is the freedom fighter distinguished from the terrorist?

We've implicitly agreed here, for instance, with a view that dominant American ideology relates success in school to good jobs afterwards as cause to effect. We've also agreed that this argument is not only insufficient as explanation but also self-serving in its mystification of the ways in which schools protect the interests of privileged groups. Finally, we've agreed with a view that the situation "in actuality" is just the reverse: socioeconomic good fortune all but assures success in school. What does our sympathy with this oppositional construction really offer beyond a view of our politics? What makes it more believable than the majority view it seeks to challenge? Freire explains what's riding on the answer to this awkward question: "we need political clarity before we can understand the political action of eradicating illiteracy in the United States or any other place" (Freire and Macedo 132). The whole point of a critical pedagogy, for Freire, is to join with students in piercing the opacity of dominant ideology—to facilitate the peasants' recognition that their living conditions are not the result of God's testing their equanimity, to support the garment workers' appreciation of the global exploitation of labor. "The unveiling of reality," Freire says, "falls within the space for possible change in which progressive and politically clear educators must operate" (126). But what are the terms of "political clarity"? Why is our view of the relationship between school success and economic success "clearer" and truer than its opposite? We can point to supportive theories and arguments, of course, to empirical and other studies, to illustrative anecdotes; but so can the other view. We can hold our ground successfully against other positions but are we really entitled to speak of greater clarity? Marxist educational arguments, Freire's included, have tended in practice to hazard the second of two poor alternatives, claiming a transcendent power of insight in favor of self-incrimination in the webs of language and ideology, well aware of the potential damage to commitment, to maintaining resolve over years of struggle, implicit in any less aggressive intellectual posture. They take the historical necessity of conflict and change as axiomatic, sorting people into the heroes who sponsor reconstruction, the villains who oppose it, and the victims who suffer from things as they are. They opt to forget their own ideological situatedness in favor of essentialism. Freire, for instance, doesn't allow for many alternatives in one's selection of a stance with respect to the political conditions of educational life. An educator can be "critical," or "naive," or "astutely naive"; there are no other categories. The "naive" educator fails to understand "clearly" how dominant ideology masks reality in its own interest—by claiming the neutrality of education, or the need to "give" learning to those who lack it, or the need to be authoritarian. The naive educator is unaware of how domination invests his pedagogy. He isn't malicious in his innocence; he may even entertain a "lyrical and idealistic" concern for the poor or the disenfranchised. But he's unaware of the extent to which his own practices conspire in the maintenance of what he may very well seek to challenge. Freire would probably call the process writing teacher "naive." The tactically or "astutely" naive educator, meanwhile, consciously assumes the dominant ideology for her own: she is authoritarian, elitist, and "consciously reactionary," so that her "innocence is purely tactical": it's in her best interests not to see reality for what it is. Either of these educators can escape the condition of naivete: it's a matter of "assuming a new critical posture," a matter of "perceiving the ineffectiveness of [their] actions by learning directly from [their] own practice," a matter of reaching "new understanding" and then "renouncing naivete" (37–46). In short, one need only grant the truth of Freire's reading of the world to be afforded the desirable status of "critical." The problem is, while Freirean Marxism believes that dominant ideology entails a concealment, a manipulation, of "reality" that critique must endeavor to penetrate, it exempts itself from the same situatedness, despite the fact that its own reasoning about class struggle and ideological contestation implies no clear light of reason for its own position.

This positivist strain of Marxist ideology runs through concepts of "false consciousness" that are frequently invoked to explain the resistance of those regarded as oppressed to the liberating efforts of critical educators working on their behalf. Ira Shor makes use of the concept in *Critical Teaching and Everyday Life*, where he defines it as "an irrationalizing force" that "conditions people to police themselves by internalizing the ideas of the ruling elite." He points out that "the great power of dominated thought is that people deny the means of their own liberation while taking responsibility for acting in ways which reproduce their powerlessness" (55). Freire invokes the same concept in *Pedagogy of the Oppressed* when he observes that "the oppressed cannot perceive clearly the 'order' which serves the interests of the oppressors whose image they have internalized." The reason for this inability, he explains, is that the oppressed are "submerged" in the "reality" of their oppression and feel "an irresistible attraction towards the oppressor and his way of life" (48). We're sympathetic to Shor's and Freire's efforts to expose the forms of "thought control" that dominant groups have at hand for manipulating public belief (television, for instance) and also their subtle analysis of victim psychology, which seems unmistakably evident, for instance, in cases of beaten wives who nonetheless defend and remain with their abusive husbands. But finally the idea of false consciousness is a dangerous one for two reasons: first, it attributes a "simplicity" to the oppressed, an innocence about their condition, that may be unwarranted and that is certainly paternalistic; second, it makes too readily available a "correct" (ideological) explanation of why other people don't always respond to liberators' "generosity" in the ways they're supposed to: indeed it explains not only the righteousness of liberatory action but also the appropriateness of ignoring the resistance it occasions—the more people resist, the more confident one can be of their false consciousness. Critical educators must surely find ways to maintain their ethical bearings and commitments, but they must also live with more uncertainty about their certainties than a notion of false consciousness allows. Oppression from the left is not preferable to oppression from the right.

Various forms of postmodern argument (we don't propose to tease apart the strands) are also contributing to critical literacy and pedagogy, but with their own distinctive attendant conundrums. If the operative concept in Marxist rhetoric is "society," the material and historical interactions of social groups or classes, the operative concept in postmodern rhetoric is "discourse," the play of power arrangements, subject positions, modes of knowing, and forms of knowledge within alternative, endlessly shifting discursive configurations. Intersubjectivity is replaced by intertextuality: language becomes not merely one of various material practices of signification through which ideology is constituted and manifested, but the very protoplasm of sociocultural life. And a tricky, mysterious stuff it is: language in postmodern rhetoric is portrayed as inherently mischievous, an endless play of signifiers, proliferating meanings without ever delivering on the promise that they point to something beyond the tangles of language. To inquire, for instance, into the meaning of a word is to discover nothing more substantial than other words, each of which leads the inquirer toward more words, and more after that, down "the chain of signifiers." Meaning, then, is endlessly deferred—"absent" in Derrida's famous characterization. The genius of language is to offer "texts" that propose fictions of "presence" appearing stable enough at first glance but revealing, on critical inspection, a "glissage," a slipperiness of reference, that sabotages any putative coherence in favor of a multitude of conflicting possibilities.

Language, in short, is a joker, forever composing and subverting the world. It is, as Terry Eagleton explains, "a much less stable affair than the classical structuralists had considered." Instead of being "a well-defined, clearly demarcated structure containing symmetrical units of signifiers and signifieds," it's more like "a sprawling limitless web where there is a constant interchange and circulation of elements, where none of the elements is absolutely definable and where everything is caught up and traced through by everything else" (129). What's true of language, specifically its figurative nature, is true of the discourses that language produces. Discourse is a practice existing within, not beyond, history; it's a site, shaped by phenomenal, shifting conditions, not a model or a code; it makes meanings but the meanings are contingent rather than determinate, dispersed rather than unified, absent rather than present, and, in the end, uncontrollably prolific. As Eagleton has put it, there's something in discourse itself, not just some forms of discursive practice, "which finally evades all systems and logics . . . a continual flickering, spilling, and diffusing of meaning [which poses] a challenge to the very idea of structure: for a structure always presumes a centre, a fixed principle, a hierarchy of meanings, and a solid foundation" (134).

The implications for critical literacy and pedagogy are plain enough. The "deconstructive" practices that have emerged from postmodern theory allow for a critique of the texts of the school world, among others, together with the discourses that serve to constitute that world, including the distribution of "subject positions"— teacher, student, administrator, parent, and others—proposed for those who participate in it. The "prose of the school" (Knoblauch and Johnston) defines who speaks and who is silent, who governs and who is governed, who knows and who is ignorant, who wins and who loses: the deploying and engaging of these subject positions comprise the power arrangements of school reality. The discourse renders those arrangements authoritatively "present" through the mystifying and coercive skill of its narration. But critical reading recalls that they are also profoundly fictitious, fraught with internal instability and contradiction, open (at least theoretically) to creative "rewriting" in pursuit of ever freer, more "dialogical" compositions. The critical practice of deconstruction examines texts, exploring the conditions and tactics that enable them to constitute themselves, the claims by which they entitle themselves to speak, the discursive continuities and disruptions in terms of which they assert their identity. It reveals ideology: the strategies by which texts deny the contingencies of their production or the plurality of their readings, the unself-conscious delimitations and preservative rhetorics that enable "traditions," "histories," "movements," and "institutions" to forget their ephemeral, problematic articulation. It reopens signification by reading texts beyond the boundaries they imagine they have set for themselves in the pursuit of their own interests. It proceeds obliquely, at the margins of those texts, at points of beginning or closure, at places of disturbance or resistance where unreconciled or barely suppressed meanings strain the effect of coherence. It reveals the secret jests lurking within even the most earnest or reverent assertions, implicitly celebrating the exuberance of language, its irreducibly—and incorrigibly—figurative disposition. It makes the critical agent aware of the foundations of discursive practices, the manner of their emergence, the modes of their action, the possibilities and impossibilities of utterance that they define, the character and dispersion of their objects and relationships, the nature of the documents that they produce, but above all the play of language that both constitutes and deconstructs those documents and ultimately the practices themselves.

By appealing to the figurativeness of language, postmodern rhetoric offers a powerful depiction of the intrinsic instability of social (read: discursive) formations and a method, in deconstruction, for its effective critique. But at the same time, the relentless skepticism of postmodern theory raises serious questions about its capacity for moral vision and its usefulness for framing or even testing the imperatives that necessarily underlie—energize—reconstructive praxis. In effect, if Marxism takes its project too seriously, postmodernism can't recover from its own bawdy laughter. If Freire appears prone to sacrifice his awareness of the ambiguities of reading political life in order to safeguard a certain purity of revolutionary commitment, the postmodern critic risks jeopardizing any commitment at all while luxuriating in the unbounded ribaldry of a theory of language. There's a relentlessly "comic" stance in much postmodern theory: we recall, for instance, Foucault's reference at the start of *The Order of Things* to a passage in Borges about a "certain Chinese encyclopaedia," a passage that occasioned "the laughter that shattered . . . all the familiar landmarks of my thought" (xv). This habitual irreverence renders it better suited for dismantling than building, despite the fact that there's little point to dismantling in the absence of a utopian dream. In postmodern theory, there's no stopping the dismantling impulse, no way to exempt the dream from the same mischievous scrutiny. Up to a point, that's how things should be: the critical educator needs to remain as skeptical of her own designs as she is the designs of others. But self-critique can become self-doubt; skepticism can become cynicism. The ethical ambivalence, if it isn't paralysis, of postmodernism may well be what subverts Sharon Crowley's arguments about deconstructive pedagogy, which we reviewed in Chapter 6. Other efforts to propose a specifically postmodern pedagogy—for instance, *Writing and Reading Differently* (Atkins and Johnson)—have displayed the identical tendency to sidestep the politics of education in favor of a restricted theory of textual critique, where one might "play" with *King Lear* or with a textbook about writing without regard for the institutional "earnestness" surrounding, and effectively trivializing, the practice. Ethical uncertainty reveals itself as political apathy.

Feminism, the third contributor to critical literacy and pedagogy, is distinguished in educational theory chiefly for its persistent focus on issues of gender, including the problems of patriarchy as a cultural norm and the persistently imperiled rights of women. It has applied arguments from both Marxism (Shulamith Firestone) and postmodernism (Toril Moi), but "realist" and "romantic" arguments as well (within essentialist movements of "radical feminism," for instance), in its pursuit of these themes, much as African American and Hispanic studies have done in examining their own, related interests. To that extent, feminism shares the difficulties attendant on the rhetorical perspectives we've already discussed, but with respect to a specific group of historically disenfranchised people and with respect to a specific marker, namely gender, of historical oppression in the West. Feminism also offers its own characteristic rhetorical turns as a result of its focus. Patrick Brantlinger has pointed out that it modifies the rationalist (not to say masculinist) preoccupation of traditional Marxism with confronting the institutions of social control, including the school, seeking instead, or as well, to alter consciousness of the cultural assumptions and attitudes imbedded in the discourses of patriarchy, an alteration that may then lead to political change. In short, subtle, persistent reeducation—"consciousness-raising"—is at least as valued a project as institutional combat. Feminist theory also maintains a practical commitment to women's rights, where it has been far more diligent in merging the intellectual and the public spheres than some brands of academic Marxism have been. Brantlinger notes that there is very little interaction in the United States between university Marxists and the working classes. Yet academic feminism has never altogether lost touch with a constituency outside the academy, even if it has too often equated "women's" rights with those of the mostly white, upper-middle-class, Eurocentric women who inhabit academe (129). A dramatic consequence of feminism's unwavering commitment to an explicit emancipatory struggle has been its extraordinary inventiveness in bringing together intellectual positions, in particular Marxism and postmodernism, that have too often remained isolated, polarized, and merely scholarly pursuits when not invoked in the service of a common, imperiled social good.

We would point, in particular, to ongoing efforts to incorporate Marxist and postmodern thinking into what is being called "materialist postmodern feminism," a project that our Albany colleague Teresa Ebert has recently discussed in a *College English* article. Ebert distinguishes between what she calls "ludic" postmodernism, with its emphasis on the "play" of language associated with Derrida, Foucault, and Lyotard, and what she calls "resistance" postmodernism, which "views the relation between word and world, language and social reality . . . not as the result of textuality but as the effect of social struggles." It's ludic postmodernism, which "addresses reality as a theatre for the free-floating play . . . of images, disembodied signifiers and difference," that encourages the damaging skepticism, the lack of political commitment that we addressed earlier. Resistance postmodernism, Ebert contends, takes its lead not from Saussure and the giddy collapse of structuralism but rather from Bakhtin and Volosinov, who view the sign as "an arena of the class struggle." Where "ludic politics," in her view, is a "textual practice" that seeks "open access to the free play of signification in order to disassemble the dominant cultural policy . . . which tries to restrict and stabilize meaning," resistance postmodernism insists on "a materialist political practice that works for equal access . . . to social resources and for an end to the exploitative exercise of power" (886–89). The reinscription of the political in postmodernity, by accounting for the instability of the sign in terms of conflicting social relations—the struggle over representations—is a bold move that entitles feminist rhetoric to claim a distinctive rewriting of Marxist and postmodern theory alike.

There are significant implications for critical pedagogy within feminist thought, not least because of the large numbers of women who toil in the nation's schools by contrast to the large numbers of male administrators and male university faculty who get to tell that predominantly female work force how to do its job. There's a broad public belief that teaching is "women's work," hence deserving of no more than women's responsibility, women's pay, and women's esteem. The power arrangements of schools along the axis of gender are plain to see, and they suggest the importance of a liberatory project not only among marginalized groups of students but also among the women teachers who primarily serve them. More of that in Chapter 8. Regrettably, however, there has been insufficient sustained attention to pedagogical issues in feminist theory, although some work has been devoted to the positioning of women within the academic world (see, for instance, Aisenberg and Harrington, *Women of Academe*). Culley and Portuges's *Gendered Subjects: The Dynamics of Feminist Teaching* and Madeleine Grumet's *Bitter Milk* remain more exceptions than the rule in the literature of critical pedagogy, where Marxist arguments have been more prolific and influential. Culley and Portuges's bibliography lists an important, but modest, smattering of articles, and only a few books. Grumet's bibliography is more extensive because of a more comprehensive theoretical listing—Barthes, Dewey, Foucault, Freire, Habermas, Lacan—but not because it has tapped a richer vein of feminist pedagogical theory. Sorry to say, if teaching is women's work, "theory" is "men's work," the currency of universities, and men's work, even for feminists in the patriarchally organized academy, doesn't generally include pedagogy as a central concern. A scholar, even a woman, writing on feminist postmodernism can win tenure, notwithstanding the bent noses of some colleagues, but a scholar, especially a woman, writing on feminist teaching practices—a "soft" issue—puts her career seriously on the line. Hence, radically feminized theories of the classroom that ought to be leading and informing pedagogical scholarship are in fact more often than not dependent on Marxist and postmodern arguments (both of which have frequently excluded issues of gender) composed mainly by men.

Not surprisingly, therefore, current feminist arguments are enmeshed in the conceptual difficulties that plague postmodern and Marxist positions in general, specifically the theoretical problem of "representation," a useful notion that we introduced cozily in Chapter 1 but that requires sterner scrutiny here. A fully self-critical feminism appropriating Marxist and/or postmodern themes inevitably confronts, for instance, the problematic nature of its own "representations" of gender and patriarchy, an issue that Mary Poovey has explored with notable subtlety. "To accept the antihumanist premises of deconstruction," she writes, "is already to question the possibility that women, as opposed to 'woman,' exist." Since postmodern argument lays open the essentialist mystification of "presence," it also denies that "either sexuality or social identity is given exclusively in or through the body, however it is sexed." A postmodern rendering posits "woman" as merely "a social construct that has no basis in nature," which then renders "the experience women have of themselves and the meaning of their social relations problematic, to say the least." Yet to concede so much is to place at risk a political project that has depended on its authority to denote and then take action against the oppression of materially and historically specific women, often particular groups of women marked by class or color. If a project based on the representation of "women's experience" is "simply another deluded humanism, complicit with the patriarchal institutions it claims to oppose," what alternative ground can there be for action against social structures that subjugate women *as* women, silence their "voices," and deny even the reality let alone the value of their differentiated "experience" (51–53)? Poovey has her notions of answers to these questions, but she concedes at the end that "if deconstruction took feminism seriously, it wouldn't look like deconstruction any more" (63).

Awkward questions arise, too, about the difference between representation and *mis*representation, and the relationship between representation and truthfulness or obfuscation, particularly within feminist appropriations of the "ludic" postmodernity that Ebert critiques. As Brantlinger suggests, if one starts from Derrida's position, where representation is taken as "the sole form of consciousness" because "absolute 'presence' is impossible," then "there seems to be no way to distinguish more or less accurate representations from misrepresentations, truth from falsehood, reality from fiction" (104–5). In a sense, for Derrida, representation is always false—a fiction of presence aiming to conceal its fictiveness. It would make little sense, therefore, to speak of "mis"representation as though it were a political manipulation, an ideological cover for the truth. There is nothing to get "behind," and therefore no incentive for critical scrutiny, let alone moral indignation. The feminist educational critic might well contest a patriarchal representation of women as, let's say, inferior to men in the field of mathematics because of a "naturally" affective rather than cognitive disposition. But her disagreement can include no ethical critique, no educative ambition: there's no grand exclusionary plot to reveal, no systematic violence to bring to public attention. What would be at stake, given Derrida's position, is little more than the power of patriarchal discourse to make its story stick at a given historical moment versus the power of the feminist opposition to claim a contrary authority. Truth belongs to whomever controls television and the academic research industry. Justice means, at best, an equal opportunity to tell lies on one's own behalf. Political struggle takes place, then, if at all, within a moral vacuum, where—as Brantlinger observes of Foucault—"there is no reason . . . to side with prisoners instead of wardens, with the insane instead of psychiatrists, or with witches instead of those who burn them" (102) beyond a "personal" preference for the underdog. To concede so much is to vitiate the moral integrity of the emancipatory project that has defined feminism from the start.

Faced with so dismal a prospect, it's tempting on the whole to prefer a Marxist reading of representation: where accusing women of genetic cognitive inferiority, for instance, would be construed as one argument within a larger network of purposeful rationales intended to naturalize patriarchal culture. The ideology of patriarchy, which seeks to conceal the interestedness of an assertion about the superiority of masculinist culture, manifests itself in representations, such as women's cognitive inferiority, that need to be critically inspected, challenged, and rewritten. We'd much prefer to imagine that we're uncovering plots than that we're playing out trivial roles within a ceaseless ebb and flow of impassive discursive arrangements. But such a view drifts back toward positivism, the assumption that "underneath" the intentional distortions of dominant culture there lies a truthfulness to which the enlightened, through disciplined critical effort, persistently aspire. Brantlinger seeks a way out of the impasse, suggesting that ideology not be construed as "a set of illusions which the rulers of a society convince the ruled to believe," but rather as "the ensemble of discursive practices—that is, of representational practices—which both structure society and are structured by it" (110). He argues for a view of ideology in which there is a "dialogical" relationship among ideas of "negotiation, consensus-formation, and degrees of truth and untruth," modeled on Gramsci's "attribution of *partial* reasonableness to 'common sense.' " Gramsci's view is that culture "is a field of struggle in which the stakes are accurate, just, and direct representation by groups and individuals instead of misrepresentations by others" (104). It's possible from this vantage point, according to Brantlinger, "to think of representation as forming a range of specific practices and instances which can be more *or less* true or false, instead of *either* true *or* false" (106, italics in original).

This appears to be a pleasing Aristotelian sort of compromise between two extremes, but it has problems of its own. For one thing, it conflates issues of truthfulness and issues of justice, arguing that the "truth" of representation is finally a matter of who does the representing: a group telling stories about itself speaks "more or less truthfully" in its own terms, while one telling stories about another group in the furtherance of a different set of interests is misrepresenting that group. By this argument, there are, to be sure, endlessly conflicting stories, but justice is fully done once each has space to assert itself without seeking to appropriate or erase some other. Given the utopian conditions of an already achieved just society, the theoretical equation of fairness and truthfulness might be plausible: points of view can differ harmlessly as every group accepts the same imperative to keep its affirming fantasies to itself. But amidst the disequilibrium of real life, the problem is to determine the "truthfulness" of claims that some groups are in fact imposing their stories on others, and that is itself a representational issue. A story is told about women's cognitive inferiority; an opposing story names patriarchy as a villainous cultural formation responsible for misrepresenting and oppressing women by means of a lie about their intelligence. Both stories "impose" on some other, the first by (mis?)representing women, the second by (mis?)representing "male" culture. Is the imposition intrinsically unjust on both sides? Perhaps not, if there's more truth to one story than the other. But both could be false, the first by confusing nature and nurture or by assigning "superiority" to what is merely "difference," the second by imputing the most sinister and broadly sustained possible motive to that "confusion." Brantlinger wants to assert degrees of truth and falsity: one story is "a little" truer than the other. But what are the terms for deciding the question? What are the rules of evidence? If feminism is entitled to debunk the cognition argument, is it also entitled to debunk it by appeal to a concept of patriarchy—a structured, self-interested plan to oppress women?

Consider the contest between the dominant educational position: "success in school leads to success in life" and the critical position: "socioeconomic standing enhances the odds of success in school." Brantlinger's argument apparently leaves the two assertions to struggle for position as best they can by appealing to whatever bodies of evidence they can assemble. In principle his position is finally empiricist, a matter of determinable degrees of truth and falsity: "particular forms of *mis*representation or ideology" can be "distinguished by comparison with alternative forms of more accurate or more truthful representation." And it's "the role of the cultural critic to make such distinctions" (104). In effect, he stands by an objectivist theory of reading: the meaning of the cultural text is "there" and the well-trained, thoughtful reader can discover it. We doubt, however, that an empirical test could resolve the dispute between the two equations regarding success in school and success in life. More important, we suspect that the issue of "truthfulness" in representation may even be something of a red herring. We could perhaps live with the conclusion that *both* equations are inadequate representations of the complexity of educational reality. But we would nonetheless argue for, and act upon, the "critical" representation because there is more social harm available from action that assumes the other, popular position to be no less truthful. We'll concede that success in school can help some people to socioeconomic improvement: there's evidence to say so. But this equation, broadly applied, also makes it easy to rationalize failure by blaming the victim, appealing to ignorance or laziness on the part of those who fail to take advantage of what school makes possible. Meanwhile, there's also evidence that prior socioeconomic standing helps ensure school success: children who are better fed, for instance, tend to do better in school—they're thinking about something other than how hungry they are. To the extent that this equation is "true," certain things follow. One is that the rich stay rich. A second is that looking to school for the reason is mystification. A third is that some students are playing to a stacked deck, disenfranchised from the start, not because of laziness or ignorance in school, but because they come from the wrong part of town or have the wrong color skin. If we find even a smallish sample of students (in "fact" the numbers are large) who are disenfranchised for this reason, there is sufficient cause for redress of grievance. And even if opponents point to "lazy" students who receive "extra privilege," we would argue that the justice done on behalf of the deserving ones more than compensates.

This position is troubled and insufficient, as it must always be. We're offering here a book full of stories and readings of stories that favor positions we've taken from the beginning. The stories are argumentative, not true or false. Are we representing functional literacy or misrepresenting it? Who gets to say? Is there more justice in the representations of its proponents than in ours? Is one story less self-serving than the other? We contest reality and our contestations are themselves contested. The alternative (which may only be conceivable rather than possible) is cultural stagnation. Readers can read our stories and agree or disagree, assisting by their subsequent judgments and actions in the renegotiation of educational life. The concern for social justice, meanwhile, which to be sure can be both well and badly pursued, is an ethical imperative beyond the dispute over representation. The goal of critical self-examination isn't to reconsider the imperative, nor is it to come up with definitive solutions to intellectual conundrums (itself a gesture mired in ideology). The goal is to pose important, even hazardous, theoretical questions, not in order to blunt the energies of reconstruction but in order to set those energies within a context of dialogue, negotiation, and intellectual humility that will continuously refine a praxis dedicated to social justice.

Chapter Eight

Teacher Inquiry
Knowing for Ourselves

Nobody would expect all teachers to be truly educated persons—persons who possessed the requisite knowledge and understanding and were also skilled to a high degree in the art of teaching. . . . That being so, what is the goal to be aimed at? It is that teachers should be on the way to becoming educated persons. . . . They should themselves be at least as well-schooled [sic] as the graduates of the schools in which they are expecting to teach. They should have completed the required course of study we have recommended. Many teachers now employed in our public schools have not themselves had basic schooling of this quality, or even of the quality now provided in our better schools.

Mortimer Adler,
The Paideia Proposal

We had thought it might prove difficult to find a published statement about teachers by some distinguished university professor that would manage to be superior, condescending, and dictatorial all at once just to help us make a point about the oppressive conditions that nonuniversity faculty confront within the hierarchical educational establishment. But it wasn't hard at all. Adler's views are quite normal among university faculty, who typically blame the schools for inade-

quate preparation of college students, who mistrust the competence
as well as dedication of practitioners (as opposed to scholars), who
believe unself-consciously in "trickle-down" theories of educational
change, and who would be shocked at any suggestion that elementary
school teachers might have the same authority to address them that
they have to speak in the schools. Adler, it's important to point out,
aims to support teachers in this passage from *The Paideia Proposal*,
wishes to encourage their continued learning after certification, sym-
pathizes with the difficult circumstances of their work, hopes to
engage them in a "common" intellectual project. But does anyone
imagine that Adler could, with the same aplomb, direct these statements toward university faculty? (Substitute the word "professor"
wherever "teacher" appears in this statement and see how it sounds.)
Would he be quite as comfortable telling his colleagues at the University of Chicago to complete "the required course of study we have
recommended"? What would their reaction be? Teachers are so invariably objects of other people's attention—politicians, parents,
school administrators, researchers—that even the most positive
statements about them within public discourse generally pertain to
their "care and feeding." Nearly everyone grants the importance of
better salaries and working conditions, for instance, but the need is
characteristically represented as something that managers "ought to
do," the noblesse oblige of plantation owners expected to "look after
our own." Of course, the understanding always is that teachers will
improve themselves, perform as they're told, put out a higher quality
(student) product, in order to merit their bosses' expanded largesse.

We're sensitive to our own complicity, as university educators,
in this state of affairs. Our graduate classes and workshops are filled
with teachers. We have ready access to publication and enough
authority in the educational world to ensure that we'll be taken
seriously, even if only in disagreement. We claim here to be addressing, among others, nonuniversity colleagues (who will not, for the
most part, have equivalent public authority to respond), and we are
plainly recommending instructional practices (critical teaching) as
well as certain attitudes toward literacy that we favor. In principle,
at least, teachers are likely to feel the same pressure from us that they
would feel from anyone else with equivalent power to speak (even if
our positions are sufficiently marginal themselves so that people
would find protection, if needed, in the strength of opposing views).
The ethical paradox here, the imbalance of power that enables us to
publish a book criticizing that imbalance yet also effectively sustaining it, cannot be explained away. We don't propose to beat our
breasts, of course, since the arguments we offer deserve no less
consideration than do others from teaching professionals who under-

stand the value, as well as the limits, of theoretical reflectiveness for informed practice. But we *are* imposing upon teachers' attention, as others are, even if the substance of our arguments constitutes a scrutiny of that imposition, an exploration of the agendas underlying alternative constructions of the school world, including our own. We trust that the teacher who feels free to reject the representations of Adler or D'Souza, Boyer or Goodman, Freire or the Department of Education because of our critique, is also the teacher who will freely reject ours as well in the process of reclaiming classroom authority. But the fact remains that we are privileged to tell our stories, while the same is not as true for every teacher who reads us.

Unfortunately, the problem doesn't lie just in the kinds of arguments that are made about the school world—some seeking a reclamation of the authority of teachers, others the maintenance of subordination. The problem lies in the nature of educational discourse, where some people get to talk and others mainly listen, where the terms of talk, the assumptions about what makes for credible statement, and the public disposition to accept some representations over others lie fundamentally outside the control of "ordinary" teachers. Motives may differ, proposals differ, degrees of identification with "the workers" differ, but ultimately everyone wants to do something "for" teachers rather than relinquish the control that denies teachers power to construct their own professional lives. As long as this circumstance remains unchanged, the conditions of teachers offer grounds for a liberatory project no less than the conditions of students, while placing similar responsibilities on those who would join their struggle. Freire observes that "no pedagogy which is truly liberating can remain distant from the oppressed by treating them as unfortunates and by presenting for their emulation models from among the oppressors. The oppressed must be their own example in the struggle for their redemption" (30). Whence the final argument we want to make here: in support of an altered educational discourse in which teachers claim power to constitute themselves as "speaking subjects" within forms of dialogue that are responsive to their distinctive experience of the school world and their distinctive ways of conceiving it. We have in mind specifically the current liberatory movement of "teacher research" or, as we prefer it, "teacher inquiry," a project of critical literacy for educators.

We would expect the majority of American citizens, including most teachers, to flinch at our seemingly melodramatic representation of teachers as an "oppressed" group. They're well educated after all; they make an adequate living by the standards of many Americans; they enjoy the advantages of The Good Life. Plainly, their oppression isn't that of the illiterate Brazilian peasants of Freire's experience. But it is, we suggest, oppression nonetheless, a subtler form of subjugation along lines of gender and class. It's the kind of oppression experienced by women in all conditions of employment: the majority of elementary and secondary teachers are women while the majority of administrators are men; women/teachers remain politically invisible in schools despite their numbers. It's the kind experienced by the American working class as a whole, alienated from its own labor by structures of socioeconomic exploitation and disenfranchisement. Boyer's politically mainstream *A Report on Secondary Education in America* concedes as much. He cites a high school teacher who comments eloquently on the structural relations between "management" and "staff" in a typical American school: "There is no teacher input into the curriculum, the scheduling, the goals, or the rules at this school. I'm allowed to make suggestions, but I don't think that anyone ever pays any attention. Even if they are implemented, I don't think it's because I suggested something" (142). Boyer cites numerous teachers who are equally eloquent on other dimensions of their present situation: "You rarely get any thank you . . . from the community, superintendent, school board, or administrators. There is no positive reinforcement for anything you do. There are no pats on the back. There's no reward system, no bonuses" (161). And again: "If a lot of us are disenchanted with the teaching profession, it's because we can't live on what we take home. I mean, how can you like what you are doing when it's not taking care of you?" (165). And again: "I'm not receiving . . . positive response from my students. . . . It's almost as if they say, 'I defy you to teach me.' I had one class of students last year with a dozen chronic behavior problems. I dreaded dealing with that class every day. It affected my whole life" (162). And again: "I go places around town collecting items for my various courses and I'm almost embarrassed to say that I'm a teacher. It's people's view of teachers as goof-offs—that they get the summer off—that really hurts" (163).

These comments and many others throughout the Boyer report paint a clear picture of the dominating conditions that teachers face: unsympathetic public attitudes; disenfranchising school policies; economic reminders of low prestige; dispirited, apathetic colleagues; unengaged and hostile students. The report was written a decade ago, of course, and there have been some modest changes since. Salaries are higher (as they are for other workers) but they differ dramatically from state to state and they aren't so high anywhere that teachers would be considered a "professional" class. (Statistics from the State Education Department of New York show for instance that in a 1991 sample of eleven suburban school districts in the capital region, seven featured a median teacher salary below the average local household income, in one case a difference of nearly fourteen thousand dollars.) School administrators insist that teachers have "been given" more authority than they used to have in matters of governance, curriculum, and textbooks. But this "generosity" is by no means universal and, in any case, is only a calculated reaction to discontent, not the sign of authentically redistributed power. There are more women school superintendents today than there were ten years ago (a promising sign), but the "improvement" must be understood in a context of the continuing dominance of male supervisors: in 1969 less than 2 percent of the superintendents in New York state were women (14 out of 763); in 1980 the figure had risen to a little over 2 percent; by 1990 the figure was 6 percent—48 out of 797; and today the number is slightly over 7 percent (Spofford, Albany *Times-Union*, October 16, 1990). Yes, things have changed since the Boyer report, but the changes have been slow in coming and grudgingly conceded. No contemporary observer of American schools will fail to hear the same complaints or notice the same conditions today that Boyer chronicled in 1983, provided a little time is taken to look underneath the pious new claims about teachers' altered professional standing.

A recent newspaper article (which we do not cite, in order to preserve the school district's anonymity) concerning shared management in one of our local school districts shows how little has really changed underneath essentially superficial concessions. Its revealing headline states that this district hopes to "expand decision making if federal grant comes through." The article explains that the district wants to involve "more" teachers in management both at "building and district levels," noting that some shared governance "structures" are already in place in two of the district's seven schools. But what, we ask ourselves, does a federal grant have to do with a district decision about who governs the schools? The answer, as anyone could guess, is the expense of training: the district can't have shared decision making without "shared decision making training." The assistant superintendent in charge of instruction and curriculum is quoted as saying that "training is the key." The two schools that have made "some stabs" at joint management have done all right, another official implies, but "we need training to make it a truly effective method." No special subtlety is required to see what's happening here: crudely put, managers are proposing to give something with one hand and take it back with the other. The grant money, which will be distributed by one set of managers at the federal level to another set in this school district, together with the top-down instruction it pays for, will effectively ensure that the assumptions, goals, values, attitudes, points of view of management are carefully introduced to "underlings" before they take part in "shared" decisions. There will be no fundamental shift of control here, only a superficial, carefully hedged "permission" to play at administration.

Teachers know their status in American life from palpable experience: the assembly-line routines of the school day, the continuous impositions of bureaucratic authority on every aspect of their work, the lack not just of curricular power but even of control over their own classrooms, the absence of time or space for professional dialogue, the modest pay (by comparison to university colleagues, let alone lawyers or doctors), the denial of community esteem, the subjection to relentless scrutiny by a growing number of citizens, "experts," and special-interest groups whose legitimate concern for the quality of education is not always quite free of overconfidence in the compelling priority of their own agendas. Teachers are members of the working class, subordinated within a social structure that mandates and maintains their limited access to power. As workers, they are assumed to require external guidance ("training") from the more enlightened managerial classes. Accordingly, their job responsibilities are carefully spelled out for them, what to teach, when to teach it, the ways to go about it, the materials to use, the preparation required, the criteria for success or failure. Curricula, textbooks, teaching practices, even daily lesson plans, are regularly devised by others—the power elite, the approved educational specialists in our society. These specialists include university scholars and researchers (the assessment establishment among them), whose entitlement to theorize, and impose theory on others, need not presume any pertinent experience at a given grade level or even teaching talent (indeed, university faculty, fully aware of the sources of their prestige, seldom refer to themselves as "teachers"). They also include textbook publishers, whose educational commitments need not always supersede their concern for the profit guaranteed by uncritical, mass-market appeal. They include politicians from federal to local level, whose educational judgment need not always transcend their most insistent constituents' convictions about beating the Japanese in technology or making English-language competence the litmus test of citizenship. And they include school administrators, who may not invariably situate the priorities of teaching and learning ahead of the priorities of bureaucratic efficiency and accountability. Of course, some scholars, publishers, politicians, and administrators do struggle along with teachers for humane, democratic educational institutions. But the point is, their positions of leadership imply no obligation to do so. In fact, their privileges, ratified by myths of credentialism and class superiority, are best defended by resisting challenges to their hegemony.

Teachers are "trained," supervised, and monitored by this array of experts, much as office or factory workers are, to ensure punctuality, obedience, efficiency, and high output—values of job performance that would presumably deteriorate to the extent that managers lacked vigilance. If the proponents of stricter oversight have their way, teachers will eventually be tested for minimal competence, a form of institutional humiliation designed to underscore the difference between managers, who are dedicated "professionals," and workers, whose abilities, not to mention motivations, are suspect because they are "just out to earn a living." While no one would deny the importance of accountability on the job, the forms of accountability are interestingly different at different levels of employment. "Professionals" are reviewed by their ostensible peers, and the rhetoric of evaluation emphasizes quality of contribution, standing in a field, and promise of future excellence. Laborers, by contrast, are evaluated by their "superiors," and not so much to judge degrees of excellence as to weed out incompetents, malingerers, and malcontents. In the professions, public concern is to hang on to the best; but in the case of workers, who are essentially interchangeable as long as they follow directions, it's to get rid of the worst.

There are additional ways of ensuring that teachers understand and accept their lower-class status. Everyone knows about them, to be sure, but seldom does anyone pause to consider their representational functions. For instance, teachers are given menial chores—hall duty, lunch-money collection, paper shuffling—which signify their position in the hierarchy as surely as the coffee-making duty of the aspiring woman executive signifies hers. Periodically, disembodied managerial voices blare from loudspeakers in the midst of class with commands, reminders, and announcements: superiors can freely interject themselves in the work of subordinates, though the reverse is not true. Teachers are "observed" repeatedly in the classroom in order to maintain "quality control": workers are not to be trusted. "Stars" from the university come in for short-term "inservice" presentations of the latest theory, reminding teachers of their permanent apprentice status as knowers and practitioners. How often are university faculty subjected to mandatory in-service presentations? How many of them would tolerate it? What chance is there that high school teachers might provide in-service at colleges?

Above all, teachers are generally denied significant managerial responsibility. The rhetoric justifying that denial turns on arguments about credentials and training—meritocratic and covertly patriarchal fictions of governance that conveniently ratify the centralization of power, thereby ensuring the retaining of the perquisites of power. Hence, the Boyer report, in one of its less benevolent observations, insists that school principals must inevitably play "the pivotal role" in effective schools, never clearly revealing why that must be so—

aside from the supposedly intrinsic value of centralization—and never fully appreciating the irony of its own statistics on principals: 93 percent male, 95 percent white, 75 percent middle-aged, and nearly all mysteriously appointed (even principals themselves often don't know what criteria have been applied) from the ranks of assistant principals and athletic directors (220). Is it simply "natural" that this group should so consistently demonstrate superior ability? Is it an accident that the credentializing process has led to so sharp a portrait of the ruling class? The closest that recent educational reports have come to a concept of "teacher authority" is the sinister, not to say cynical, suggestion that some teachers, designated as "masters," be encouraged to believe they should oversee others, replicating the foreman/laborer split among factory workers, a means of conquering by dividing. The comparatively dovish Boyer report recommends no less energetically than the hawkish *A Nation at Risk* that school authorities establish "career ladders" among teachers, a reproduction within the dominated class of the same hierarchic social order responsible for the domination. Keep them busy climbing over each other and they won't pause to question why they aren't climbing over their managers.

No wonder, in light of this systemic professional disenfranchisement, that many teachers become clock-punchers, listlessly exchanging a day's work for a day's pay because there is no incentive to do anything more or to think in other terms. Such behavior reintroduces the plausibility of Freire's "false consciousness," the submergence in and irrational acceptance of an oppressor's reality, which leads to a measuring of one's own value by the oppressor's yardstick (48–49). But fortunately, this isn't the whole story. If some teachers have been defeated in the ways that Freire suggests, and Shor as well in his own representations of "false consciousness," others have not been. Moreover, the subjugative practices that work to maintain a lower-class status for teachers are neither universally applied nor universally effective. A crucial fact pointing the way to institutional change is that structures of domination are never as monolithic, efficient, or impervious as they appear to be. Resistance to them from within, the challenging of their necessity, the posing of alternatives, and a subsequent reconstituting of educational reality are not impractical dreams but concrete, ongoing social processes. Many teachers creatively resist their professional displacement by teaching, however surreptitiously, by the dictates of their own knowledge and experience, despite the collective effort of curriculum monitors, classroom observers, and state testing apparatuses to enforce their own priorities. Politically conscious, "critical" teachers are present on local school boards, present at educational union activities, present as active voices (not just passive listeners) at scholarly conventions. Those voices gain additional power through such publishing houses as Heinemann, Boynton/Cook, and Bergin & Garvey, which have demonstrated a commitment to educational change in the face of economic disincentives that are well understood and prudently side-stepped by mainstream publishers. Teachers are finding sympathetic principals, superintendents, and other administrators—because they are always there to be found—with the political standing and will to support a struggle to change the conditions of schools. They're finding parents and even an occasional politician responsive to their concerns and no less dedicated to change. Teachers are also forming their own collective will—in literacy education, for instance, within such reform-minded programs as the National Writing Project, the Bread Loaf School of English, and the Center for Educational Improvement Through Collaboration in Michigan, all featuring cooperative efforts among elementary, secondary, and college teachers to improve the quality of educational practice. However large and long the struggle to claim their due measure of authority in schools, the sustaining awareness that teachers can bring to it is a knowledge of the progress they've already made.

It's in the contemporary context of these promising possibilities and signs of change that we wish to situate the practices of teacher "research" or "inquiry." In the simplest, indeed self-evident terms, teacher research is educational investigation that is carried out by teachers themselves rather than by educational researchers (typically from universities) for whom that work, in a certain form, is a central professional activity. The concept of teachers becoming inquirers in their own classrooms has been gaining stature for more than a decade through the efforts of Vito Perrone, formerly of the University of North Dakota; Dixie Goswami and the teachers at Bread Loaf; Jay Robinson and the teachers of Ann Arbor, Detroit, and Central Michigan; Capital District teachers in New York working at the Center for the Learning and Teaching of Literature; and Ann Berthoff, Nancie Atwell, Glenda Bissex, and numerous others with a commitment to educational change. There are various rationales advanced for teacher inquiry and more than one argument for the appropriate means of conducting it. The perspective we prefer is one most commonly associated with Goswami's work (see Goswami and Stillman, *Reclaiming the Classroom*) and that of Glenda Bissex (see Bissex and Bullock, *Seeing for Ourselves*). Philosophical explanations of teacher inquiry are found in Parts 1 and 2 of *Reclaiming the Classroom* and in Part 1 of *Seeing for Ourselves* as well as in a variety of recent scholarly articles (Hoagland; Knoblauch and Brannon, "Knowing Our Knowledge"; and others). Useful reviews of practical questions of method in teacher research include Part 3 of *Reclaiming the Classroom* and Marian M. Mohr and Marion S. MacLean's *Working Together*.

Teacher research looks in several directions for its goals and justifications. It's concerned, as is all educational inquiry, with the constructing of knowledge about the practices of teaching and learning—in this case a knowledge distinctively enhanced by the insiders' understanding of the classroom that teachers can provide. But it's also concerned with the special advantages that accrue to teachers who engage in that inquiry themselves instead of remaining content with traditional arrangements in which university scholars do research and pass its conclusions along to teachers, with or without recommendations about practice. Goswami and Stillman summarize the advantages for teachers in their Preface:

1. Their teaching is transformed in important ways: they become theorists, articulating their intentions, testing their assumptions, and finding connections with practice.

2. Their perceptions of themselves as writers and teachers are transformed. They step up their use of resources; they form networks; and they become more active professionally.

3. They become rich resources who can provide the profession with information it simply doesn't have. They can observe closely, over long periods of time, with special insights and knowledge. Teachers know their classrooms and students in ways that outsiders can't.

4. They become critical, responsive readers and users of current research . . . and more authoritative in their assessment of curricula, methods, and materials.

. . .

6. They collaborate with their students to answer questions important to both, drawing on community resources in new and unexpected ways. . . . Working with teachers to answer real questions provides students with intrinsic motivation for talking, reading, and writing and has the potential for helping them achieve mature language skills. (vi)

Teacher research, then, is a program of critical literacy, aiming to construct new knowledge of educational life from the vantage points of its primary participants—teachers and students. It also aims to enfranchise teachers as authentic makers of that knowledge in order to enhance the quality of their participation in curricular planning, resource development, instructional change, and other areas of educational administration to which they have legitimate and beneficial contributions to make. Not least, it intends to improve the quality of teaching and learning by engaging teachers as well as students more intensively, more self-consciously, in the processes of inquiry and reflection that enable effective teaching and learning in the first place. The project is, in short, overtly political—intended, as Goswami says, to "reclaim the classroom." But it's more than merely self-serving. Connections between teacherly knowledge and the development of teaching ability are no less important than connections between the authority to make knowledge and the acquisition of political power. Indeed, the two sets of relations are complexly interwoven. The proximate goal of teacher inquiry is for teachers themselves to improve the quality of their work by improving the qualities of attention and reflection they bring to their classroom experience. Representing and sharing classroom insight through the formal vehicle of "research," typically rendered in narrative form, establishes a basis for self-scrutiny and conversation that can lead to more informed, more flexible, more critical instructional choices. At the same time, the progress of that organized conversation (through computer networking, for instance, or publication) can promote the solidarity among teachers that will be essential if they are to gain genuine access to the political power necessary for curricular authority. Demonstrating the legitimacy of classroom knowledge, both by appeal to the special vantage point that teachers enjoy in the school world and by appeal to the heuristic power of the narratives they construct to represent it, can help create the conditions of access to power—specifically, public confidence in the value of teacherly insight and enough support within the communities of university researchers and school administrators to enable the applying of that insight in curricular decisions. Bringing formal teacherly knowledge to bear through collective action can enhance school life and other social spheres as well.

What claims can be made for the validity and usefulness of teacher inquiry? We've written elsewhere about the intellectual justifications that can be offered, including its starting point in phenomenal experience—the world of everyday life–as opposed to the schemas and other abstractions of formal science, its typically narrative rather than experimental or statistical mode, its frank repudiation of myths of objectivity, and its impressive conceptual heritage, not just in philosophical traditions ranging from phenomenology to postmodernism, but also in the arguments against positivism mounted within contemporary sciences from quantum mechanics to anthropology (Knoblauch and Brannon, "Knowing Our Knowledge"). It's unfortunate that the reflexive and seemingly "subjective" nature of teacher inquiry creates such suspicion among other educational researchers, working within traditions of empirical science, and also in the public at large, conditioned to associate the making of knowledge restrictively with quantitative and ostensibly "objective" methods. There are, to be sure, real differences of philosophy and method between teacher research and empirical educational study, but the belief that only one of them can claim reliability is erroneous and mischievous. Teacher research has its own justifying rhetoric, its own methodological preferences and forms of representation. We'll grant its ideological colorings, but with the stipulation that naive suggestions of political innocence or sociocultural transcendence should be erased from all characterizations of "research," not just those of marginalized groups. Meanwhile, several features of teacher research require highlighting and explanation in view of the misunderstandings and simplifications that cause the devaluing of its knowledge.

1. Teacher research presumes that its knowledge is neither "objective" nor "subjective" but that, like any form of knowledge, it is "interpretive."

Teacher research accepts the philosophical principle, well understood among the founders of quantum mechanics and now acknowledged (we trust) in all reflective research communities, that there is always an interdependence between observer and object observed (see Heisenberg; Planck). Human beings are not privileged to perceive their world from a vantage point outside or beyond it. They belong to the world: "nature" is observable only through humanly designed instruments that are themselves part of nature; human practices and institutions are known, indeed knowable, only through the mediation of other such practices and institutions. There's no question, then, in thoughtful research, of objectivity versus subjectivity, for neither of these concepts is adequate separate from the other. The isolated concept of subjectivity falsely reifies consciousness and tends toward solipsism, separating human understanding from the material world that conditions its character. The isolated concept of objectivity falsely reifies understandings that are always, necessarily, products of human inquiry and human efforts to articulate—always, in other words, interpretations. Human beings construct the world and themselves through the mediation of languages—forms of signification—that enable acts of interpretation. Those languages can include mathematics, music, dance, the plastic arts, and other forms besides natural language. All enable distinctive modes of interpretation, each in a particular way reconciling subjectivity and objectivity within a particular form of discourse (see, for instance, Langer).

In *The Interpretation of Cultures*, the anthropologist Clifford Geertz explains that the concept of culture he espouses "is essentially a semiotic one. Believing . . . that man is an animal suspended in webs of significance he himself has spun, I take culture to be those webs, and the analysis of it to be therefore not an experimental science in search of law but an interpretive one in search of meaning. It is explication I am after, construing social expressions on their surface enigmatical" (5). Teacher research shares with Geertz's version of anthropology an essentially hermeneutic understanding of the study of culture. That is, it seeks to "read" the world of educational life—its "webs of significance"—and make interpretive statements about it. Teacher research construes meanings and constructs them as texts, seeking a richer understanding of the classroom world in terms of the distinctive practices of that form of discursive inquiry. Its readings are as plausible, careful, responsible, sensitive, and compelling as any, although its methods and their products are different—its discursive practices are not the same as those of experimental science.

2. Teacher research is phenomenological in its aim, not abstractive or generalizing.

Arthur Eddington points out in *The Nature of the Physical World* that physicists can characterize an elephant sliding down a grassy hillside by means of force vectors, computations of mass, and coefficients of friction, and that the resulting representation will be both accurate and useful. But its limitation, Eddington adds, is that the elephant and the grassy hillside will have disappeared from the merely schematic rendering (251–52). Teacher research seeks, as it were, to retrieve that elephant, that grassy hillside, and the world of meanings surrounding them, as a material presence. Geertz argues that "culture" is composed of "interworked systems of construable signs," and that, as such, it is best regarded not as an entity, an objective power "to which social events, behaviors, institutions, or processes can be causally attributed" but rather as a "context" in which these "can be intelligibly—that is, thickly—described" (14). Cultural analysis for Geertz is "microscopic" (21), emphasizing the thickness, the details and textures, the colorations and ambiguities, of everyday life in its "phenomenal" immediacy. Culture is a context of particularities, existing only in and through them. The controls and intentional exclusions of experimental method are for Geertz inappropriate to an expression of the reality of culture, because "it is not in our interest to bleach human behavior of the very properties that interest us before we begin to examine it" (17). Similarly, the models, statistical averages, and general rules that experimental research seeks to articulate are inadequate as *evocations* of culture (however useful they may be for other purposes) because they offer the austere fictions of a merely intellectual portrayal of life in place of the dramatic fictions—such as those of literature—that result from its sensuous rendering. Teacher research is concerned with the culture of the classroom, aiming to depict, to evoke, what phenomenologists such as Heidegger and Gadamer have called 'the life world'—that palpable, tactile, kaleidoscopic, mysterious reality that constitutes our material rather than merely intellectual existence. Teacher research seeks to retrieve the intuitive understandings, the oblique awarenesses, the ambiguities and paradoxes, of life as it's lived, not because that's the only way to see life but because it's a way that other forms of inquiry tend to neglect, sometimes at peril to our recollection of life's richness and complexity.

3. Teacher research views the cultural reality of the classroom from a vantage point within it instead of outside it.

Geertz's anthropologist is an outsider, possessed of the advantages of that status—the ability to see what is "ordinary" (to insiders) as something strange and different, the ability to comment on a way of life detached from its habitual claims to insiders' attention and therefore free from its enveloping rationale as a necessary way of being in the world. The outsider has the distance to recognize otherness, and therefore what is distinctive about a given social reality, while also escaping the illusion, woven by that reality, that it's timeless, inevitable, unchangeable, and right. The teacher researcher's initial challenge as an insider is to defamiliarize the classroom world, to make what is usually thought to be normal, natural, and ordinary into an object of altered attention, where its rationales, practices, and institutions become available to critical scrutiny and no longer simply compel belief. Having met this challenge (a crucial first step in becoming aware of the possibilities of educational change), the special knowledge of the insider can enhance understanding of the classroom world. Motives, assumptions, intuitive awarenesses, the "felt sense" that insiders have about the character of their reality, which is unavailable except as hearsay to the outsider, are now accessible, lending firsthand richness to its portrayal. When alert, critical teachers "read" their own practices or those of other teachers, they represent them from the sympathetic vantage point of people who understand what it feels like to be in the classroom, who know the potentials and peculiarities of children at a certain age, know the political realities that inform educational practice and govern its shape. They can compare what they do in their classes to what they see in others, their experience to that of their colleagues—possessing a basis for critical judgment that the outsider lacks.

The point is not that the insider alone has exclusive access to knowledge, but only that the insider *has* legitimate knowledge, different in kind from that available to the outsider and valuable as such. Given the power of positivist concepts of "objectivity" in contemporary American life, that's no simple point to win. A common assumption is that only an outsider, such as the university research specialist, has the distance, the purity of motive, the methodological control, to undertake "reliable" inquiry. We certainly have no interest in claiming some such purity for teachers—because it's finally the positivist concept of "objectivity" that is flawed, making estimates of who is capable of achieving a pure vision irrelevant. The professional researcher is no freer than the teacher of a range of motives, ideological commitments, and methodological biases influencing both what is seen and what is concluded from what is seen. The outsider's very "outsideness" is a barrier to insight, however elaborate the means of gaining "information." Seeing is always an interpretive act, a constituting of the "thing seen," always incomplete, subject to revision, regardless of the rhetorical trappings (epistemological justifications, training rituals, procedural safeguards, rules of evidence, authoritative claims) that give privileged forms of sight, such as the scientific experiment, their cachet at a given cultural moment.

   4. Teacher research relies less on conventional academic argument than on narrative—the story (in a loose sense), the representative anecdote—as its means of articulating what it has come to understand. There are pluses to each method: neither is intrinsically more "reliable" than the other. Each invites the reader to assume a particular stance, to effect a particular quality of attention. The story is concrete, immersed in the lifeworld, intent upon richness of event, where the traditional research report is aloof and generalized. The first aims to evoke, the second to simplify. The first brings the reader actively into the process of construing meaning; it can't insist on its own valid or invalid readings. The second asserts compelling proofs. Discursive argument aims to compose "propositional" knowledge, which is abstract (a generalization from data), conclusive (a judgment supported by evidence), potentially replicable or falsifiable (through additional data gathering and the making of new statements), and cumulative. Propositional knowledge displays itself as such to readers, a conclusion for our evaluation, a contention that something is or isn't so. In the case of stories, however, motifs, patterns, tendencies emerge for attentive readers (including the writer): themes are construed as details of the story unfold and suggest their meaningfulness in an evolving context—just as, for Geertz, "culture" is construed from the details of social life. Themes aren't announced by narrators; they're sought by readers within a story's details, and once they become visible they have the effect of proposing a coherence for the text. But two readers won't compose the same themes. Moreover, no such interpretive judgment will permanently reduce the complexity of the story itself: it's reread for new insights, altered meanings. Stories endlessly modify other stories; readings endlessly modify other readings. Literature offers a helpful comparison: critics may judge that the awakening of guilt and the effects of that awakening constitute a theme of *Crime and Punishment*, but they reach that conclusion, as active readers, by reflecting upon the details of the story, not by seeing it explicitly affirmed by Dostoevsky's narrator. Meanwhile, there's no serious argument that Dostoevsky's portrait of Raskolnikov is somehow less "reliable" than a psychologist's report on the "guilt mechanism."

In principle, the stories teacher researchers have to tell are crafted with the formal care, attention to detail, and a felt sense of evolving theme that readers expect from any skilled storyteller. But they needn't, and usually don't, reflect the practiced artistry of a professional writer, nor need they result in an aesthetic experience. That isn't their function. Examples in the Goswami collection, in the North Dakota pamphlet series, and in the stories published by the Center for the Learning and Teaching of Literature at the University at Albany, SUNY, suggest that teachers are fully able to transcend the uncritical "lore" of their work, the self-serving anecdotes, the easy repetition of common knowledge that the scrupulous and the patron- izing alike throw up as inevitable barriers to reliable inquiry among "untrained amateurs." Teachers are as capable as anyone else of close observation, problem posing, conversation with others, careful read- ing and writing—all the usual capacities associated with "deliberate learning" (Garth Boomer's understanding of research) or "seeing and seeing again" (the dialectic of observing and reflecting that Ann Berthoff has in mind when she uses the term). These are the qualities that matter in teacher inquiry; when they are present in teacher narratives the consequence is always generative, and sometimes moving, for other teachers, who readily see in the stories versions of themselves, their students, and their own circumstances.

What can be learned from teacher-researcher narratives? Since stories dramatize the lifeworld, rather than abstracting from it, the learning that stories offer is inductive and intuitive, an improved quality of understanding that comes from the attentive reading of details and the construing of themes. Such narratives offer glimpses of actual life in the classroom, impressions of what it's like, without removing the complexities, uncertainties, contradictions, and para- doxes of life as it's lived. Since stories don't lead to general conclu- sions, they don't offer quantitative advances in the store of knowledge or a systematic development of some analytic argument to which a slow succession of other studies has already contributed.

They may remind one of other stories, inviting comparison, but they don't point to necessary conclusions when they bring to mind similar themes any more than they falsify each other when they are different. Stories improve the quality of knowledge without increasing the content of information. They remind readers that people and situations and actions are not simple. They cause readers to pay attention to the phenomenal character of life. They provoke reconsiderations of settled beliefs, attitudes, and judgments. They create contexts for reflection. They offer images of the possible and even reclaim what has appeared to be impossible. They make room for the knowledge that resides in ambiguity. At their best, they articulate feelings, hunches, dispositions, awarenesses, doubts, desires, that lie too deep in readers to be effectively touched by other forms of representation. They give voice to hopes and imaginings. Whatever individual readers see in stories is something to share with others who may well have learned something else or more from the same texts. The value of the stories lies finally in the fact that they offer a context for conversation among teachers. The fuller that conversation, the more stories available to sustain it, the greater the gain in a qualitatively improved awareness of the meaningfulness of classroom life. By reproducing the lifeworld of school teaching and learning apart from the immediacy of teachers' actual engagement in that world, classroom narratives create the tranquil, objectified conditions needed for reflection while still retaining teachers' intuitive recognition of the complexities of their experience. Stories don't tell teachers what to do; they simply portray people doing, and also thinking and feeling. Watching others in action, readers see themselves. Discovering personally meaningful themes in the stories, readers find coherence and support for their own professional work.

Teacher research, then, has its own definition, its own agenda, and its own intellectual validation. Advocates don't, for the most part, suggest that teachers wish, or should wish, to become partners of the educational research establishment (what Garth Boomer calls big-R research) by adopting equivalent methods in order to conduct equivalent inquiries. Berthoff, Goswami, and Atwell have all insisted, on the contrary, that the goal of teacher research is decisively not to reproduce official (typically empirical) knowledge, partly because it fails to capture the teacher's sense of classroom reality and partly because the effort to reproduce it could only constitute a misguided, even rather pathetic effort of dependent children to emulate the least responsive forms of parental behavior. Its goal is to give a distinctive teacherly knowledge accessible objective form in order to ground instructional and curricular choices in shared, authoritative renderings of the classroom world. At the same time, there's no claim among advocates of teacher inquiry that it should supplant the knowledge of other research communities, specifically those of the empirically based educational establishment. The issue is validation of a pertinent, but hitherto marginalized, knowledge that can help to improve the quality of teaching and of classroom life. The issue, too, is a share of policy-making responsibility based on access to a legitimate knowledge that ought to be invoked in the development of policy.

Unfortunately, of course, the problem teachers ultimately face in claiming authority is less intellectual than political. Prevailing notions of how to improve schools depend on the assumption that those "in charge" of teachers must find The Way and pass it along for dutiful application. Claims of teacher authority, however resourcefully advanced in philosophic terms, eventually imply a threat to privileged interests. Accordingly, the scholarly critiques of teacher inquiry carry evident political intent, as the educational research establishment argues firmly for a philosophy of "research" that has worked long and well toward preserving its social standing. Consider, for instance, the statement by Arthur Applebee, then editor of *Research in the Teaching of English*, titled "Musings . . . Teachers and the Process of Research," which appeared in the April 1987 issue. The essay is not overtly offensive to teachers—in fact far from it: Applebee makes every effort to acknowledge the particular competence of teachers, even as he makes an equivalent effort to distinguish theirs from that of the scholar. He's determined to show the "different professional expertise" of the "researcher," specifically the "disciplinary rigor" that characterizes research. The teacher, he says, "is inevitably an imperfect researcher," because she or he lacks both a "detached, observational stance" and the requisite "methodological and disciplinary skills." Applebee's argument clearly proceeds from the *topos* of "separate but equal," a tactic commonly applied whenever the more equal are addressing the less equal. Intellectually, the argument presumes implausibly clear-cut distinctions between the value of teacher knowledge and that of researcher knowledge, while also relying on concepts of "detached observation" and "methodological skill" that belong at least as much to the self-serving rhetoric of educational research as to its practice. We don't suggest that there's anything villainous, or even immediately conscious, about the effort to keep university scholars at the top of the educational heap: it's a natural response to potential disequilibrium in the hierarchy. Nor do we wish to load a disproportionate share of criticism upon Applebee's argument, coming as it does from one whose work with and for teachers is a matter of record. But the political facts are plain: the editor of a powerful research journal has published in a lead article of that journal his personal judgment on the matter of teacher research. His voice is going to be heard very clearly by those whose interests are most clearly served by what he has to say. If it's also heard by those whose position in the order of things is less privileged, it should at least be heard with its rhetoric critically visible for their inspection.

The best political response to opposition from the research establishment is simply to carry on the work, perfecting its rationales to be sure, but mainly telling more stories and creating outlets for their dissemination. That's what has been happening at the Center for the Learning and Teaching of Literature (CLTL), where groups of teachers have been working on various projects of teacher inquiry. Incidentally, one of the center's directors is Arthur Applebee, who first approved and continues to approve the funding for this work, a fact that should help to avoid demonizing any individuals in the process of mounting a nonetheless rigorous objection to the politics of educational research. Since 1988 a group of English teachers from districts in and around Albany, New York, has been producing portraits of high school literature classrooms. Participants include Doris Quick, Ann Connolly, Carol Forman-Pemberton, Roseanne DeFabio, David Marhafer, Tricia Hansbury, Susan Burke, and John Danaher, each of whom has composed one or more narratives published by CLTL. Each of these researchers is an experienced professional and each has been observing the work of other area teachers, considered to be equally accomplished in presenting literature to high school students, in order to produce narrative representations of what actually goes on today in English classrooms. (More recently, some of them have begun to portray their own classrooms as well.) The portraits, taken as a whole, are celebrations of the work of high school teachers, but they are also critical inquiries into the conditions of teaching in secondary schools, and into the relationships between schooling and other aspects of American life. As such, they don't shrink from issues of gender, race, and class, issues of managerial relations in the schools, problems of curricular reform, and the socioeconomic circumstances that continue to affect quality of life in the school world.

Details about these teachers' methods of inquiry are available in research reports from the center (Knoblauch and Brannon, *Teaching*). It's sufficient to explain here that the group has spent considerable time examining the heritage of "phenomenological inquiry," the complexities of observing the lifeworld of the classroom, and the narrative techniques available for writing accounts of observation. They are well read in the literature pertaining to "ethnographic" and "naturalistic" inquiry (see, for instance, Mishler; Kantor) as well as

that from other efforts of teacher research, including published stories from projects similar to their own (Bissex and Bullock; Goswami
and Stillman). They understand the epistemological and hermeneutic questions that surround practices of observing and writing about
complex human settings, the necessarily interpretive nature of classroom or any other observation, the effect of their presence on what
is seen, the selectivity and slant of observational notes, the necessary
but simplifying reduction of experiential detail to judgments, characterizations, conclusions, and other "statements"—in general the
interrelationship between observer and object observed as finally
constituted in the textual record of some experience. The teacher
researchers share a pervasive self-consciousness about interpretation, a desire to offer richness of detail in place of clear-cut generali-
ties, a concern for discussing "readings" of the classroom with the
largest possible number of people (the teachers and students involved as well as the other researchers), a preoccupation with concepts of "storyteller," "theme," "plot," and "character," more typical
of literary study than of empirical research.

Through the course of inquiry, researchers and their "subject"
teachers have collaborated to create "stories" of classroom life: their
viewpoints converge and diverge in intricate ways that the resulting
narratives don't attempt to conceal. The researchers are "narrators"
who don't seek to render themselves invisible in what they write,
whose voices are distinctive and important to the meaningfulness of
the stories. The teachers and students are "characters" who come to
life according to the ways in which they have been conceived by the
narrators, but they also speak freely, having had authority throughout
the drafting of the narratives to critique the ways in which they and
their classrooms were being represented. Each story is organized—
has plot—according to the themes that emerged for each writer over
the course of observation and dialogue with the teacher subjects,
their students, and the other teacher researchers. Since the "stories"
enact the philosophical assumptions discussed earlier, they don't
lend themselves to tidy summary or to collective generalization. Each
reflects the vantage point of one researcher, albeit a perspective that
has been extensively modified by the responses of others; each is
about a particular teacher who has composed a particular classroom
suited to his or her own personal and professional instincts; each is
about individual students from specific backgrounds who have
formed a class with its own distinctive "personality." Nothing in the
reality that any one story strives to depict is likely ever to be the same
on another occasion (as experienced teachers well understand). Little, if anything, in the rendering of another researcher would precisely replicate the observations, emphases, details, or themes that

make this story the symbolic object that it is. Each story, in fact, comprises a complicated layering of prior texts, creating not just interpretations but interpretations *of* interpretations—the texts of transcribed verbal interactions (supported, sometimes, by a camera's "text" of classroom events); the text of a teacher subject's impressions of a class; the texts of student impressions, the texts of conversations among the researchers. The process of making meaning here is not one of simply matching language to events, but rather one of applying one statement about events to another. Readers in their turn must apply their statements to the ones recorded in the narratives. In this way meanings are proliferated, negotiated, contested.

The stories themselves move back and forth from local details of daily classroom encounter to broader focuses on the social, political, and economic circumstances impinging on teachers, students, and others within (and beyond) the school. At one moment, a story will depict the teacher subject scrutinizing her own performance, worrying about the disengagement of student A, the eagerness of B, the laziness of C, the change in mood of D, wondering about new books, better assignments and activities, more effective ways to use time, looking for ideas, tricks, things that will work. At another moment, the story will feature the narrator reflecting on pros and cons of different teaching styles: this teacher is a performer, capturing attention from the front of the room; that one down the hall is a nurturer, waiting, with seeming unobtrusiveness, for students to initiate activity and then supporting their tentative or awkward beginnings; the narrator herself is more like a coach, showing the way, inspiring, goading, needling, whatever it takes. The narrative will shift again to a discussion between the two teachers concerning literary critical vantage points and the purposes of instruction: is the text an expression of cultural values? a means to political awakening or social consciousness? a catalyst for understanding the self? Should the texts be mainly canonical? Should they be chosen because they match student interests even if they lack "literary" esteem? What is "literary" anyway? These emphases, and others reflecting the specific professional concerns of teachers, understandably receive a lot of attention. But although the classroom is always in clear focus, neither the narrator nor the teacher subject in any story is unaware of the larger issues of curriculum, pedagogy, literary theory, and educational philosophy of which these local preoccupations are emblematic.

Nor are the stories reluctant to contextualize shop talk with social and political themes. For instance, narrators notice and sometimes pay considerable attention to the fact that not all classrooms are created equal. The narrator's own class is located in a suburban school catering to upper-middle class students, most of whom are as serious as adolescents can be about doing well in school, most of whom are college-bound, most of whom are competent readers and writers, most of whom have interested parents in business and professional careers. Her school is reasonably well funded and well outfitted, her colleagues not only motivated to teach and interested in improving their craft but also possessed to some degree of administrative and curricular authority: they choose their readings, design elective courses, work in some cases with relatively small numbers of students. The teacher subject works in the inner-city with children of the underclass, teaching remedial reading in the face of high truancy rates, disciplinary problems, drug addiction, early parenthood, unemployment, low self-esteem. She's thinking of leaving the profession. The conditions in her building reflect the tax base and social standing of the community. She works with a lockstep curriculum and has little control over its substance. Since the teacher inquirer and the cooperating teacher subject rarely come from the same school, and often come from vastly different ones, questions about what constitutes "good teaching" in dramatically diverse social settings can't help but arise to complicate limited technical issues of method.

In some stories even darker themes of school life begin to emerge (especially as inquirers become more expert, more sensitive, at observation): teachers who are beaten down by the demands of their work, alienated by bureaucracy, caught between the conflicting agendas of parents, administrators, educational researchers, and local politicians; schools that reveal the racism, sexism, and classism of the communities in which they are located; administrators who don't care about anything other than discipline, accountability, and results—who sometimes don't even live in the districts they supervise; colleagues who actively sabotage efforts to initiate curricular or pedagogical discussions; students who are far too disaffected by the circumstances of their lives and previous schooling to be reached any longer by even the most inventive educational appeal; realities of poverty and discrimination; realities of gender bias in relations between typically male administrators and typically female teachers; local and state governments reducing educational expenditures year after year while increasing demands for "better" schools; conservative politicians calling for "basic skills," competency testing, longer hours in ever more desolate teaching and learning environments, and most recently teacher testing. These themes and others begin to situate circumstances "inside" particular classrooms in terms of public spheres beyond them, so that the stories are no longer just "safe" shoptalk. Conversation becomes at once richer and more difficult, compelling but also emotionally jarring, provocative but also politically jeopardizing. By the end, an attentive reader has eavesdropped on complex, frequently moving, sometimes angry or tense professional conversations of experienced high school teachers, as well as the talk of many of their students, learning not just about the daily circumstances of school life but also about the social realities framing the work of schools. The result isn't a clear sense of rights and wrongs, or dos and don'ts, or successes and failures, but rather an altered, an enriched sensitivity to the multifacetedness of teaching, learning, and classroom life. The result is also a new understanding of the politics of education, seen from the perspective of "workers" who are frequently underserved by the hierarchical and discriminatory structures of schooling.

Is the consequence of all this work a revolutionary new educational world in which critical teachers, authorized to speak within discourses that they've helped to constitute, now undertake radically transformed reading and writing instruction in order to produce politically, no less than intellectually, responsible contributors to tomorrow's America? Obviously, an important part of the answer is no. Even if this entire, still continuing project were an unqualified success, it would remain a small effort by a handful of committed teachers to change massively resistant school (and still larger) realities that run evidently counter to everything they've tried to do. And the project has in fact not been an unqualified success: some of the teachers who served as subjects have felt enormously vulnerable about the intrusions of others in their classrooms, have felt uncomfortable, even occasionally dismayed, over their representations in stories; some teacher inquirers have been no less uncomfortable about their seeming complicity in the research agendas of the academic establishment (altered discursive modes notwithstanding); some principals and other administrators have reacted with nervousness or annoyance to "readings" of the school world that differ (not surprisingly) from their own. In retrospect, the project might have been better off from the start had teacher inquirers been content to view themselves rather than other teachers as research subjects, so that the dangers of appropriation, the darker complexities of motive, the jeopardy that attends critique of any kind could have been somewhat reduced. Teacher inquiry does, for that reason, usually entail classroom autobiography. Our efforts at something else, at biography, paid off in a distancing that enabled certain issues to surface (for instance, the implicit racism or classism of some remedial and honors programs) that would have been too painful or explosive had they been raised in the first person. But the gain wasn't worth one portion of the cost: some teachers, represented in the third person, feeling used, despite their favorable portrayal, in stories that aimed to look critically at the conditions in which they work.

Part of the answer, however, to this stern question about social change is also yes. Teachers who had been silent previously are silent no longer. Institutions that had not previously been critiqued from within have been critiqued. Stories that would have had no publisher a decade ago are now published, so that the voices and the critiques have gained a public visibility, an authorization, that somewhat alleviates their loneliness. What happens in these teachers' classrooms can no longer be what it once was, has been affected by an altered self-awareness energizing a newly politicized "way of being" in the schools. As a result, what happens outside their classrooms can't remain quite what it once was either. Other liberatory movements in the United States have followed similar paths after similarly modest, similarly determined beginnings. A century ago American women were not allowed to vote; they were denied the property rights that men enjoyed; they suffered from discriminatory marriage and divorce laws; they were largely confined to the home, had only limited access to higher education, were barred (socially if not legally) from much professional work and exploited in the workplaces to which they had access; they faced a double standard of morality, along with a double standard of merit and achievement, in the social codes of the day. There is justice in the argument that these conditions are by no means fully ameliorated, even that the larger cultural circumstances of women continue essentially unchanged notwithstanding the fact that laws and overt discriminatory practices have been modified. But no one can say that authentic, far-reaching, and permanent social changes on behalf of women have not occurred over the past century.

The reasons for these changes in broad habits of gender discrimination have nothing to do with abrupt, massive, revolutionary change, and still less to do with a sudden enlightenment of the dominant, male population. They have everything to do with small numbers of women, even at first individuals, performing acts of critical intervention amidst political and economic realities organized against their best interests. Small numbers have grown slowly but persistently into larger numbers with new trust in their solidarity and new hope of reconstituting the power arrangements of American life. The historical track of critical pedagogy, leading by small increments toward an increasingly engaged citizenry unwilling to accept the subordination or other mistreatment of any of its members, will resemble the track of women's rights far more than the catastrophic movement of the Russian or American revolution. It will be defined by local, determined interventions into teaching life, as in the case of teacher inquiry, just as it's defined by such interventions into student learning. The project is utopian to be sure, the ends unreachable in their perfected envisioning, the missteps along the way as inevitable as the victories. But the utopian ends guide a practical project that has substantial capacity—and will—to yield concrete results. A poem by Judy Grahn, from her collection *The Work of a Common Woman*, strikes us as pertinent in this regard. It invokes the project of women's rights, but it could as easily apply to the political efforts of teachers, the majority of whom below college level remain women, to constitute themselves as speaking subjects. Teaching *is* in the best sense women's work; and it *is* a women's issue. The poem reads, in part:

> Solemnly swearing, to swear as an oath to you
> who have somehow gotten to be a pale old woman;
> swearing, as if an oath could be wrapped around
> your shoulders
> like a new coat:
> For your 28 dollars a week and the bastard boss
> you never let yourself hate;
> and the work, all the work you did at home
> where you never got paid;
> For your mouth that got thinner and thinner
> until it disappeared as if you had choked on it . . .
> for your persistent nerve
> and plain white talk—
> the common woman is as common
> as good bread
> as common as when you couldnt go on
> but did.
> For all the world we didnt know we held in common
> all along
> the common woman is as common as the best of bread
> and will rise
> and will become strong—I swear it to you
> I swear it to you on my own head
> I swear it to you on my common
> woman's
> head

Bibliography

Acevedo, America, et al., eds. *Our Mural of Cultures.* New York:International Ladies Garment Workers Union Worker-Family Education Program, Locals 89-22-1 and 10, n.d.

Adler, Mortimer J. *The Paideia Proposal: An Educational Manifesto.* New York: Macmillan, 1982.

Aisenberg, Nadya, and Mona Harrington. *Women of Academe: Outsiders in the Sacred Grove.* Amherst: University of Massachusetts Press, 1988.

Applebee, Arthur N. "Musings . . . Teachers and the Process of Research." *Research in the Teaching of English* 21 (February 1987), 5–7.

———. *Tradition and Reform in the Teaching of English: A History.* Urbana, IL: National Council of Teachers of English, 1974.

Aristotle. *On Interpretation.* Trans. H. P. Cooke and H. Tredennick. Cambridge: Harvard University Press, 1973.

———. *Rhetoric.* Trans. Lane Cooper. Englewood Cliffs, NJ: Prentice-Hall, 1932.

Aronowitz, Stanley, and Henry Giroux. *Education Under Siege: The Conservative, Liberal, and Radical Debate over Schooling.* South Hadley, MA: Bergin & Garvey, 1985.

Atkins, G. Douglas, and Michael L. Johnson, eds. *Writing and Reading Differently: Deconstruction and the Teaching of Composition and Literature.* Lawrence: University Press of Kansas, 1985.

Atwell, Nancie. *In the Middle: Writing, Reading, and Learning with Adolescents.* Portsmouth, NH: Boynton/Cook, 1987.

Bailey, Richard W., and Robin Melanie Fosheim, eds. *Literacy for Life: The Demand for Reading and Writing.* New York: Modern Language Association, 1983.

Barriers to Excellence: Our Children at Risk. Board of Inquiry Project. Boston: National Coalition of Advocates for Students, 1985.

Berthoff, Ann E. *The Making of Meaning.* Portsmouth, NH: Boynton/Cook, 1981.

Bissex, Glenda, and Richard H. Bullock, eds. *Seeing for Ourselves: Case-Study Research by Teachers of Writing.* Portsmouth, NH: Heinemann, 1987.

Bloom, Allan. *The Closing of the American Mind.* New York: Simon and Schuster, 1987.

Bloomfield, Leonard. *Language*. New York: Holt, Rinehart and Winston, 1933.

Boomer, Garth. "Addressing the Problem of Elsewhereness: A Case for Action Research in Schools." In *Fair Dinkum Teaching and Learning: Reflections on Literacy and Power*. Portsmouth, NH: Boynton/Cook, 1985.

Bormuth, John. "Literacy Policy and Reading and Writing Instruction." In *Perspectives on Literacy*, eds. Richard Beach and P. David Pearson. Minneapolis: College of the University of Minnesota, 1978.

Bowles, Samuel, and Herbert Gintis. *Schooling in Capitalist America*. New York: Basic Books, 1976.

Boyer, Ernest L. *High School: A Report on Secondary Education in America*. New York: Harper & Row, 1983.

Brantlinger, Patrick. *Crusoe's Footprints: Cultural Studies in Britain and America*. New York: Routledge, 1990.

Britton, James, et al. *The Development of Writing Abilities (11–18)*. London: Schools Council Publications, 1975.

Brodkey, Linda. "Tropics of Literacy." *Journal of Education* 168 (1986): 47–54.

Cameron, Deborah, ed. *The Feminist Critique of Language: A Reader*. London: Routledge, 1990.

Campbell, Jeremy. *Grammatical Man: Information, Entropy, Language, and Life*. New York: Simon and Schuster, 1982.

Cassirer, Ernst. *Language*. Trans. Ralph Manheim. Vol. 1 of *The Philosophy of Symbolic Forms*. New Haven: Yale University Press, 1955–57.

————. *The Philosophy of the Enlightenment*. Trans. Fritz C. A. Koelln and James P. Pettegrove. Boston: Beacon, 1951.

Chomsky, Noam. *Language and Mind*. New York: Harcourt Brace Jovanovich, 1972.

Cicero. *De oratore*. Trans. E. W. Sutton and H. Rackham. 2 Vols. Cambridge: Harvard University Press, 1976–77.

Crowley, Sharon. *A Teacher's Introduction to Deconstruction*. Urbana, IL: National Council of Teachers of English, 1989.

Culley, Margo, and Catherine Portuges, eds. *Gendered Subjects: The Dynamics of Feminist Teaching*. Boston: Routledge, 1985.

Daniels, Harvey. *Famous Last Words: The American Language Crisis Reconsidered*. Carbondale, IL: Southern Illinois University Press, 1983.

Derrida, Jacques. *Of Grammatology*. Trans. Gayatri C. Spivak. Baltimore, MD: Johns Hopkins University Press, 1974.

Descartes, Rene. *Discourse on Method* [1637] and *Meditations* [1641]. Trans. Laurence J. Lafleur. Indianapolis: Bobbs-Merrill, 1960.

Dixon, John. *Growth Through English: Set in the Perspective of the Seventies.* Huddersfield, Yorkshire, UK: NATE, 1975.

D'Souza, Dinesh. *Illiberal Education: The Politics of Race and Sex on Campus.* New York: Free Press, 1991.

Eagleton, Terry. *Literary Theory: An Introduction.* Minneapolis: University of Minnesota Press, 1983.

Ebert, Teresa L. "The 'Difference' of Postmodern Feminism." *College English* 53 (December 1991):886–904.

Eddington, Arthur. *The Nature of the Physical World.* Ann Arbor: University of Michigan Press, 1958.

Elbow, Peter. *Writing Without Teachers.* New York: Oxford University Press, 1973.

Ellsworth, Elizabeth. "Why Doesn't This Feel Empowering? Working Through the Repressive Myths of Critical Pedagogy." *Harvard Educational Review* 59 (August 1989):297–324.

Fader, Daniel N., and Elton B. McNeil. *Hooked on Books: Program and Proof.* New York: Putnam, 1968.

Fausto-Sterling, Anne. "The Myth of Neutrality: Race, Sex, and Class in Science." In O'Malley et al., *Politics of Education*, 207–18.

Firestone, Shulamith. *The Dialectic of Sex.* London: Women's Press, 1979.

Foucault, Michel. *The Order of Things: An Archaeology of the Human Sciences.* New York: Random House, 1970.

Frankenstein, Marilyn. "A Different Third R: Radical Math." In O'Malley et al., *Politics of Education*: 219–29.

Freeman, Deidre, and Maureen LaMar. *ILGWU Worker-Family Education Program Curriculum Guide, 1990–91.* New York: International Ladies Garment Workers Union, 1991.

Freire, Paulo. *Pedagogy of the Oppressed.* Trans. Myra Bergman Ramos. London: Penguin, 1972.

Freire, Paulo, and Donaldo Macedo. *Literacy: Reading the Word and the World.* South Hadley, MA: Bergin & Garvey, 1987.

Geertz, Clifford. *The Interpretation of Cultures.* New York: Basic Books, 1973.

Gelb, I. J. *A Study of Writing.* Chicago: University of Chicago Press, 1952.

Giroux, Henry. *Ideology, Culture, and the Process of Schooling.* Philadelphia: Temple University Press, 1981.

———. *Theory and Resistance in Education: A Pedagogy for the Opposition.* South Hadley, MA: Bergin & Garvey, 1983.

Goodman, Kenneth S., and Olive S. Niles. *Reading: Process and Program.* Urbana, IL: National Council of Teachers of English, 1970.

Goswami, Dixie, and Peter Stillman, eds. *Reclaiming the Classroom: Teacher Research as an Agency for Change.* Portsmouth, NH: Boynton/Cook, 1986.

Gould, Stephen J. *The Mismeasure of Man.* New York: Norton, 1981.

Grahn, Judy. *The Work of a Common Woman: The Collected Poetry of Judy Grahn, 1964–1977.* New York: St. Martin's, 1978.

Gramsci, Antonio. *Prison Notebooks.* New York: International Publishers, 1971.

Grumet, Madeleine R. *Bitter Milk: Women and Teaching.* Amherst: University of Massachusetts Press, 1988.

Guthrie, John T., ed. *Cognition, Curriculum, and Comprehension.* Newark, DE: International Reading Association, 1977.

Heisenberg, Werner. *Physics and Philosophy: The Revolution in Modern Science.* New York: Harper, 1958.

Hirsch, E. D., Jr. *Cultural Literacy: What Every American Needs to Know.* Boston: Houghton Mifflin, 1987.

Hoagland, N. "On Becoming A Teacher-Researcher: An Introduction to Qualitative Research." *The Writing Instructor* (1984):55–59.

Hunter, Carman St. John, and David Harman. *Adult Illiteracy in the United States: A Report to the Ford Foundation.* New York: McGraw-Hill, 1979.

Hurlbert, C. Mark, and Michael Blitz, eds. *Composition and Resistance.* Portsmouth, NH: Boynton/Cook, 1991.

Johnston, Peter H. *Constructive Evaluation of Literate Activity.* New York: Longman, 1992.

Kantor, Kenneth J., Dan R. Kirby, and Judith P. Goetz. "Research in Context: Ethnographic Studies in English Education." *Research in the Teaching of English* 15 (1982): 293–309.

Kimball, Roger. *Tenured Radicals: How Politics Has Corrupted Our Higher Education.* New York: Harper & Row, 1990.

Knoblauch, C. H. "Critical Teaching and Dominant Culture." In Hurlbert and Blitz, *Composition and Resistance*: 12–21.

———. "Literacy and the Politics of Education." In *The Right to Literacy*, eds. Andrea A. Lunsford, Helene Moglen, and James Slevin. New York: Modern Language Association, 1990: 74–80.

———. "Rhetorical Constructions: Dialogue and Commitment." *College English* 50 (1988): 125–40.

Knoblauch, C. H., and Lil Brannon. "Knowing Our Knowledge: A Phenomenological Basis for Teacher Research." In *Audits of Meaning: A Festschrift for Ann E. Berthoff*, ed. Louise Z. Smith. Portsmouth, NH: Boynton/Cook, 1988: 17–28.

———. *Rhetorical Traditions and the Teaching of Writing.* Portsmouth, NH: Boynton/Cook, 1984.

————. *Teaching Literature in High School: A Teacher-Research Project.* Report Series 2.2.(April). Albany: Center for the Learning and Teaching of Literature, 1989.

Knoblauch, C. H., and Peter Johnston, "Reading, Writing, and the Prose of the School." In *Developing Discourse Practices in Adolescence and Adulthood*, eds. Richard Beach and Susan Hynds. Norwood, NJ: Ablex, 1990, 318–33.

Kozol, Jonathan. *Illiterate America.* New York: Anchor/Doubleday, 1985.

Kuhn, Thomas S. *The Structure of Scientific Revolutions.* Chicago: University of Chicago Press, 1970.

LaMar, Maureen, and Emily Schnee. *Excerpts from "The Global Factory" (Activities #1–#5).* New York: International Ladies Garment Workers Union, 1991.

Langer, Susanne K. *Philosophy in a New Key.* Cambridge: Harvard University Press, 1963.

Livingstone, David W., ed. *Critical Pedagogy and Cultural Power.* South Hadley, MA: Bergin & Garvey, 1987.

————. "Upgrading and Opportunities." In Livingstone, *Critical Pedagogy:* 125–36.

Locke, John. *Essay Concerning Human Understanding* [1689]. New York: Macmillan, 1965.

Lyotard, Jean-Francois. *The Postmodern Condition: A Report on Knowledge.* Trans. Geoff Bennington and Brian Massumi. Minneapolis: University of Minnesota Press, 1984.

Mackay, Donald M. *Information, Mechanism, and Meaning.* Cambridge: Massachusetts Institute of Technology, 1969.

MacKinnon, F. D. "The Law and the Lawyers." In *Johnson's England: An Account of the Life and Manners of His Age,* Vol 2, ed. A. S. Turberville, 287–309. Oxford: Clarendon, 1952.

Mailloux, Steven. *Rhetorical Power.* Ithaca: Cornell University Press, 1989.

Miller, James E. *Word, Self, Reality: The Rhetoric of Imagination.* New York: Dodd, Mead, 1972.

Miller, Susan. *Rescuing the Subject: A Critical Introduction to Rhetoric and the Writer.* Carbondale: Southern Illinois University Press, 1989.

Mishler, Elliot G. "Meaning in Context: Is There Any Other Kind?" *Harvard Educational Review* 49 (1979):1–19.

Mohr, Marian M., and Marion S. MacLean. *Working Together: A Guide for Teacher-Researchers.* Urbana, IL: National Council of Teachers of English, 1987.

Moi, Toril. *Sexual/Textual Politics: Feminist Literary Theory.* London: Methuen, 1985.

A Nation at Risk: The Imperative for Educational Reform. U.S. National Commission on Excellence in Education. Washington, DC: Government Printing Office, 1983.

O'Malley, Susan Gushee, Robert C. Rosen, and Leonard Vogt, eds. *Politics of Education: Essays from 'Radical Teacher'.* Albany: State University of New York Press, 1990.

Orwell, George. "Politics and the English Language." In *Shooting an Elephant and Other Essays.* New York: Harcourt, 1950.

Planck, Max. *The Philosophy of Physics.* New York: Norton, 1936.

Plato. *Phaedrus.* Trans. W. C. Helmbold and W. G. Rabinowitz. Indianapolis: Bobbs-Merrill, 1956.

———. *Republic.* In *Great Dialogues of Plato,* eds. Eric H. Warmington and Philip G. Rouse, trans. W. H. D. Rouse. New York: Mentor, 1956.

Poovey, Mary. "Feminism and Deconstruction." *Feminist Studies* 14 (Spring 1988):51–65.

Robinson, Jay L., et al. *Conversations on the Written Word: Essays on Language and Literacy.* Portsmouth, NH: Boynton/Cook, 1990.

Saint Augustine. *On Christian Doctrine.* Trans. D. W. Robertson, Jr. Indianapolis: Bobbs-Merrill, 1958.

Shor, Ira. *Critical Teaching and Everyday Life.* Chicago: Chicago University Press, 1987.

———, ed. *Freire for the Classroom: A Sourcebook for Liberatory Teaching.* Portsmouth, NH: Boynton/Cook, 1987.

Spofford, Tim. "More Women Getting Top School Jobs." Albany *Times-Union,* October 16, 1990.

Sporn, Pam. "Teaching the VietNam War at a South Bronx Alternative High School." In O'Malley et al., *Politics of Education:* 78–86.

Strunk, William, and E. B. White. *The Elements of Style.* New York: Macmillan, 1979.

Stuckey, J. Elspeth. *The Violence of Literacy.* Portsmouth, NH: Boynton/Cook, 1991.

Sullivan, Edmund V. "Critical Pedagogy and Television." In Livingstone, *Critical Pedagogy:* 57–75.

Trevelyan, G. M. *English Social History.* London: Penguin, 1967.

Volosinov, V. N. *Marxism and the Philosophy of Language.* Trans. Ladislav Matejka and I. R. Titunik. Cambridge: Harvard University Press, 1973.

Von Humboldt, Wilhelm. *Linguistic Variability and Intellectual Development* [1836]. Trans. George C. Buck and Frithjof A. Raven. Philadelphia: University of Pennsylvania Press, 1972.

What Work Requires of Schools: A SCANS Report for America 2000. The Secretary's Commission on Achieving Necessary Skills. Washington, DC: U.S. Department of Labor, 1991.

Williams, Raymond. *Marxism and Literature*. London: Oxford University Press, 1977.

The World's Women 1970-1990: Trends and Statistics. New York: United Nations Publications, 1991.